The Accountable Corporation

The Accountable Corporation

CORPORATE GOVERNANCE
VOLUME 1

Edited by
Marc J. Epstein
and
Kirk O. Hanson

Praeger Perspectives

Westport, Connecticut
London

Library of Congress Cataloging-in-Publication Data

The accountable corporation / edited by Marc J. Epstein and Kirk O. Hanson.
   p. cm.
  Includes bibliographical references and index.
  ISBN 0-275-98491-5 ((set) : alk. paper)—ISBN 0-275-98492-3 ((vol. I) :
alk. paper)—ISBN 0-275-98493-1 ((vol. II) : alk. paper)—ISBN 0-275-98494-X
((vol. III) : alk. paper)—ISBN 0-275-98495-8 ((vol. IV) : alk. paper)
  1. Corporate governance. 2. Business ethics. 3. Social responsibility
of business. I. Epstein, Marc J. II. Hanson, Kirk O.
  HD2741.A282 2006
   174'.4—dc22   2005025486

British Library Cataloguing in Publication Data is available.

Library of Congress Catalog Card Number: 2005025486
ISBN: 0-275-98491-5 (set)
       0-275-98492-3 (vol. 1)
       0-275-98493-1 (vol. 2)
       0-275-98494-X (vol. 3)
       0-275-98495-8 (vol. 4)

First published in 2006

Praeger Publishers, 88 Post Road West, Westport, CT 06881
An imprint of Greenwood Publishing Group, Inc.
www.praeger.com

Printed in the United States of America

The paper used in this book complies with the
Permanent Paper Standard issued by the National
Information Standards Organization (Z39.48-1984).

10 9 8 7 6 5 4 3 2 1

Contents

Introduction

MARC J. EPSTEIN and KIRK O. HANSON

The complex relationship between the modern business corporation and the society in which it operates has evolved continually since the modern corporation emerged in the United States during the last third of the nineteenth century. The corporation initially enjoyed significant autonomy. Gradually, in the Progressive Era, in the New Deal, and in the 1970s rush of consumerism and environmentalism, the corporation became subject to an increasing set of laws and expectations that changed its character and its behavior. But we believe that the first years of the twenty-first century represent the most intense change in the corporation's relationship to its environment ever experienced.

This set of volumes is designed to explore the new and changed state of this relationship. We believe the most important change in the role of the corporation is that, to a degree never before achieved, the corporation is subject to new controls on its behavior. The recent months and years have seen the rise of the Accountable Corporation.

Whereas one might have simply cataloged legislation and counted regulations to evaluate whether the corporation had been made more accountable, today one must examine a much wider range of social and economic controls. Traditional regulation represents only one form of making the corporation accountable. Advances in communications and information technology have made information about the behavior of corporations much more available than ever before in history. Reporters and producers are using investigative reporting and lightweight video cameras to "get" stories they never would have gotten before. The modern press and media can track the behavior of corporations as they never have before.

At the same time, the outlets for media stories have exploded. The coming of cable television has greatly expanded the space and demand for programming. Mass access to the Internet as well as the ability to use e-mail to gather more information have revolutionized the "always on" availability of information about corporations. And, New York attorney general Eliot Spitzer has shown how forensic examination of past e-mails can document corporate behaviors that before would never have come to light.

The capabilities of the Internet have also mobilized the growing cadre of citizen activists who have followed Ralph Nader's footsteps in examining and publicizing corporations' misbehavior. Today, on very short notice, activists by the thousands can be mobilized to march in the streets of Seattle against the actions of global corporations. But activism itself has changed. Whereas activism has been associated more with the longhaired Vietnam War protester, social activism today is more frequently embodied in the rise of the "social entrepreneur." A substantial new cadre of individuals has embraced a personal vocation to produce significant social change by pressuring—or starting— businesses. These social entrepreneurs, some of whom are being trained in business schools such as Stanford and Oxford, want to make corporations more responsive to the needs of society, or want to create new types of businesses that are more responsive.

We believe the modern corporation has entered a decidedly different era, one in which it must dedicate substantially more resources to being accountable, and to demonstrating to a skeptical society that it is actually more accountable. This series documents many aspects of this transition to the Accountable Corporation, presenting the state of the art of Corporate Governance (Volume 1), Business Ethics (Volume 2), Corporate Social Responsibility (Volume 3), and Business-Government Relations (Volume 4).

We hope the portrait presented in these volumes helps those leading the modern corporation to guide their institutions to become more accountable. We believe the success of the corporation in the twenty-first century depends upon how the corporation can satisfy this new reality.

We also hope this portrait can aid scholars of the modern corporation to understand how significant this disjuncture in corporate history is, and to identify avenues of research that will aid the corporate executives and citizen activists of the twenty-first century to shape the Accountable Corporation.

THE IMPACT OF GLOBALIZATION

During the last two decades of the twentieth century, American-style capitalism and democracy made great strides around the world. With the collapse of Eastern European communism in the late 1980s, free market capitalism and its vanguard—the modern global corporation—have become ubiquitous around the world. McDonald's, KFC, and now Starbucks have achieved a global presence. As if to illustrate how far things have come, Starbucks even opened a store inside Beijing's Forbidden City in 2001, only to have the Chinese Communist Party expel it after a month.

The globalization of business has helped set the stage for the intense debate over the accountability of the corporation. World Trade Organization riots in Seattle and Genoa demonstrated a pent-up frustration with the behavior of corporations and the dark side of free markets. Is globalization removing the tenuous ties corporations have had to the welfare of even their own home nations and local communities? Are global corporations now accountable only to themselves? The workings of global capitalism are seen as broadening, not narrowing, the substantial gap between the developed and less-developed world.

It is in the midst of this unease that the financial manipulations and frauds perpetrated by Enron executives and those at so many other large corporations shocked American citizens. The scandals in the United States were sadly mirrored by corporate meltdowns in Italy and France, and even in Sweden and Switzerland, where corporations were thought by many to operate with a greater rectitude.

The scandals of 2002–2005 set off a debate in the United States over how to rein in corporate malfeasance and make the corporation accountable. The Sarbanes-Oxley Act of 2002 was adopted by the United States Congress and led to extensive changes in corporate procedures, controls, and reporting. The collapse of Arthur Andersen as well as enactment of the Sarbanes-Oxley Act stiffened the backbone of the remaining large accounting firms in the United States, perhaps making them more like the watchdogs they were meant to be. In the European Parliament and in legislatures around the world, politicians are seeking the right levers to control the increasingly powerful local and global corporations.

But what are the most effective levers of accountability? Many politicians and critics of business are convinced that only draconian legislation can keep corporations in line. Others are shaping voluntary codes of behavior—on an industry, national, or global basis. Corporations themselves are creating policies and programs that express a new commitment to ethical behavior and corporate responsibility. New internal mechanisms and strategies of responsibility and accountability are being forged for the corporations themselves. But the balance between internal and voluntary standards on the one hand and compulsory legislated standards on the other is yet to be determined. And should standards be national, regional, or global, undoubtedly the balance will be struck somewhat differently from country to country and from company to company.

VOLUME 1: CORPORATE GOVERNANCE

Though we have seen accounting scandals and other violations of trust throughout corporate history, only recently have these scandals begun to impact larger sectors of the population. With increased individual stock ownership and the increased ownership of pensions and retirement funds, many more people are affected when companies fail. It is not just the wealthy, but an increasingly broad spectrum of the society that is harmed. Among these are large and small investors, employees, customers, governments, and communities.

The recent flurry of very public failures including Enron, WorldCom, Global Crossing, Adelphia, Arthur Andersen, and others have caused intense activity by government regulators, industry associations, and individual firms to correct deficiencies in corporate governance and accountability.

Given the severe reaction to recent scandals, there is no longer any choice for companies. Increased external transparency and improved internal governance are required. The Sarbanes-Oxley Act along with new regulations at the stock exchanges have mandated that. Further, increased enforcement of existing regulations and more frequent investigations of corporate behavior have caused corporations and their directors to focus far more on the responsibilities they have both to the corporation and its stakeholders. The chapters in Volume 1 address all of these issues in depth. They address how boards should evaluate their responsibilities in this new environment. The history and development of the roles and responsibilities is examined in both the United States and internationally, and current activities and trends in enforcement are discussed. Further, eminent researchers and practitioners in corporate governance both from a legal and management perspective describe the challenges for corporate directors and prescribe ways to improve corporate governance, transparency, and accountability.

Generally, we think of boards of directors as having three primary responsibilities: a) strategic oversight and guidance, b) accountability to corporate stakeholders, and c) evaluation, selection, and succession of senior management. But, how corporations can better meet those responsibilities is often the challenge. Though some have criticized various new regulations and enforcement as being more burdensome than necessary to correct deficiencies, it is clear that this has encouraged some very positive changes. For some companies, the regulations only caused a formalization of existing practices, but for many others they caused a new reexamination and dramatic changes in governance and internal controls. Recent developments have also caused corporate directors to carefully reexamine their roles and responsibilities and the processes in place in the corporations to protect the company from crises and to provide better corporate oversight and accountability.

At Enron, for example, we saw that an overreliance on trust caused cataclysmic governance problems. The board was, in our view, guilty of lax oversight of both corporate activities and the CEO. Excessive trust also caused the board of directors to relax their scrutiny of the company's operations and its financial statements. The directors were seduced by a rising stock price and impressive financial performance that they believed validated their trust. In other cases there is additional evidence that just complying with regulations may not be enough. Ticking boxes on issues of board composition or process is not enough. Corporate boards must follow the rules but must also have underlying principles of accountability guiding their actions. They must put processes in place to more effectively implement and evaluate better board performance. And, they must provide increased transparency to both corporate actions and the actions of the board. Good corporate governance improves both the reality of better corporate performance as well as the market's perception of better performance.

Though regulation may provide the outline of a solution, there is much more that needs to be done. This will require a careful reexamination of these inputs and processes that will drive improved governance. Companies need to be focused on improving accountability including both internal corporate governance and external transparency. This volume provides the latest thinking of corporate governance leaders in industry, law, and academia as to the way forward to improve the performance of both corporations and their boards.

VOLUME 2: BUSINESS ETHICS

The ethics of business has been debated since the first railroad corporation in the 1870s engaged in questionable practices. But the debate over business ethics in the United States and the deliberate management of ethics in the corporation dates from the late 1970s. Two major corporate scandals dominated the decade's attention: illegal corporate contributions to the Nixon re-election campaign in 1972, and bribery by American corporations seeking business around the world. Over 100 large American corporations confessed to making illegal political contributions, many of them "laundered" through accounts in Mexico. Over 200 large American corporations that investigated their own marketing practices abroad in the late 1970s disclosed patterns of bribery. In the wake of these two scandals, American businesses began to think deliberately about managing ethical behavior, and American business schools began to introduce the formal study of business ethics.

Throughout the 1980s, despite major insider trading, savings and loan, and defense scandals, most companies continued to believe the problem of ethics was one of insuring that lower-level employees toed the line and followed legal and other compliance standards. Rarely was it thought that the executive suite faced ethical problems. A few companies, however, notably Johnson & Johnson, reached back in their histories for statements of values, and ethical standards, and promulgated them for all employees to follow—from the executive suite to the shop floor to follow.

In the defense industry, congressional and public pressure led to the creation of the Defense Industry Initiative on Business Ethics and Conduct in 1986, which in turn led to the hiring of the first generation of "ethics officers" in many American companies. Their learning informed the work of newly appointed ethics officers and staff in other industries. Throughout the 1990s, corporate ethics programs and the ranks of ethics officers grew, but the debate between compliance programs and values programs remained unresolved.

The scandals of 2002–2005 changed the shape of the debate over business ethics in significant ways. There was no doubt in the cases of Enron, WorldCom, and Tyco that it was the ethics of the executive suite and not the shop floor that was the problem. In the Sarbanes-Oxley Act and in other standards promulgated by the SEC and the stock exchanges, efforts were made to make the individual CEO, CFO, and corporate director personally responsible for the integrity of the company's accounts and behavior. The Federal Sentencing Guidelines, the rules by which judges determine fines for corporations and jail sentences for individuals, were revised in 2004 to give credit for ethics programs and for companies that did such things as assess the ethical risk in their systems and organizations. In business schools, a second wave of curriculum development on ethics and management more firmly established these topics in the required curriculum.

Business ethics was less easily embraced in cultures beyond the United States. In Western Europe, academics and a small number of corporate executives in the 1980s established the European Business Ethics Network and several national business ethics organizations, but the continent-wide debate focused more on corporate responsibility and such concepts as the "triple bottom line." In Asia, business ethics had a particularly hard time gaining a foothold in Confucian cultures or in the economic giant Japan. A few individual executives and academics there promoted business ethics based on particular religious or spiritual values.

The future of business ethics is clearly being driven by globalization and the global reach of giant corporations. There is a realization that national regulation must be aided by the corporations' own internal values and management of their behavior. The second force is the growing understanding of the debilitating effects of corruption. In the mid-1990s, World Bank studies demonstrated clearly that business and governmental corruption held up development. This led the World Bank, the world's largest lender for economic development, to establish an office and program to fight corruption. In particular countries, the problem of corruption has led to national government and business ethics reform efforts. Even in China, the problem of corruption has led the Communist Party to sanction the establishment of the first national center on business ethics and "eastern wisdom" in Beijing.

VOLUME 3: CORPORATE SOCIAL RESPONSIBILITY

The concept of corporate social responsibility (CSR) has gone through several major transitions in the past fifty years. Though the discussion over what the appropriate nature and level of corporate involvement with its community continues, the discussion about whether companies have a responsibility and whether they should be engaged with their stakeholders is reasonably settled for most senior managers and researchers. The question is no longer should companies include stakeholder concerns in their decision-making processes. The question is how to do it.

Companies question the appropriate level of engagement, how to integrate issues of corporate social responsibility into capital investment and operational management decisions. They are challenged by the real difficulties of integrating societal issues into their organizational systems and structures. They are looking for ways to better institutionalize it in both the internal and external reporting platforms and to find ways to better identify and measure the impacts of the company on society. This then leads to questions about whether social responsibility expenditures should be examined based on societal impacts or on long-term profitability, or on both. That is, when there are win-win situations, the answers and the decisions are easy. We have learned, for example, that there remain many win-win situations in business where companies can reduce environmental waste, thereby both reducing societal costs and increasing corporate profits. But what happens when companies are faced with products, services, processes, or other activities where the benefit to the company is high and there is significant cost to society? Can these externalities be voluntarily internalized? Will this occur in the short term or long term? What will be the impact on corporate reputation, and will that impact corporate profitability? How should companies measure the payoffs to both the company and the community?

Thus the discussions on CSR included in this series focus primarily on the nature of the engagement, and how to implement CSR in the corporation. The chapters provide an overview of the arguments and the development of CSR. They describe the dimensions of CSR. But, they also look forward at the future of the concept, the challenges to implementation, and the opportunities for corporate involvement in solving societal challenges.

Though there have been various starts and stops in the development of CSR, companies have recently recognized that they have no choice regarding whether to integrate stakeholder concerns into the management decision-making process. The consequences of ignoring these concerns are just too great.

As companies move forward to better integrate CSR into the fabric of the organization, the focus has become how to improve the formulation of a social responsibility strategy and how to develop the plans, programs, structures, systems, performance evaluations, rewards, and culture necessary to implement the strategy effectively. There is increased focus on how companies must more effectively engage their stakeholders and identify, measure, monitor, and report the impacts of the company's products, services, processes, and other activities on society. Both the definition of stakeholders and the analysis of the impacts must be broadly defined. To effectively implement CSR, companies must find ways to help managers better evaluate, integrate, and make the trade-offs necessary for making improved corporate decisions. Understanding how various stakeholder reactions will likely impact corporate performance and anticipating these reactions when designing and committing to corporate investment is critical.

Senior corporate managers have the opportunity to make important advances in improving the long-term welfare of both society and the corporation. They can be forward-looking and anticipate factors in the external environment that will likely affect corporate success. They can also anticipate how corporate activities will affect their various stakeholders. Through more effective management of the impacts of corporate activities on society, both social welfare and corporate performance can be enhanced.

VOLUME 4: BUSINESS-GOVERNMENT RELATIONS

The relationship between business and government in the United States has always had distinct characteristics. Put simply, most business executives have never trusted, perhaps because they have never understood, their government and its workings. Big business and the modern corporation grew up in the United States before the emergence of big government in the New Deal. A sizable segment of business executives has argued that they should be free of any government regulation and even of any taxation. Small businesses, represented in Washington by such groups as the United States Chamber of Commerce and the National Association of Manufacturers, has had a distinctly conservative tone, opposing almost all regulation and business taxation, and much of the social legislation of the last half of the twentieth century.

There are signs that American business is emerging from this dark nay-saying period. Corporations are more frequently involved in collaborative efforts to find solutions to social and business issues rather than stonewalling as before. In 1954, President Dwight D. Eisenhower called a group of business executives to the White House and urged them to create an organization to educate businesses about government and about the opportunities to be involved in influencing government decisions. As the turn of the century approached, corporations more frequently supported regulatory or tax legislation, even proposing more effective ways to achieve the social goals behind the regulation. Companies partnered with traditional enemies, including unions and activists, to support or oppose particular legislation. In industries where regulation played a major role in shaping business opportunities, CEOs were hired who had a more sophisticated understanding of government and had the skills to operate in Washington.

Following the scandal over illegal political contributions by corporations in 1972, new legislation made it unambiguously legal for corporations to sponsor "political action committees," entities that could solicit funds from company executives and other employees and then contribute them to election campaigns. The result was that corporations dramatically increased their legal political and campaign activities, and corporate staffs in Washington grew apace. During the 1990s a backlash against the large amounts of corporate contributions flowing to candidates and political organizations emerged, and many different forms of legislation were proposed to reduce corporate influence. Efforts to substitute public funding for corporate and individual contributions to campaigns foundered, but pressure on corporate influence continued.

In the twenty-first century, the debate over business-government relations will address such questions as limits on corporate lobbying and contributions, and detailed disclosure of these. One of the most difficult questions concerns the impact of conflicts of interest on the ability of individuals and corporations to function as a legislator or regulator, or as a business executive.

The chapters in Volume 4 explore both the present and future shape of business-government relations in the United States.

CONCLUSION

It is our hope that the reader of these volumes will discover new insights into the future of the corporation. We are grateful to the authors of the many chapters in these volumes for their wisdom and for these contributions to all of our learning. We also have trust that the wisdom and resourcefulness of regulators, activists, and above all, corporate management itself, will shape a healthy future for the modern *accountable* corporation.

I
FOUNDATIONS AND PERSPECTIVES
OF CORPORATE GOVERNANCE

—————— 1 ——————

A Perspective on Corporate Governance: Rules, Principles, or Both

IRA M. MILLSTEIN

The need for appropriate corporate governance has existed since the birth of the corporation, which became the paramount form of business organization, not by fiat, but by meeting needs: the need to accommodate the explosive demand for capital, and the consequential need to protect diffused investors. Corporate governance exists to meet both needs, and its core has remained constant, even though the rules, principles, and practices by which it is expressed continue to evolve over time. The dominant initiation of corporate governance reforms may swing between regulation (rules) and voluntary private sector action (principles and practices), but the goal is always to protect investors while attracting their capital.

Corporate governance rests on three intersecting visions. The first has its roots in the Jeffersonian ideal expressed in the Declaration of Independence that "all men are created equal ... endowed by their creator with ... inalienable Rights, that among these are Life, Liberty, and the pursuit of Happiness [and] [t]hat to secure these rights, Governments are instituted among Men, deriving their just powers from the consent of the governed."[1] This ideal recognizes each person's right to be left alone in a world of opportunity, where success or failure will be decided by his or her own individual abilities and desires. The role of government is limited to assuring and sometimes providing opportunities, and protecting those who have failed. The rights of the individual provide the foundation on which the market economy rests. The second vision is the "market," where participants are motivated to interact by self-interest.

Aggregated, individual decisions in the market should result in greater public good than should state planning. The third vision recognizes fundamentals of justice and mercy that must temper individual rights and free markets, and so we must all strive to "do the right thing" as ethical people. For the Judeo-Christian world, this vision has its origins in the prophecies of Micah, who placed responsibilities on the essential character and behavior of people rather than on proscribed sacrifices and burnt offerings.[2] The first two visions were articulated in the same year, 1776.[3] The third is a bit older. They all seem to be universally applicable.

Together, these visions place the government as the protector of individual freedom and the market, but in exchange place responsibilities on the individual. In this sense, individual rights and free markets are not free goods. In this soil, corporate governance defines what is expected of the people who populate the corporate world—the managers and directors (and the investors who put them in place and entrust them with their assets). According to Adam Smith, people are expected to have the virtues of "prudence, justice and beneficence,"[4] "temperance, decency, modesty and moderation,"[5] and should be "scrupulous . . . never either to hurt or offend."[6] This was his "moral philosophy" and was a foundation for his market theory. But he knew this vision would never be fully achieved,[7] and he was right. So he, and we, seek mechanisms to make up for the shortfall.

In fact, people cannot always be relied upon to live up to Adam Smith's vision. The historical corporate governance examples of this failure are plentiful—from Dutch tulips[8] to South Sea bubbles,[9] to the use of inside information at Texas Gulf Sulphur,[10] to the inclusion of false and misleading information in the proxy statements of BarChris Construction Corporation,[11] to the near-collapse of Chrysler[12] and the frauds at Equity Funding.[13] These corporate governance failures largely occurred as a result of something far less than "temperance," "prudence," and "beneficence" on the part of managers and boards. But such failures focused attention on board and management performance, and what could be done to improve that performance, either through self-help, regulation, or both.

With the evolution of widely dispersed owners and professional managers—the modern separation of ownership and control as described by Bearle and Means in the 1930s[14]—the board came to be recognized as the focal mechanism for protecting investors against managers' failure to live up to moral sentiments such as those espoused by Micah and Smith. Management failures are increasingly likely as ownership and control become increasingly separated, because of the inherently flawed nature of humans and their tendency to act in their own self-interest. This is the perpetual "agency" problem. Governance practices, both self-created and legislated, have evolved to position the board to monitor this agency problem as well as the performance of managers generally. This evolution is continuing and is apparent in practices relating to director independence from management and director involvement in key issues such as director nomination and recruitment, evaluation, compensation, and, where necessary, removal of management, and the integrity of audit and financial reporting.

Board responsibility for key tasks has been an active topic of interest since the 1930s for reform proponents in the private sector and academia.[15] State corporate law provides that the corporation is to be managed and directed by the board.[16] However, the statutes do not provide significant guidance as to what responsibilities this entails. If the board's role is to act as a surrogate for the owners of the corporation and this requires the board to oversee management's performance in the interests of maximizing long-term shareholder value—the polestar of profit maximization—the board must also pay attention to "social responsibilities" such as employment conditions and the interaction of the company with the communities in which it operates. The reform movement since the 1930s has addressed these issues, urging that directors be informed and able to make objective decisions with due care and in the best interests of the company, to assure optimal corporate performance.

Early reform efforts by the private sector placed great faith in the board's ability, and willingness, to fulfill these critical responsibilities. Much of the impetus for corporate governance reform from the 1970s through the 1990s was driven by the private sector (albeit to some extent in an effort to forestall further regulation). Important roles were played by groups such as the Business Roundtable, which commented on board composition in 1978[17] and corporate responsibility in 1981,[18] and the American Law Institute, which published its *Principles of Corporate Governance: Analysis and Recommendations* in 1994[19] after fifteen years of preparation and widespread consultation. In the late 1980s, as pension funds became active and organized, the interest in reform intensified. Corporations responded by increasing board independence, heightening board focus on corporate performance, and encouraging more board participation in strategic planning. Self-help best practices, such as those articulated in guidelines by the board of General Motors in 1994,[20] became widespread when the California Public Employees' Retirement System (CalPERS) distributed the General Motors guidelines to the three hundred largest public companies and asked those companies whether they adopted similar policies, then published "grades" based on the corporate responses.[21] While the private sector was the dominant architect of reforms during those years, there were also regulatory steps being taken by the Securities and Exchange Commission (hereinafter SEC) and the stock exchanges, and by some specific congressional action, for example, the Foreign Corrupt Practices Act of 1977. These regulatory steps ranged from the imposition by the New York Stock Exchange of audit committees with some independent directors in the 1970s[22] to the SEC removing restrictions on shareholder communications in the 1990s.[23]

These private sector efforts were aimed to position boards to address their complex but essential responsibilities. Leaving corporate governance architecture to the private sector through adoption of voluntary best practices came into serious question after failures such as Enron, WorldCom, and Global Crossing entered the public consciousness earlier this decade. Those scandals removed the sentimental barriers to federal corporate governance legislation among the general population, enabling the United States Congress to enact the Sarbanes-Oxley Act of 2002 (hereinafter Sarbanes-Oxley). Sarbanes-Oxley, together with SEC-issued enabling rules and related revisions to the listing rules of the New York Stock Exchange and NASDAQ, attempt to institutionalize corporate accountability at the board level by converting what were previously voluntary "should have" best practices into "must have" minimum standards for board structure, composition, and, to some extent, responsibility.[24] The failure of Adam Smith's "man" to "do the right thing" resulted in the reform pendulum swinging from the private sector to the regulators.

A serious lesson has been learned—again. Scandal begets regulation. This time it was Congress—in a major way. The lesson is, either improve via self-help, or more regulation will follow. Now, the private sector must work to swing the pendulum back.

The private sector's new focus should be on recasting board members— collectively Adam Smith's "men"—as people whom shareholders, employees, suppliers, customers, and communities can trust to "do the right thing." In this regard, corporations, academics, and practitioners will, hopefully, look beyond structural and process requirements for the board in an effort to understand the substantive issues underlying board performance. Now, instead of focusing on issues such as how many independent directors are sitting on a board—important as they are—the emphasis should be on the individual board members' trustworthiness and ethics; these are central to the directors' fiduciary duties of good faith, loyalty, and care, and are at the heart of corporate governance.

The new corporate governance environment has intensified focus on the board as the key decision-making organ of the corporation on behalf of the shareholders.[25] Together with new legislated structures, and new and old legislated responsibilities, the board is surely the repository for ultimate corporate power. It always was, but directors did not act as if they were; now they are directed to understand. That this must be the case is clear. In a publicly traded company, the owners of corporations—the shareholders—have entrusted the management of their investment to a group of people they do not even know. Why? Because investors who wish to commit capital to an enterprise cannot know, and therefore cannot trust, one another to keep that capital safe from the competing agendas of different investors. So they cede the power to oversee the corporation to a board, which they must trust to do the right thing for a disparate group of "owners."

Investor trust in the board as an institution is fostered in a number of ways. At a macro level, corporate governance rules engendering trust in the board are essential to the evolution and growth of efficient capital markets because potential investors will not invest in a company they do not trust. To encourage investment, particularly in developing countries, legislated rules of corporate governance and corporate law need to sit alongside other investment safeguards such as property ownership protections, contract law, enforcement mechanisms, and accounting and auditing standards. People will be more likely to invest in a market that has a transparent, stable, and predictable investment climate.[26] These are features that investors in developed countries take for granted. But they are often nonexistent in developing countries and are among the reasons why investors might shy away from committing their capital in those markets.

At the individual company level, the trustworthiness of the board in the eyes of investors is critical, notwithstanding enabling laws, regulations, and climates. The "locked-in" capital theory, developed by Professor Margaret M. Blair, is based on the idea that investors have no basis for trusting fellow investors.[27] According to Professor Blair, this theory explains the dominance of the corporation as a form of business organization. The "locked-in capital" theory is explained as follows. Investors contribute capital to the company in return for newly issued shares. That investment becomes part of the capital of the company and is "locked away" from the investors in the sense that they are denied any sort of meaningful access to it—they do not have the right to demand a dividend or a repurchase of their stock or any other return of capital. However, in the event that the investors wish to leave the corporation, they can sell their shares for value. From the perspective of the company, the capital contributed by investors and "locked away" from them can be drawn upon to enable the corporation to enter into long-term commitments to employees, customers, and suppliers. These features, along with perpetual life and limited liability, distinguished the emerging corporate form of organization from the partnership and similar vehicles, and led to the corporation's present dominance as an organizational form.

The board is responsible for making decisions in the best interests of all the investors in the utilization of "locked-in" capital. The structure is conducive to accumulating large amounts of capital because investors no longer need to know or have faith in the reputations of their fellow investors. However, investors *do* need to trust in the willingness and ability of the board to make decisions on behalf of all.

Therefore, going forward, corporate governance must recognize the dominance of the board and the absolute need for it to be trusted to "do the right thing." The law of fiduciary duties already provides a firm formulation on which to build greater trust. These duties are dealt with in depth elsewhere in this volume.

At a basic level, fiduciary duties prescribe what directors must do in order to fulfill their responsibilities as the custodians of other people's money. These duties require directors to act in good faith and with due care, loyalty, and candor.[28] Specific applications have been developed by the courts in the United States on a case-by-case basis, ensuring that optimal flexibility can be maintained in molding the scope of the duties to actual factual situations. The Delaware Court of Chancery and its Supreme Court are especially adept at shaping the duties to reflect the prevailing exigencies of business. Delaware General Corporation Law utilizes an "enabling model" of corporate law that provides a "skeletal framework" for corporate law, thereby allowing the judiciary to develop the rules in response to the demands of the day.[29] This enabling model can be compared to a "rules-based system" that attempts to cover the field with specific rules enshrined in legislation rather than leaving the judges to work out the specifics. Compelling the responsiveness of the judiciary in developing the law of fiduciary duties is the fact that shareholders in states such as Delaware can bring derivative suits on behalf of the company against a director for breach of fiduciary duty,[30] a mechanism that ensures that cases are brought before the bench for analysis.

The common law approach to fiduciary duties, a case-by-case application leading to principles to follow, fills in the gaps. No legislation can cover every business situation.

The ongoing development of the law of fiduciary duties combined with the structural requirements mandated by Sarbanes-Oxley, the new exchange listing rules, and earlier law and regulations, provide an essential base for ensuring that companies are able to achieve best-in-class standards of corporate governance. However, even a cursory examination of the scandals occurring in corporate America prior to the recent wave of reforms indicates that all of this was not enough. A prime example is precollapse Enron, whose board of seventeen consisted of fifteen nonmanagement directors with exemplary reputations, including lawyers, academics, CEOs, and former regulators. A former dean of the Stanford Graduate School of Business was chairman of the audit committee.[31] Surely they had the structure and process in place—but even so—something went terribly wrong.

The perception is that corporate governance practice descended into ticking the right boxes, while substance was missing. This perception is leading to a shift in thinking about what makes for good governance. An example of the perils of box-ticking, and the need for substance, can be found in the area of executive compensation.[32] It is difficult to see how a director who is "doing the right thing" could approve some compensation schemes that are at astronomical levels. Payments of tens if not hundreds of millions of dollars for average or below-average performance and option stock increasing in value to similar levels purely because of a rising stock market are not justifiable. Yet directors continue to engage in box-ticking to justify extreme remuneration and incentive packages, for example, by holding meetings and discussing information obtained from compensation consultants. Current corporate governance thinking should now focus on encouraging the sort of culture that will ensure that directors instinctively know how to "do the right thing," so that governance measures in areas such as executive compensation do not merely represent box-ticking, or "burnt offerings" in the language of Micah. In this regard, Chairman William H. Donaldson of the SEC has advocated that the board, the CEO, and senior management should try to set the right "tone at the top" of the organization, by emphasizing high standards of ethics and business conduct through internal communications.[33] In his view, a good approach to corporate governance should be so ingrained in the culture of an organization so as to become "part of their companies' DNA."[34]

An example of a company setting the right "tone at the top," with encouragement and monitoring by a board, is Tyco International, Ltd. (hereinafter Tyco). As part of the corporate governance reforms instituted in the wake of the corporate malfeasance of then-CEO Dennis Kozlowski and other senior members of management, Tyco's new CEO, Ed Breen, with the encouragement and support of the board, made it clear at the outset that he would insist on the highest standards of business practices and ethics from each of the 260,000 Tyco employees worldwide. The new management team at Tyco created a comprehensive *Guide To Ethical Conduct,* which set forth rules of conduct relating to harassment, conflicts of interest, compliance with the law, and fraud.[35] The *Guide To Ethical Conduct* was translated into fourteen languages and published worldwide. In addition to stating the rules, the *Guide To Ethical Conduct* offered employees vignettes on problematic situations and was supplemented by short videos dramatizing the scenarios. The *Guide To Ethical Conduct* was rolled out in mid-2003 and distributed and explained to employees worldwide. If the "tone at the top" was so articulated to 260,000 employees, the board could do no less than be a model for them and the stockholders.

In addition to drawing up structural requirements and setting the right "tone at the top," to "do the right thing" directors need access to the information required for them to exercise wise business judgment as custodians of "locked-in" investor capital. The need for directors to be adequately informed links into the fiduciary duties framework, as directors should make decisions only after receiving and processing relevant information in order to act as true fiduciaries. The requirement to be informed is exactly the same for management and nonmanagement directors, even though nonmanagement directors lack meaningful access to information and are reliant on management in providing it.

The difficulty in nonmanagement board members becoming informed enough to make those good faith decisions on behalf of the company is exacerbated by the fact that most boards meet infrequently and usually for short periods of time. To overcome these obstacles, each board needs a leader who will set the agenda for each meeting and coordinate information dissemination for each director. The board should ideally be led by an independent director for a number of reasons. First, the interests of the board and management may diverge in many respects, so management cannot necessarily be relied on to tell the board everything it needs to know, particularly when problems and failures are involved. Second, the function of evaluating senior management is entrusted to the board, so it follows that this process should be led by someone who is independent from management. Third, the activities of board committees and meetings of independent directors in executive session should, as a matter of logic, be coordinated by a director who is independent from management. Finally, companies require independent judgment and a level head, particularly in times of crisis, and boards need to be steered through those times by someone who is separate from a likely source of the crisis—management.

At present, the board leader at many companies is also the CEO of the company. This situation is unsatisfactory for the reasons noted above. However, stripping the CEO of the chairman title may send a negative message to investors and regulators that the directors do not have confidence in management. Instead, the issue of independent leadership should be dealt with in succession planning and implemented in time through the succession process.

But fiduciary duties, new structures and processes, tone at the top, information flow, and independent leadership do not fully assure us of the trust we need that directors will "do the right thing" when faced with the inevitable tough issues, such as compensation.

Corporate governance must, and will, move beyond focusing on structural requirements to the more amorphous concepts such as honesty, loyalty, integrity, and ethics. This will occur because the passage of time has shown that laundry lists of "must do's" can never spell out how a director should respond to every situation presented. Corporate governance best practice should, and will, require directors to be hardwired to "do the right thing" in every aspect of decision-making. The three visions articulated at the outset as the soil of good governance require this to be so. Individual rights, such as corporations and their boards and managers enjoy in the market, require significant personal individual responsibilities. Board structures and processes are necessary but not sufficient. Proscribed "burnt offerings"—box-ticking—will not substitute for character.

The challenge going forward will be how to identify whether each person being nominated and elected as a director possesses the character and individual "moral compass" to allow him or her to do what is best for the company, its investors, and the broader community. Armed with this fresh "moral compass" perspective, the private sector and corporate governance scholars now need to think hard about how such directors can be identified objectively. Once this occurs, the pendulum can safely begin a swing back to Adam Smith's ethical "man" as the primary safeguard of efficient markets, a situation infinitely more preferable than markets capsizing under the weight of more and more government regulation. Directors who have demonstrable moral compasses have little to fear in the courtroom, as the courts are inclined to seek out and identify ethical qualities and are less likely to impose liability upon a person who is thought to possess them.

We may fail in this endeavor to engender reasons to trust, and if we do, we can be sure of another crisis in governance, followed by even more intrusive regulation.

NOTES

Special thanks to Weil, Gotshal and Manges LLP associate Rebecca C. Grapsas and partner Holly J. Gregory for contributing valuable input and insights to the preparation of this chapter.

1. The Declaration of Independence (1776), paragraphs 2–3.

2. The Grace Institute (February 5, 1998), *Micah,* at http://www.gcfweb.org/institute/prophet/micah.html

3. The Declaration of Independence (1776); Adam Smith (1776), *The Wealth of Nations.*

4. Adam Smith (1759), *The theory of moral sentiments.*

5. Ibid.

6. Ibid.

7. Ibid.

8. Peter M. Garber (1989), Tulipmania, *J. Pol. Econ.,* 97, 535.

9. Larry E. Ribstein (2002), Market vs. regulatory responses to corporate fraud: A critique of the Sarbanes-Oxley Act of 2002, *J. Corp. L.,* 28, 1, 19.

10. *S.E.C. v. Texas Gulf Sulphur Co.,* 401 F. 2d 833 (2d Cir. 1968).

11. *Escott v. BarChris Const. Corp.,* 283 F. Supp. 643 (S.D.N.Y. 1968).

12. A chrysler crisis for IOU's (1979, August 20) *Business Week,* 112.

13. *Dirks v. S.E.C.,* 463 U.S. 646 (1983).

14. Adolph Berle and Gardiner Means (1932), *The Modern Corporation and Private Property.*

15. See, for example, William O. Douglas (1934), Directors who don't direct, *Harv. L. Rev.,* 47, 1305; The Business Roundtable (1978), Statement on the role and composition of the board of directors of the large publicly owned corporation; The Business Roundtable (1981) Statement on corporate responsibility; The Business Roundtable (1983) Statement on the American Law Institute's proposed "Principles of corporate Governance and Structure: Restatement and Recommendations"; Winthrop Knowlton and Ira M. Millstein, Can the board of directors help the American corporation earn the immortality it holds so dear? in *The U.S. business corporation: An institution in transition* (1988), 169, as well as the Institutional Investor Project at the Center for Law and Economics, Columbia University School of Law, which commenced in 1987.

16. See, for example, Delaware General Corporation Law, Del. Code Ann. Tit. 8, sec. 141(a) (2004).

17. The Business Roundtable (1978), Statement on the role and composition of the board of directors of the large publicly owned corporation.

18. The Business Roundtable (1981), Statement on corporate responsibility.

19. American Law Institute (1994), *Principles of corporate governance: Analysis and recommendations.*

20. General Motors Board of Directors (1994, January), *Corporate governance guidelines on significant corporate governance issues.*

21. CalPERS (1995, May 31), press release, CalPERS announces results of governance survey.

22. New York Stock Exchange Listed Company Manual (1986), sec. 3.03.

23. SEC Rule 14a-2(b), 17 C.F.R. sec. 240.14a-2(b) (2003).

24. For example, boards of public companies in the United States must be comprised of a majority of directors who fulfill certain independence requirements. At a basic level, these independence criteria focus on the existence of contractual, employment, and familial relationships that could reasonably be expected to result in a conflict of interest. In addition, boards must have at least three standing committees—an audit committee, a compensation committee, and a nominating and corporate governance committee. Each of these committees must be comprised entirely of independent directors and must have a written charter setting out enumerated responsibilities. Audit committee members bear an especially large workload, ranging from approving the financial statements and internal controls to whistle-blowing and risk management. The board is also the repository of other, legislated responsibilities. These mainly relate to the making of significant decisions affecting the company, including whether a dividend should be declared, whether the company should merge with another company, and whether the company should be dissolved. See Sarbanes-Oxley (2002), sec. 301; New York Stock Exchange Listed Company Manual (2003), sec. 303A; NASD Rules (2004), sec. 4350; Delaware General Corporation Law, Del. Code Ann. Tit. 8 (2004), secs. 170, 251, 275.

25. The restructure of the board of the Tennessee Valley Authority (TVA) provides a recent example of renewed focus on the board. The changes included converting the board from part-time to full-time, expanding it from three members to nine, giving the board authority to choose its own chairman and CEO, and requiring that seven board members reside in the TVA's service area: Conference report on H.R. 4818, Consolidated Appropriations Act of 2005 (Tenn.); TVA board restructured under omnibus appropriations bill (2004, November 29), *Daily Report for Executives,* A-2.

26. United Nations General Assembly (2002, March 1), Draft outcome of the International Conference on Financing for Development: Monterrey consensus, 5.

27. Margaret M. Blair (2004), Reforming corporate governance: What history can teach us, *Berkeley Bus. L.J., 1,* 1; Margaret M. Blair, Locking in capital: What corporate law achieved for business organizers in the nineteenth century, *UCLA L. Rev., 51,* 387.

28. E. Norman Veasey (2004, October 14), *Juxtaposing Best Practices and Delaware Corporate Jurisprudence,* Second Annual Directors' Institute on Corporate Governance, Practicing Law Institute, New York, N.Y.

29. Ibid.

30. Delaware General Corporation Law (2004), Del. Code Ann. Tit. 8, sec. 327.

31. Andrew Osterland (2002), Board games: Board reform is essential. Too bad it may backfire, *CFO, 18* (12), 34.

32. Mark van Clieaf (2004), Executive accountability and executive compensation: A new test for director liability, *The Corporate Governance Advisor, 12* (6), 1.

33. William H. Donaldson (2003, March 24), *Remarks at the 2003 Washington Economic Policy Conference,* National Association for Business Economics, Washington, DC, at http://www.sec.gov/news/speech/spch032403whd.htm

34. William H. Donaldson (2003, July 30), *Remarks to the National Press Club,* Washington, DC, at http://www.sec.gov/news/speech/spch073003whd.htm

35. Tyco International, Ltd. (2003), *Tyco Guide To Ethical Conduct,* at http://www.tyco.com/pdf/tyco_guide_to_ethical_conduct.pdf

2

The Rise of Corporate Governance

SIR ADRIAN CADBURY

It is natural to begin any discussion of the rise to prominence of corporate governance, as a major economic and political issue, by asking why its emergence should have been so recent. It is the power and accountability of corporations that lie at the heart of corporate governance, and corporations have been exercising power with or without accountability since the seventeenth century. In earlier years, nations relied on statutory regulation to control corporations and prevent the abuse of monopoly power. While writers like Adam Smith recognized in the eighteenth century the threats posed by the corporate form,[1] the governance of business did not effectively begin to attract the attention of politicians, economists, or the wider public until after the First World War.

It is not as if corporate fraud and financial disasters were uncommon in those formative years, but they do not generally seem to have been attributed to lapses in governance. The South Sea bubble of 1720 is an example from Britain of the way in which it was the promoters of speculative enterprises rather than those who directed them who were held responsible when they failed. This spectacular financial scandal was promoted by the Tory government of the day and involved the South Sea company taking over part of the national debt. Robert Walpole for the Whig opposition spoke against the proposal in Parliament in words that have a modern ring: "The great principle of the project was an evil of the first magnitude; it was to raise artificially the value of the stock, by exciting and keeping up a general infatuation and by

promising dividends out of funds which would not be adequate for the purpose."[2]

South Sea stock rose from 128 to 300 in three months and by June 1721
reached 1,050 before collapsing as Walpole had foretold. Corrupt politicians
and speculative mania were held to blame, not the directors of the company.
While there was an ineffective regulatory response in the form of a Bubble Act,
the reaction to the scandal probably reflected a generally robust view that it
was up to investors to judge the competence and honesty of those with whom
they placed their money, not the authorities. In addition, investing in companies was limited to those with the means to do so. It is when the fortunes of
large and representative masses of the public are in the balance, as they are
with today's pension funds, that the governance of companies has to become a
significant political and social matter. As a footnote, Robert Walpole bought
stock and sold out before the crash and became prime minister on the strength
of his reputation for financial competence.

It was in the nineteenth century that company law in Britain began to introduce regulations concerning the formation and structure of companies. The
Joint Stock Companies Act of 1844 required unincorporated companies to
register and be brought under some degree of control to protect those investing
in them. The key change, however, came with the introduction of the concept
of limited liability in 1862. This enabled the members of a company to limit
their liability to their stake in the business and not to be exposed to claims
beyond their stake in the event of disaster. The logic of this change had everything to do with encouraging investment and putting the savings and increasing wealth of the country to productive use. It was an economic measure
designed to promote enterprise, although it did require directors to accept
certain responsibilities in their conduct of their companies. These restrictions,
however, still left directors with a fairly free hand, and therefore their power to
govern their businesses well or ill, honestly or dishonestly, did not give rise to
political challenge.[3]

That challenge first appeared in Europe with the introduction of the supervisory board structure in Germany. In 1870, Bismarck had the Companies
Act Amendment Act passed, which made supervisory boards compulsory for
joint stock companies. Although today, the German two-tier board tends to be
associated with employee representation that was a development of the 1950s.
The fact that, at a later date, the two-tier structure enabled employees to be
represented at the board level is nevertheless an interesting reflection on the
adaptability of this significant governance initiative. However, the supervisory
board system was devised specifically to strengthen the control of shareholders, particularly banks, over the companies in which they had invested. It
developed into a means of clearly separating the control function of the supervisory board from the executive function of the management board. It
represented the first overt political move in Europe to curb corporate power.

There are a number of reasons why corporate governance could not be expected to figure to any great extent on the political agenda of the eighteenth and nineteenth centuries. National goals would have been to encourage enterprise and the creation of wealth, not to impose restrictions on those who were expected to achieve these goals. There was also surely the view in less regulated days that it was up to investors to judge those whom they should trust with their money; they after all had most to gain or lose. The role of the state was to provide a relatively open legal framework that would nevertheless give investors some recourse against duplicity. More generally, the influence of corporations in the past was much less widely significant than it became in the last century.

By the 1920s, however, corporations whose shares were quoted on the stock market were economically important in the United States and in Britain, and their fortunes were beginning to affect broader constituencies. The debate about their governance really got under way when Berle and Means in *The Modern Corporation and Private Property*[4] drew attention to the increasing separation of the ownership of corporations from their management. Their concern was with the growing power of large corporations, which they felt might one day challenge the power of the state, and with the inability of shareholders to exercise effective control over boards of directors whom they nominally elected. This lack of accountability arose not simply because ownership had become divorced from management, but because that ownership was dispersed.

The Liberal Party in Britain set up an inquiry into the country's economy at much the same time and came to similar conclusions about the lack of corporate accountability, due to what they referred to as "diffused ownership." They described the governance situation as one in which boards of directors played little part: "The truth is that a strong and possibly efficient management rather likes to have an ineffective Board which will know too little to have views or to interfere; and the ineffective Board enjoys its fees."[5]

In both countries, therefore, the governance picture could be summarized as one of weak boards, powerful executives, and shareholders unable to hold either boards or executives effectively to account. Shareholders did, however, have the ability to sell their shares in companies in which they had lost confidence. This constituted a degree of market regulation and was, in a sense, an advantage of dispersed ownership whatever its other drawbacks. It is also probable that individual executives rather than boards were perceived to be in charge, and thus the success or failure of their enterprises would be put down to their abilities or lack of them. The remedy would then be more one of selecting the right executives, "strong and possibly efficient managers" to quote the Liberal inquiry, than of attending to the governance structure of the corporation itself.

THE RELEVANCE OF QUOTED COMPANIES

This is an appropriate point at which to be reminded that publicly quoted shareholder-owned enterprises were and are the exception in terms of corporate form around the world. Family firms are the dominant form of business internationally, and they continue to hold that position in Asia, the Pacific, and much of Europe. In Europe outside Britain, banks provide capital on a larger scale than investors, and many quoted corporations have a single controlling or block shareholder, which again is common in Canada. In addition, there is still a degree of state involvement, although that has been reduced through privatization, which in turn has added to the ranks of shareholders. At the time of the report on corporate governance in the Netherlands, only two countries had a stock exchange capitalization greater than their GDP: Switzerland and the UK. This compares with figures of 19 percent for Italy, 24 percent for Germany, and 32 percent for France.[6]

While the United States, Britain, and Australia are exceptional as regards the significance of shareholder-owned corporations in their economies, it is nevertheless logical to focus on their contribution to corporate governance. It was those countries and their corporations that set the pace in the development of corporate governance structures and processes. Not only that, but it was the governance standards that they established which corporations in other countries in the end had to match regardless of their sources of finance.

Corporations everywhere work within boundaries. Those boundaries are set by laws, regulations, their own constitutions, their sources of finance or their shareholders, and by public opinion. These frameworks, derived from history and culture, vary country by country, and their boundaries change through time. The growth in the importance of the issue of corporate social responsibility in many countries is an example of a boundary change driven by public opinion. The movement to raise standards of corporate governance is directed at strengthening the accountability of corporations within whatever national frameworks they carry on their activities.

In shareholder-owned corporations, the governance focus is on boards of directors. Boards are the bridge between the providers of funds and those who put those funds to use. It is their task to appoint the executives and ensure that they act in the interests of the investors. They are also the link between the corporation and the outside world; they are responsible for the reputations of their corporations, and they are the guardians of the values of their corporations. The UK committee that I chaired defined corporate governance as "the system by which companies are directed and controlled."[7] It is the function of the board to govern, that is to direct and control. The distinction between direction, which is the job of the board, and management, which is the task of the executives, needs to be crystal clear in any form of organization, if its governance is to be effective. If that distinction is not understood and maintained, it is not possible to know where authority lies within an organization nor who can be held accountable for decisions.

WHAT PUT GOVERNANCE ON THE AGENDA?

Governance became an issue through two routes. First, financial sectors in some countries, like Britain, became concerned about investors and the public losing confidence in the integrity of their markets, when publicly owned companies collapsed without warning. Such failures raised questions over the reliability of reports and accounts, over the value of audits, and over the effectiveness of accounting standards. Boards of directors are collectively responsible for the financial control and reporting of their corporations, therefore the spotlight in those cases turned on how adequately they were discharging their responsibilities.

Second, shareholdings began to become more concentrated and moved into the portfolios of institutional investors. These investors had the resources to monitor board performance and to gain access to board members when dissatisfied with the way the companies in which they had invested were being run. The era of the active investor had begun. The first answer to dissatisfaction with corporate performance, notably in the United States, was to encourage another management group to bid for the corporation concerned and take control of it.

To its proponents, the takeover was the answer to the problem of inefficient governance. A free market in the control of assets was the magic bullet. It would restore accountability, provided the takeover was wholly or mainly for debt, and it would improve performance given that the successful bidder could self-evidently make better use of the assets involved. The peculiar attraction of the takeover approach, as a means of raising levels of performance, was that it put all boards that might be bid targets on notice to raise their game. For a number of reasons, however, takeovers did not fully live up to the claims of their advocates and at times they were simply an expensive and disruptive means of bringing about changes in top management.

THE INVESTING INSTITUTIONS

The next stage, with the United States in the lead, was for some investing institutions to use their voting power and influence by engaging directly with boards. Their interventions were usually targeted at bringing about changes in corporate strategy or board leadership. U.S. institutions, for example, caused some of the largest and apparently most powerful corporations, like General Motors and IBM, to change their board structures and replace their chief executives. They brought about these changes by bringing pressure to bear on the outside, nonexecutive members of these boards, prodding them to take action. At least some boards were being made to govern.

The focus on the duties of boards intensified when, in 1970, Penn Central collapsed without warning. It was the sixth-largest U.S. corporation at the time, and the Securities and Exchange Commission was sufficiently alarmed to institute an inquiry into its failure. One of their conclusions was: "The somnolent Penn Central board . . . was typical of most giant corporations' boards in the post-war period."[8] Too many boards were in effect sleeping partners, not actively directing and controlling their corporations. Power lay in the hands of the executive managers rather than in those of the board.

As the institutions emerged as the largest owners of shares in mature markets, they had on the one hand the power to make their influence felt, but on the other hand they were no longer able collectively to walk away from board problems by selling their shares. Around 80 percent of the shares of British corporations are in the hands of institutions, and pension funds alone own about one-third of those shares. The institutions as a class are becoming increasingly locked in. The only way even for indexed funds to improve their returns is to ginger up the laggardly performing boards of corporations whose shares they hold in their portfolios.

THE UK CORPORATE GOVERNANCE COMMITTEE

In addition to the impact of the growing concentration of share ownership, there were the concerns of the financial sector, in centers like London, that corporate failures were undermining confidence in the reliability and accuracy of financial reporting. The UK corporate governance committee that I was asked to chair was established by the London Stock Exchange, the Financial Reporting Council (responsible for UK accounting standards), and the accountancy profession. All of them had a direct interest in raising standards of corporate governance, which had been put in question by significant corporate failures.

Two of the corporations whose collapse gave cause for concern were Polly Peck and Coloroll. It was not so much that they had collapsed, as that their reports and audited accounts just prior to their failure appeared to give no indication of the true state of their financial affairs. The London Stock Exchange was concerned about business moving to competing exchanges whose reporting standards might be thought to be higher, while the main accounting firms were concerned with their reputations and with the doubts being cast on the value of their audit statements. The Financial Reporting Council was concerned with loose accounting standards allowing boards too much scope to manipulate their results to meet the expectations of the stock market.

It may be useful to say something about the way in which the first UK corporate governance committee came to its conclusions and drew up its Code of Best Practice, given the number of other countries that have followed a similar path. The committee was asked to report on the nature of the problems of corporate governance and recommend what action needed to be taken to restore confidence in the country's corporate system. Although the committee was set up specifically to deal with the financial aspects of corporate governance, it had hardly started work before the Bank of Credit and Commerce International failed, with reverberations that are still being felt more than ten years later, and the Robert Maxwell scandal broke. The need to take the lessons from these disasters into account widened the committee's remit beyond the financial aspects of corporate governance to that of corporate governance itself.

The committee reported to the three sponsoring institutions that funded its work. Although the UK government was not directly involved, they shared the concern about the country's governance standards and seconded a senior civil servant to be the committee's secretary. The committee's definition of corporate governance, to which reference has already been made, was, "the system by which companies are directed and controlled." The committee began its work in May 1991 by asking interested organizations and individuals to give them their views on what they saw as the deficiencies in existing governance structures and processes and on what actions needed to be taken to remedy them. The committee received a good response to its call for evidence, much of which pointed to the need for greater clarity over the role of corporate directors, collectively and individually.

The committee, therefore, worked at drawing up a brief code of best practice for boards of directors, backed by a more detailed report[9] that explained the reasoning lying behind the committee's code recommendations. In addition, the report made recommendations to institutional investors and to the accounting profession. The recommendations to institutional investors were that they should use their votes and declare their policies on the way in which they used them. The accounting recommendations centered on ways to increase the effectiveness and value of the audit process.

CODE OF BEST PRACTICE

It was the Code of Best Practice, however, that lay at the heart of the report. Its nineteen recommendations, which were set out on two pages, were addressed to boards of directors. While the code was primarily directed at the boards of publicly quoted companies, the report encouraged as many other companies as possible to aim at meeting its requirements. The code itself was literally based on best practice, on the practice of companies that were generally accepted as being well run. It was a statement of principles for boards to follow in ways that made sense in their particular circumstances and that carried the support of their shareholders. The code was in four sections, the first of which dealt with the role and responsibilities of the board. It covered board composition, the need for a formal schedule of matters to be reserved to the board for decision, and procedures for directors to take independent professional advice. It also addressed the question of whether the chief executive should be the chairman as well.

The second section dealt with the role of outside or nonexecutive directors. The recommendations here related to the need for the majority of them to be independent and for them to be selected by a formal process involving the board as a whole. The third section related to executive directors and made recommendations on how directors' pay should be determined and disclosed.

The final section focused on the board's responsibilities for reporting and controls. A key recommendation here was that boards should appoint audit committees made up of at least three outside, nonexecutive directors. Audit committees were not only important in themselves, and their establishment followed the U.S. lead in the matter, but this recommendation set the minimum number of outside directors that boards were required to have to comply with the code. Other recommendations included the board's duty to present a balanced and understandable assessment of its company's position and to report on the business as a going concern.

The recommendation also in this section that boards should report on the effectiveness of their system of internal control caused difficulty over its wording and raised concerns that it might unintentionally increase the legal liabilities of directors. The aim of the recommendation was that boards should not only have appropriate control systems in place, but that they should ensure they were working effectively. The debate over the wording of this recommendation has been resolved in the current guidance for boards contained in the UK Combined Code, which came into force in July 2003. This states that the board "should at least annually conduct a review of the effectiveness of the group's system of internal controls and should report to shareholders that they have done so."[10]

The corporate governance committee's intention was to strengthen the UK's unitary board system and improve its effectiveness, not to replace it. The objective was to make what was already in place work better and function more in accord with the theory on which it was based. The classical governance model for publicly quoted corporations was that the shareholders elected the directors, the directors appointed executives to run the corporation in the interests of the shareholders, and they answered to the shareholders in general meeting. In addition, the shareholders elected auditors who in the same way reported to them on the board's stewardship at the annual general meeting. The gap between theory and practice needs no underlining.

The aim of the code was to render boards of directors more accountable to shareholders and at the same time encourage shareholders to participate more actively in the governance of the companies in which they had invested. In the words of the report:

> The widespread adoption of our recommendations will turn in large measure on the support which all shareholders give to them. The obligation on companies to state how far they comply with the Code provides institutional and individual shareholders with a ready-made agenda for their representations to boards. It is

up to them to put it to good use. The Committee is primarily looking to such market-based regulation to turn its proposals into action.[11]

COMPLIANCE

Given that the committee's code, in common with the majority of similar codes around the world, did not have statutory backing, why should corporations comply with it? In the UK, the London Stock Exchange made it an obligation for companies listed on the exchange to report annually how far they complied with the Code of Best Practice's recommendations and state their reasons for areas of noncompliance. Listed companies did not have to comply with the code, but they did have to disclose the degree to which they complied. Compliance itself was left as a matter between boards and their shareholders.

The committee was clear that its job was to recommend a set of principles or guidelines for boards to follow, not to act as judge over whether corporations were adequately following those guidelines. Implementation was for the market to determine. That approach could only work, however, provided the market had accurate, intelligible, and up-to-date information on which to make its judgments. Equally, it required investors to play their part in the process, and to accept that they had both an interest in and a responsibility for standards of governance.

There were sound reasons for companies to comply with the UK code. It was genuinely based on best practice, and therefore following it helped boards to meet those standards. In the same way, companies that complied could expect compliance to be taken into account in their valuation by the market and possibly be reflected in their cost of capital. This in turn gave shareholders an incentive to persuade companies in which they had invested to comply. There was also the potential threat that market regulation of this kind might be displaced by statutory regulation, unless companies were seen to be acting on the code's recommendations.

The committee's Code of Best Practice was published in December 1992 and came into effect from the middle of the following year. In May 1995 the committee issued a study of compliance and then disbanded.[12] The study monitored compliance in relation to individual code recommendations and did so by size of company. Unsurprisingly, compliance was highest among larger companies, but the degree of compliance just less than two years after the code came into effect was encouraging. To give one example, the code included a recommendation that there should be an agreed procedure for directors to take independent professional advice in the furtherance of their duties. Only a few leading companies had such a procedure in place when the code came out, but by May 1995, 94 percent of the top five hundred companies had complied with this provision.

A further example concerns the question of whether the chief executive should also be chairman. The code was not prescriptive on the matter, because it was literally based on best practice, not on theoretical notions of best practice, and there were examples of highly regarded companies where the two posts were combined. The committee's report stated that, in principle, the posts should be separate because the two jobs were distinct and different. The code recommendation, however, concentrated on the safeguards that needed to be in place where the two posts were combined. It turned out that this was a matter on which institutional investors had clear views and one on which, unusually at that time, they were prepared to act. As a result, although in 1989 half of the top one thousand UK listed companies had a combined chairman and chief executive, by 1994 that proportion was down to less than one-quarter, as a result of investor pressure. Here was an example of the code providing a lead, but with the market making its own judgments and putting them into effect. This was the way in which market regulation was intended to work.

The approach that the committee adopted was christened "comply or explain." It was important to establish that these were accepted alternatives, and that it was not a case of "comply or else." Provided companies explained why they were not following a recommendation and carried their shareholders with them, this met the requirements of the code. That remains an accepted option, and a number of companies retained shareholder support for not fully complying with the code. The comply-or-explain approach has been adopted widely and taken up by the European Commission in its consultation on the role in listed companies of nonexecutive or supervisory directors.

THE REPORT IN RETROSPECT

Clearly a question that does arise is whether with hindsight the committee would have acted differently. For myself, I would still advocate the comply-or-explain approach and reliance on the market, with one exception, which relates to the recommendation on audit committees. My view now would be that there is a case for making the establishment of a properly constituted audit committee a statutory requirement for any organization that takes public money.

Other issues the committee dealt with in its report were the "quarantining" of the audit function from other services provided by audit firms and the compulsory rotation of audit firms. Both were raised in the context of the need to strengthen the objectivity of the audit process. The committee's recommendation on quarantining was that companies should disclose in their annual reports the total cost of services, other than audit, which their auditors had provided worldwide. The UK Companies Act requirement was related solely to services provided in the UK; this did not necessarily give shareholders the information they needed in order to judge the degree of independence of their auditors. The committee was again relying on the market, in the shape of shareholder influence, to monitor auditor objectivity. On compulsory rotation, at that stage the only evidence of this in practice was from Italy, and the evidence was not encouraging. I would expect the committee to remain today of the same mind over compulsory rotation, but that the question of the provision of services other than audit by auditors would be likely to result in a stronger recommendation, in the light of all that has happened since the publication of the report.

THE REGULATORY BALANCE

The point of principle that needs to be addressed, in reflecting on the committee's approach, is where the balance between statutory and market regulation should lie. Clearly both forms of regulation are needed. However, the governance framework within which corporations work varies country by country and, for a range of reasons, the United States could be expected to tilt the balance more in the direction of statutory regulation than Britain. Equally, there is a longer tradition of market or self-regulation in Britain than elsewhere in Europe. The UK Panel on Takeovers and Mergers, for example, has no statutory backing, but its rulings are accepted because those subject to them regard this form of regulation as being preferable to a statutory equivalent.

The advantages of using nonstatutory bodies of this kind are normally their speed of judgment, their relatively low cost, and their ability to deal with new issues as they arise; none of which are attributes of the statutory approach. A further benefit of nonstatutory regulation is that it can promote compliance, not just with the letter of the law, but with the intention behind it, thus setting a higher standard. Statutory regulation on the other hand has the advantages of relative certainty, enforceability, and therefore of fairness, since its decisions apply equally to all. Its capacity to regulate is, however, costly.

There are particular advantages in market regulation in the field of corporate governance, because important aspects of governance are not easily reduced to legally enforceable rules. The committee's Code of Best Practice referred, for example, to "non-executive directors of sufficient calibre."[13] This requires a qualitative judgment. It is one for which shareholders and financial commentators have shown themselves ready and able to make, but it would be difficult if not impossible to frame a legal regulation to the same end. Quite apart from the need for qualitative judgment in a number of governance areas, codes of best practice can in some instances be more effective in achieving their purpose than an equivalent law. For example, the committee's recommendation on the necessary safeguards should the chief executive of a company also be its chairman was worded as follows: "There should be a clearly accepted division of responsibilities at the head of a company, which will ensure a balance of power and authority, such that no one individual has unfettered powers of decision. Where the chairman is also the chief executive, it is essential that there should be a strong and independent element on the board, with a recognised senior member."[14]

If it were a legal requirement that the posts should be split and that companies should have both a chairman and a chief executive, the intent of the law could be subverted by appointing a cipher in one or the other post. The letter of the law would have been followed, but its purpose frustrated. No follow-up by investors would be possible, because the response would be that the board concerned had met its legal obligations. The code reference to a clear division of responsibilities, however, enabled shareholders, financial analysts, or the media to pursue the matter by asking precisely how responsibilities were divided and to press the point until they received a satisfactory answer.

Statutory regulation and market regulation both have their part to play in matters of governance; the balance between them will change through time and be driven by the perceived issues and priorities of the day. If codes of best practice lack any kind of teeth, the risk is that they will be followed by the well intentioned and ignored by the less conscientious, those whom above all the codes aim to influence. The UK committee's code would not have achieved the degree of compliance that it did if it had not had the authority of the London Stock Exchange behind it. The only obligation on listed companies was to disclose how far they complied with the code and to explain areas of noncompliance. It was hard for boards to justify nondisclosure, and in that sense the compliance requirement was not onerous.

The consequence of disclosure, however, was that it gave shareholders and financial commentators the basis for judging whether a company's governance structure was acceptable, or in need of strengthening in some way. Equally, it provided them with the information they required in order to enter into a constructive dialogue with the company concerned. Thus compliance with the disclosure requirement of the London Stock Exchange enabled the Code of Best Practice to achieve its aims without having to be enforced by further sanctions. The power of the code lay in opening up an informed debate between the principals, the boards, and their shareholders, and in setting an agenda for that debate.

GOVERNANCE CODES

Generalizing from the UK experience, what has been the part played by codes in the development of corporate governance? National codes of best governance practice have now been published in many countries around the world, a situation summed up by the headline in the February 2000 issue of the international newsletter *Governance*, "Code Epidemic Hits Portugal."[15] They have been initiated by industry associations, by governments, and by a variety of professional and financial organizations. They share certain characteristics. They do not have the force of law and typically their recommendations are couched in terms of governance principles to be followed by boards in ways that meet their particular circumstances and that carry the support of those who provide them with funds. Some degree of flexibility is needed to cater for the differences between corporations and between boards.

The principle on which governance codes are based is that of disclosure, or transparency. Codes aim to encourage boards to explain how they direct and control their enterprises. This enables all those with rights or responsibilities towards corporations to exercise those rights and responsibilities in an informed way. Disclosure is as much an opportunity for corporations to establish their business aims and principles as it is a means of enhancing their accountability. All else apart, openness is the basis of public trust in the corporate system. Justice Brandeis of the United States summed up the case for disclosure with his customary insight and authority when he wrote: "Sunlight is said to be the best of disinfectants: electric light the most efficient policeman."[16]

Another characteristic of governance codes is that they call for appropriate checks and balances in the governance structure of corporations, especially at the board level. Many headline corporate scandals have arisen because too much power was in too few hands. Quite apart from the importance of building in checks on individual power, there is also a positive need to involve boards as a whole, collectively, in the process of decision-making. It is essential for the proper working of boards that they should not become rubber stamps dominated by one powerful personality.

This leads on to the question of board composition. What kind of mix of individuals should boards and their chairmen aim to include? It is characteristic of codes that they include provisions for the appointment of board members who are free of the ties of management and can exercise independent judgment. There are inevitably possible conflicts between the interests of the executives and those of the corporation over such matters as executive pay, whether top management succession should be from within the company or from outside, takeover bids, and how the free cash flow should be apportioned between dividends to shareholders and reinvestment in the business, arguably to the benefit of the executives. As well as potential conflicts of interest, there is also the question of who is to judge the performance of the executive team. This can only be done by board members who are not involved in the management of the business. In the end, all these have to be decisions of the board as a whole, but independent outside directors are best placed to guide the board in taking decisions where personal interests could be in conflict with corporate ones.

INDEPENDENCE

The drawing up of codes has required some definition of what independence means and of who is independent. The UK committee defined independence as being "free from any business or other relationship which could materially interfere with the exercise of their independent judgment."[17] This meant that outside directors who were bankers or lawyers would not be classed as independent, nor would former executives, although they could all be valuable board members in their own right. While the exclusion of those with potential business interests and of those who have served as executives is clear cut, I am less convinced about arbitrary rules over length of board service or age debarring outside directors from being classed as independent. Independence at the end of the day is as much a state of mind as a function of age or service. My preference would be to treat such rules as guidelines and to leave the final decision on independence to shareholders. Shareholders can make such judgments only if they have full and relevant information about directors coming up for election. In the provision of that information, the United States is ahead compared with other countries, bringing us back once again to the overriding importance of disclosure.

There is a more general point to make about independence, and that relates to the manner in which outside directors are selected. Traditionally in Britain, chairmen put forward possible names to their boards, and their preferences normally prevailed. The drawbacks of this method of selection are self-evident. Directors tended to be drawn from too shallow a pool. They owed their position on the board largely to their chairmen, which to that extent undermined their independence, and the consequence was that boards were too much like clubs, and gentlemen's clubs at that. The UK code recommendation was that directors should be selected through a formal process, and that this process and their appointment should be a matter for the board as a whole. By a formal process, the committee meant that boards should consider their current balance of skills, backgrounds, age, and experience, and purposefully search for candidates who could fill gaps and thus bring additional value to the existing mix of board members. The object of involving the board as a whole was to get away from chairmanly patronage. Old habits die hard, but the great majority of UK boards have established nomination committees and have brought their selection process in line with the code recommendation, which carried strong shareholder support from the outset.

The selection of outside directors in the United States had similar consequences for independence, arguably to an even greater extent. Here given that the posts of chief executive and chairman were normally combined, it was possible for chief executives more or less to pick their outside board members. Once again the result was to draw outside directors from a shallow pool of those with similar backgrounds. It also made it difficult for them to challenge the person who had effectively appointed them, even when it might be in the corporation's interest to do so. As shareholder influence has grown, the matter of who is appointed to the boards of U.S. corporations and how they are selected has become a far more open issue.

It is worth commenting at this point on the differences between U.S. and UK boards. Using the same word to describe both bodies papers over those differences. Jonathan Charkham in his book *Keeping Good Company*,[18] which is a comparative study of corporate governance in the U.S., the UK, France,

Germany, and Japan, quotes Herzel and Shepro's description of a U.S. board meeting. "The CEO would probably be the chairman of the meeting and completely in charge. Generally, he controls both the agenda and the flow of information to the directors. He dominates the meeting and the board plays a quite secondary role."[19] Whatever the degree of realism in that description, it brings out the power relationship between the chief executive and the board when he or she is also chairman. In the UK, the board would normally be in charge, and the board is essentially a collegiate body reaching its decisions by consensus under an independent chairman, with the chief executive reporting to it. In a way it mirrors the differences in the political structures of the two countries. There is presidential rule in the United States and cabinet rule in the UK, even if some prime ministers edge toward a presidential role. The key points are, however, that the same governance labels do not necessarily mean the same thing in different countries, and that the unitary board structure can accommodate different governance models.

What contribution have codes of best practice made to the development of corporate governance in general? First and foremost, they have put corporate governance firmly on the board agenda. Boards had structures and processes in place for directing and controlling their corporations before, but it was unusual for boards to have brought together these two elements, which tended to be seen as separate, and thereby to have reviewed their governance system as a whole. However willingly or reluctantly boards around the world reacted to the advent of governance codes, they gave thought to the manner in which they needed to respond to them, and this put corporate governance squarely on the business map. The fact that national codes of best practice addressed the governance issues that were relevant to the countries concerned and therefore differed in detail was no drawback. The central issues of disclosure, of clarity over the role of the board, of the need for checks and balances in the governance structure, and for having an effective independent element on the board were common to all codes. The later emergence of generally accepted governance principles applied internationally was fostered by the growing influence of international institutional investors and by the increasing importance of international capital markets. It marks the next step in the development of corporate governance.

Reflecting more generally on the manner in which corporate governance has developed, codes of best practice would seem to have been devised more in response to the demand for higher and more consistent governance standards, than to have been in themselves the driving force to raise those standards. In that sense, they were more an effect than a cause of the way in which corporate governance has developed.

INTERNATIONAL CODES

The next major step in the development of corporate governance came when codification moved from the national to the international stage. The

Organisation for Economic Co-operation and Development (OECD) asked a business sector advisory group under the admirable chairmanship of Ira Millstein of the United States to prepare a corporate governance report. The report, published in April 1998, was titled *Corporate Governance: Improving Competitiveness and Access to Capital in Global Markets.*[20] The report sets out guidelines for countries establishing their own corporate governance frameworks, but makes it clear that there is no question of "one size fits all." Every country has to start from where it stands in matters of governance, and from its existing balance of law and market regulation. It then has to decide on the measures necessary to bring its governance standards up to those that will meet the requirements of international investors. The reason this marks a new stage of development is that national codes were basically aimed at raising corporate governance standards to improve the performance of individual corporations and to make them more accountable to their shareholders or their providers of funds. International codes have the broader task of encouraging investment and enabling funds to flow where in the world they can be best put to use and promote economic growth.

The OECD report made the point that there was no single universal model of corporate governance and that, therefore, experimentation and variety should be expected and encouraged. It set out, however, some fundamental parameters:

- Increasingly, it is accepted that the corporate objective is maximizing shareholder value, which not only requires superior competitive performance but also generally requires responsiveness to the demands and expectations of other stakeholders.
- Increased transparency and independent oversight of management by boards of directors are the central elements of improved corporate governance.
- Board practice should be subject to voluntary adaptation and evolution, in an environment of globally understood minimum standards.
- There are certain areas in which the adoption of universal rules is preferable (such as in accounting).[21]

Two points, referred to in those parameters, are examples of the way in which corporate governance was beginning to broaden its scope. First, the essential part that accounting standards played in governance was becoming fully recognized. There had been a general appreciation of the need for national accounting standards to be tightened in parallel with the development of governance principles in order to raise standards of financial reporting and control. Here, however, we have a cautious call for a move toward one set of internationally recognized accounting standards. Universal rules were seen to aid transparency and the efficient allocation of capital. Adoption of internationally accepted accounting standards is now firmly on the world governance agenda.

The second point is the reference to stakeholders. It is important to recognize the philosophical difference between the U.S./UK concept of market capitalism and the variations on that model that are seen in many other parts of the world. Oversimplifying the differences and comparing Britain with much of the rest of Europe, quoted corporations are regarded in Britain as enterprises based on the capital invested in them by their shareholders. The key relationship in a capitalistic enterprise of this kind is between owners and managers, hence the emphasis in Britain on the rights and responsibilities of shareholders.

In countries like France, Germany, and the Netherlands, the accent is more on corporations being basically partnerships between capital and labor. Corporations are seen as being coalitions of interests and as serving a wider social and economic purpose beyond that of providing a return to shareholders. Emphasis is therefore placed on the relationships with employees, on the place of corporations in the community, and on their contribution to the cohesion of society. This is in contrast to the rights of shareholders, especially minority shareholders, which have in the past received scant consideration.

The broader Continental European concept of the place of corporations in society emphasizes that the success of capitalistic enterprises, particularly in the medium to long term, depends on more than the support of their shareholders alone. Employees, customers, suppliers, bankers, creditors, and the community all have a part to play in determining the fortunes of corporations. They are referred to as stakeholders, although that is not an entirely accurate description, and constituencies would seem to be a more appropriate designation. The question that arises is: What should the relationship be between corporations and the constituencies they serve?

The OECD reference to stakeholders encompasses both the U.S./UK approach to capitalism and the Continental European or Japanese models. In practice those models are tending toward convergence. Taking Europe as an example, competition has forced Continental European corporations to focus more sharply on their financial objectives and their rates of return on capital. In the same way, their need for funds has led them to give greater consideration to providing value to their shareholders. Shareholder groups have sprung up in Continental Europe, where previously investors had no collective voice, and they are having an increasing influence on corporate policies. Corporations have even had to back down on deals that overrode the rights of minorities. The importance of the role of corporations in society continues to be recognized, but it is tempered by giving greater recognition to the place of shareholders in the corporate framework.

Equally, what appeared in the UK to be an exclusive focus on returns to shareholders has been broadened to take account of the increasing interest in the issue of corporate social responsibility. While accountability remains legally to shareholders, corporations accept that they have responsibilities to the constituencies on whom they depend for success, and that these include the societies they serve. Institutional investors take the same view. Hermes, a leading UK pension fund, has set out in its statement of general principles: "A company run in the long-term interests of its shareholders will need to manage effectively its relationships with its employees, suppliers, and customers and with regard to the common weal."[22]

The Business Sector Advisory Group's report recommended that regulatory intervention should be directed and limited to ensuring fairness, transparency, accountability, and responsibility. The report's recommendations were followed up by the OECD itself appointing a task force representative for all member states. The task force set out to develop a nonbinding statement of core principles that each country could then adapt to its own particular needs and values. These were:

- Protection of shareholder rights.
- Equitable treatment of all shareholders, including foreign and minority shareholders.
- A corporate governance framework that would recognize the rights of stakeholders as established by law and encourage active cooperation between companies and stakeholders in creating wealth, jobs, and sustainable enterprises.
- The framework should ensure disclosure of timely and accurate information on the financial situation, performance, ownership, and governance of the company.
- The framework should ensure strategic guidance and effective monitoring by boards and board accountability to the company and its shareholders.

The task force report was published as *OECD Principles of Corporate Governance* in 1999.[23]

Another international body, the Commonwealth Association for Corporate Governance, also drew up guidance on corporate governance for the countries that they represented, at much the same time as the OECD. Their stated aim was to establish capacity "in all Commonwealth countries to create or reinforce institutions to promote best practice in corporate governance; in particular, codes of good practice establishing standards of behaviour in the public and private sector should be agreed to secure greater transparency, and to reduce corruption."[24]

The CACG guidelines extend the influence of the corporate governance movement in two ways. First, until these guidelines were framed, governance had largely been seen as a matter for corporations in the private sector, with their publication the public sector was to be included as well. This is salutary, both because of the importance of the public sector in many countries and because the public sector is often less effectively accountable than the private sector. The second development lay in the specific promotion of best practice in corporate governance with the aim of reducing corruption. This brought an ethical as well as an economic dimension into the guidelines, and again the question of standards of behavior remains an issue as much for the public as for the private sector.

The third international body to promote higher standards of corporate governance has been the World Bank. The bank's president, James D. Wolfensohn, notably declared in 1999: "The proper governance of companies will become as crucial to the world economy as the proper governing of countries."[25] The World Bank through its Global Corporate Governance Forum is following James Wolfensohn's lead by offering practical help and guidance to countries on ways of raising their standards of corporate governance. The forum provides relevant training material in a variety of forms and encourages the spread of best governance practice through seminars and conferences. The World Bank emphasizes the role that corporate governance can play in promoting economic and social development. The forum's publication in its Focus series, *Corporate Governance and Development,*[26] concludes that there is a positive relationship at the level of the firm between good governance and good performance. On this rests the economic case for helping countries, especially those in the course of development, to improve their standards of corporate governance.

The World Bank is equally concerned about the ability of developing countries to attract the investment they need if they are to make the most of their opportunities. Private capital has become the prime source of funds for investment worldwide. That investment is to an increasing extent in the hands of institutions that act as intermediaries. In that role, a role that incidentally raises issues about their governance and accountability, they place the funds for which they are responsible wherever in the world they consider those funds will earn acceptable returns. They are seeking a spread of risk and reward and, in coming to a judgment on this, standards of corporate governance have a measurable part to play. It is recognized that resources will flow to those countries whose corporate governance frameworks inspire trust. The World Bank thus has a direct interest in promoting best practice in governance as part of its mission to alleviate poverty and raise standards of living and the quality of life throughout the world.

CONVERGENCE

There is another aspect of the role of institutional investors in governance. They represent one of the forces that are bringing about a degree of international convergence in corporate governance standards. International institutional investors look for the same levels of board effectiveness, transparency, accountability, and financial probity wherever in the world they invest. As a consequence, countries and corporations have to meet their governance standards. The capital markets of the world are the other force for convergence. Expanding corporations, wherever they are situated, are likely to need to tap international capital markets, either because they have outgrown their domestic sources of capital or in order to raise their funds on better terms. They will be able to access international capital on favorable terms only provided that they meet the disciplines of the market in respect of the accuracy and transparency of their financial reporting and the adequacy of their systems of financial control.

As a result, institutional investors and capital markets are between them bringing about a degree of governance convergence worldwide. It is, however, a convergence of standards, not of structures. There is no call for corporations all to adopt the same governance forms, provided that they achieve the same governance aims. Institutional investors have had a further part to play in influencing corporate governance standards, first at a national and then at an international level. The guidelines published by Hermes, a leading UK pension fund, have already been mentioned, in connection with their reference to the need for companies to manage their external relationships with regard to the interests of society. Their publication explains that the guidelines set out the policies that Hermes will normally apply in respect of its clients' holdings: "We do, however, accept the need for flexibility and that application should be governed by the spirit rather than the letter of the various codes. These guidelines therefore will be applied by Hermes pragmatically taking into account the specific circumstances of individual companies."[27]

TIAA-CREF and CalPERS are leading U.S. pension funds that have a track record of active engagement with the corporations in which they have invested. They have also published guidelines for companies at home and abroad in which they are potential investors. TIAA-CREF's *Policy Statement on Corporate Governance* concludes: "While this statement is intended primarily for domestic corporations, we will endeavour to apply comparable principles, as appropriate, in voting proxies on the foreign corporations in our portfolio."[28] CalPERS heads its statement, *CalPERS Global Corporate Governance Principles*,[29] but went further in publishing country-specific guidelines, which took account of the governance regime in each of the countries concerned. The major investing institutions were, therefore, lending their support to the application of governance codes that were in force nationally and at the same time by applying their principles internationally they were assisting the process of bringing about governance convergence around the world.

CORPORATE SOCIAL RESPONSIBILITY

A different aspect of governance has come into prominence with the emergence of corporate social responsibility as a public and shareholder issue. It focuses on the external relations of corporations, on the relationships they have with the society of which they are a vital and integral part. One reason for the wider interest that corporate social responsibility is attracting is that markets have become global. Multinational corporations are seen as no longer being subject to a single jurisdiction, and this has raised questions over their accountability; they also operate in politically sensitive industries such as energy, mining, and pharmaceuticals. The transfer of activities abroad by corporations is another outcome of the increasingly global scale of operations. All of which raise questions about the nature of the responsibilities that corporations have to their employees, their shareholders, and the communities affected by their decisions. A further reason for this sharper focus on the responsibilities of corporations stems from concerns about the environment. These range from domestic awareness of the problems of pollution, waste disposal, and the need for energy conservation to broader questions of economic sustainability and of the future of the planet.

All of these elements of social responsibility are being forcefully drawn to the attention of corporations and the public by well-organized special interest groups. At the same time, corporations are acutely aware of the risk to their reputations, unless they are perceived as having dealt correctly with matters where social responsibility is involved. The governance development in this area of corporate affairs has been the search for ways for corporations to report usefully on their social and environmental policies.

On the environmental front, a body of institutional investors, environmental groups, and corporations have formed CERES—Coalition for Environmentally Responsible Economies. The corporations that have joined have endorsed a set of principles covering such fields as reducing waste, saving energy, and minimizing health and safety risks to employees and the community. They have agreed to report publicly on their progress in implementing these principles. Out of the CERES principles has come the Global Reporting Initiative, or GRI. This initiative aims to design a corporate reporting system under three headings: economic, social, and environmental. At present, the GRI has made more progress with its environmental than with its social and economic indicators. A difficulty on the economic side is how to express concepts like human and intellectual capital in a world where fixed assets are diminishing in importance and human assets are the opposite of fixed.

Investor interest in corporate social responsibility has resulted in the formation of funds specifically directed to promoting that objective. In addition, under the UK Pensions Act regulations, trustees of UK occupational pension funds have to disclose in their statement of investment principles "the extent (if at all) to which social, environmental and ethical considerations are taken into account in the selection, retention and realisation of investments."[30] As a result, guidelines for listed companies say that companies should state in their annual reports whether their boards take regular account of the significance of social, environmental, and ethical matters in their business decisions, and whether they have identified and assessed the significant risks involved in this field.

The need for corporations to report on their approach to social responsibility is an example of the way in which the concept of corporate governance has broadened its scope in the space of a few years. Reports and accounts were traditionally backward-looking, based on historic figures and facts. Boards are increasingly being expected to look ahead and opine on future opportunities and risks. At the same time, they are being asked to account for the impact that actions taken in the interests of their shareholders may have on society in its widest sense. To illustrate this development, it may be helpful to quote from the current UK review of company law, which proposes that companies should extend their reporting to include an operating and financial review, to be known as an OFR.

> We, therefore, propose that all companies of significant economic size should be required to produce, as part of their annual report and accounts, an OFR. This would provide a review of the business, its performance, plans and prospects. It would include information on direction, performance and dynamics (capital projects, risks, etc.) and on all other aspects which the directors judge necessary to an understanding of the business, such as key business relationships and environmental and social impacts. The requirement to produce an OFR would improve the quality, usefulness, and relevance of information available to the markets and to everyone with an interest in the company. As such, we expect it to lead to improved understanding of business performance and prospects, as well as promoting accountability and encouraging responsiveness and high standards of business practice.[31]

This proposal brings out the manner in which, what began as a means of improving the governance of corporations in the interests largely of their shareholders, has spread to encompass the role of business in society. It is noteworthy that the proposed OFR would apply to "companies of significant economic size," not simply publicly quoted companies, and that the accent is on future prospects rather than past performance. All this is a pointer to at least one direction in which corporate governance is likely to develop.

THE DEVELOPMENT OF CORPORATE GOVERNANCE

This is therefore a logical point at which to arrive at some conclusions about the development of corporate governance as a field since the 1990s and about its standing today. It originated as a response to perceived problems in the manner in which individual corporations were directed and controlled. In particular, governance codes aimed to use market forces to extend best practice as widely as possible throughout the corporate sector. In addition, accounting standards were tightened and market regulation was backed by statutory regulation where necessary. Market regulation, however, could only be effective provided the market played its part in the process. The key to effective market involvement was the concentration of shareholdings in the portfolios of institutional investors. It changed the balance of power between boards, managers, and shareholders. The capacity of institutional investors to influence and intervene as a result of their collective shareholding power has been the single most important factor in the development of corporate governance to date.

   The ability of institutional or individual investors to influence and intervene effectively is dependent on their understanding of the manner in which corporations are being directed and controlled. Disclosure, therefore, is the basis on which the practice of corporate governance has been built, and disclosure remains fundamental to its further development. There is no doubt that, as best practice has spread and standards of governance have been raised, corporations have become more accountable to shareholders and to society. In particular, corporations have become more accountable to the institutional investors who own such a high proportion of their shares. The loose end in the chain of accountability is to whom are those investing institutions accountable and to whom should they be? Looking ahead, this is likely to be an issue that will move up the corporate governance agenda.

Perhaps the most striking aspect of the development of corporate governance has been the way in which its scope, its impact, and its possibilities have broadened. The first governance codes were aimed at improving the way in which corporations were directed and controlled by spreading best practice. Their focus was on boards of directors, and they had a measurable impact on national corporate governance standards. Building on that experience, corporate governance extended its influence in two directions. It developed international governance guidelines in addition to national ones, and its aims widened to include those of encouraging economic growth and the free flow of capital. Through these developments, corporate governance has become more than a means of enabling corporations to be better directed and controlled to the general benefit. It is now concerned at its highest and broadest level with holding the balance between economic and social goals, and between individual and communal goals. The governance framework is in place to encourage the efficient use of resources and equally to require accountability for the stewardship of those resources. As a consequence, corporate governance is developing into a means of aligning as nearly as possible the interests of individuals, corporations, and society. This is a remarkable transition.

CONCLUSION: THE WAY AHEAD

Having summed up where corporate governance stands today, it is worth touching briefly on how it might develop in the future. Regulatory frameworks and codes of best practice are broadly in place, but what further steps would assist in raising corporate standards of accountability and performance? Public expectations of corporate behavior could not yet be said to have been met, and those expectations continue to rise. While there will always be financial scandals, how can the likelihood of their incidence be further reduced and the level of public confidence in the corporate system be further raised? My personal views on possible ways forward are no more than that; they are offered primarily in the context of publicly quoted corporations in Europe and North America with the proper caution that the levers of power to maintain improvements in governance vary by country and by corporation. Where does that power lie? I would suggest that there are four main players on the governance stage that have the power and the responsibility to raise confidence in the corporate system. They are the regulators, the corporations themselves, those who invest in them whether as shareholders or as lenders, and those broader constituencies that have the ability to influence corporate behavior.

I would be cautious in most jurisdictions in expecting more from regulation. The thrust of recent regulation, especially in the United States, has been to increase the penalties for inaccurate or misleading information on those responsible for financial reporting. Throughout I have argued that the foundation of sound corporate governance is full and honest disclosure by boards of directors. There are, however, a number of balances that regulators need to consider in this field. One is the need to encourage risk-taking, which is the lifeblood of enterprise. Risks need to be understood and assessed, but opportunities should not be shelved through too great a fear of penalties for error. Another balance is between the rewards for attaining high executive office as against its potential liabilities. Then there is the need to distinguish between intentional deception and honest error, given, for example, that the figure for corporate profits in any one year is a matter of judgment, possibly between quite wide margins. There is value in the approach advocated in the UK company law reform proposal for boards to publish an operating and financial review. Such a review puts more emphasis on boards assessing the opportunities and risks that lie ahead than on overreliance on the precision of figures for past performance.

The primary risk that members of corporate boards run is to their reputations. The moment that trouble strikes, the cry goes up, where were the directors? That threat to reputation applies with equal gravity to their auditors. Business news, and especially bad business news, is today headlined by the media in all its forms. The public spotlight is to an unprecedented extent on those who carry corporate responsibilities. Their exposure to reputational risk should be taken into account by regulators in establishing appropriate penalties for misfeasance.

This leads on to the question of steps that corporations might take to further improve the standing of business in the eyes of investors and the public. There is the straightforward need to meet reasonable expectations on timely and accurate financial reporting, on effective internal controls, and on the management of risk. This is simply good housekeeping. In addition, boards should look at their own governance structures. Boards are the bridge between those who have invested in corporations and the executives who run them day to day. That bridge needs to be kept in good repair. The key to sustained corporate success is an effective board. It is the board that forms the corporation's strategy, appoints the chief executive to carry it out, and monitors the performance of the executive team. The choice of the chief executive is crucial, and is the responsibility of the board.

Arguably, the direction that governance is already taking, prompted by codes of best practice, is to emphasize the importance of the leadership role of boards and of their collective responsibility for the future of their enterprises. Boards should be powerhouses on which chief executives can draw for advice, constructive challenge, and support. Where the posts of chairman and of chief executive are split, it is chairmen who are responsible for the effectiveness of their boards. They take the lead in the board evaluation process and in taking action on the outcome of that evaluation. Where the chief executive is also the chairman, it is the lead director, or senior outside director, who will play that part. This will involve meeting with the other outside directors in executive session as necessary and ensuring that the performance of the board collectively, and of its members individually, is thoroughly assessed and addressed.

Effective leadership by boards is not at the expense of leadership by chief executives; it adds to it. A capable and supportive board is the greatest asset a chief executive can have. The board's task involves both direction and control. The directors are responsible for achieving the business results expected of them and they are accountable for how those results are achieved. They need to be accelerators or brakes, depending on the circumstances, and to have the capacity to fulfil either role equally. The two-tier board structure separates supervision from execution and in that separation it is the management board that is responsible for strategy. The unitary board, on the other hand, combines responsibility for strategy with responsibility for monitoring its execution. A potential strength of the unitary board is that it is a forum where strategy can be debated and formed, drawing both on the depth of knowledge of the business of the executive directors and on the broad experience of the outside directors.

The effectiveness of boards turns on the caliber of their members and the skill of their chairmen. A central issue for corporations, therefore, is the composition of their boards. It requires experience and judgment to select the right board members, and it takes a skillful chairman to get the best out of them as a team. There is the question of size. A board should be no larger than is necessary to bring together an appropriate mix of knowledge and experience, which means that selection has to be a considered process. Board selection should follow on from board evaluation, because the evaluation will point to any gaps in the backgrounds of existing board members, gaps that might usefully be filled. The search for new board members then becomes purposeful. Boards that are seen to be conscientious about assessing their own effectiveness and about explaining how their proposed board candidates will add value will inspire confidence in those they serve.

It is a feature of many corporate failures that too much power was in the hands of individuals and not enough was in those of their boards. As more is expected of boards, so more is expected of their directors. The outside directors have to be capable of both directing and controlling. Sufficient of them need to be independent to be able to determine objectively where the best interests of their corporations lie. In an increasingly turbulent world, independence alone or high reputation gained outside business are no longer in themselves sufficient. Independent outside directors have to acquire an appropriate understanding of the nature of the businesses whose direction they share. It follows that a characteristic of effective boards is that their members are carefully selected, regularly briefed, and encouraged to continue their directorial development throughout their period of office.

This leads on to the part that investors can play in raising standards of corporate performance and accountability. There is no particular role to assign to individual investors, each of whom will have their own objectives, ranging from day-to-day trading on price movements to investing for the long term. Institutional investors, however, have a central role, not only because of the weight of their investments, but also because of their duty to act solely in the interests of their clients. This calls for them to engage with boards, which are not serving their investors as well as they might. There are notable examples of pension funds that discharge this duty; there is also as yet a silent majority.

While statutory regulation sets the governance framework, it is market regulation that provides the momentum within it. For market regulation to function, the market has to play an active part in governance. Those who invest for others are responsible to them for promoting corporate performance. How can investing institutions best serve their clients in this regard? They have first to ensure that the corporations in which they have placed their clients' money understand what as investors they expect in terms of results. They should, for example, engage with boards, if they consider that shareholders' funds are being wasted through pursuing aggrandizement at the expense of returns to investors. They should, in particular, take a proper interest in board composition and in the nomination of directors. This is their function, and it should be their contribution to the strengthening of the collective leadership of corporations by their boards.

While the nomination of candidates for board membership is the responsibility of chairmen and boards, institutional investors can put forward their own proposals to widen the field from which those nominations are made. They should at all times exercise their votes; the power to vote is an asset for which they are responsible. They should use their votes in the election of directors, so that their assessment of board candidates is disclosed. Ira Millstein has recently put forward a reasoned proposal that would strengthen confidence in boards and in their membership. His proposal is that, if directors fail to get a majority vote, taking into account votes withheld, the board concerned should have to find another nominee who will satisfy the majority of shareholders. As he puts it, "This would be a mechanism that would cause boards to be more careful in the nomination process."[32] The nomination process is one of the most direct ways in which investors can exercise their responsibilities in the cause of strengthening board effectiveness.

There is, however, a further fundamental issue on which it has to be in the interests of the investing institutions to take a lead, on behalf of those whose savings they are investing. The liabilities of pension funds in particular extend into the future. Their target must, therefore, be a future stream of earnings on which they can depend to meet those extended liabilities. Sustained profit performance and a consistent dividend policy are required to meet pension demands in the years ahead. Short-term movements in share prices may provide trading opportunities, but sustainable earnings are the goal. It is, therefore, in the interests of institutional investors to ensure that the structure of corporate rewards, such as bonuses, share options, and incentive schemes of all kinds, focuses executive attention on results over at least the medium term, and that these rewards have to be earned against suitably challenging targets.

This shift in time horizons from the short to the medium term is a matter for boards themselves and for institutional investors. It requires the institutions to clarify their expectations in terms of performance, and it requires boards to recognize their accountability in this regard. The aim is to achieve as close an alignment as possible between the objectives of corporations and those of their major shareholders. Pressure to make incentive payments dependent on measurable improvements in results over a reasonable time period would have the added benefit of reducing the scope for offensive and inappropriate executive rewards.

A further point in the part that the investing institutions can play in governance improvements is related to their need to strengthen their accountability to those whose funds they are investing; it is those funds that give them both the duty and the power to promote the interests of their clients. They do, however, need to determine what those interests are, because the interests of pensioners, for example, may extend to the quality of the life into which they are retiring as well as to the quantum of their pensions. Here the UK company law reform proposal, that the dialogue between corporations and their shareholders should be on line, could become significant. Such an advance in communications would open up the possibility of a more direct and positive relationship between boards and their shareholders, and likewise between investing institutions and their clients.

The last group that has some responsibility, if less directly, to encourage good governance is broadly based. It is made up of those who contribute to the corporate debate and who influence the expectations of a whole range of investors. It includes the media in all its forms, financial advisers, analysts and commentators, financial institutions, and the body politic. We have seen the impact on expectations that they can exert, when their combined influence focuses on a single short-term indicator, such as the share price of an individual corporation. So long as the share price is rising, they cheer it on and encourage investors to believe that riches are within their grasp provided they join the bandwagon. The majority of the cheerleaders are well aware that rising share prices do not necessarily equate with rising shareholder values, the goal on which they should be encouraging boards and investors to focus. This delusion becomes only too clear when the rising share price succumbs to gravity and the bubble bursts. Some responsibility for the inevitable collapse rests with those who fan the speculative flames by raising "artificially the value of the stock, by exciting and keeping up a general infatuation," to use Robert Walpole's words.

In conclusion, if the collective leadership of wisely chosen boards is strengthened, and if corporations and the investing institutions lengthen their time horizons, corporate governance standards will continue to rise and trust in the corporate system will be enhanced. Much has been achieved through the emphasis that has been put on the benefits of good governance, by boards themselves, by investors, by governments, by international agencies, and by informed commentators on financial matters. The test of what has been achieved in response to various pressures is how well it holds if the economic climate were to become more equable. Governance, like liberty, is the price of eternal vigilance.

NOTES

1. Robert A. G. Monks (2001), *The new global investors*, Oxford: Capstone, 4.

2. Winston S. Churchill (1957), *A history of the English-speaking peoples*, vol. 3, London: Cassell, 93.

3. R. I. Tricker (1994), *Corporate governance*, Aldershot: Gower, for an account of the development of corporate structures.

4. Berle and Means (1932), *The modern corporation and private property*, New York: Macmillan.

5. Ernest Benn (publisher) (1928), *Britain's industrial future*, London, 91.

6. Peters Committee (1997), *Corporate governance in the Netherlands,* 42.

7. Gee Publishing, Ltd. (1992), *Report of the committee on the financial aspects of corporate governance,* 15.

8. Ira. M. Millstein (1998), *The evolution of corporate governance in the United States,* Egon Zehnder International, 14.

9. Gee Publishing, Ltd. (1992), *Report of the committee on the financial aspects of corporate governance.*

10. Financial Reporting Council (2003), *The combined code on corporate governance,* FRC site, www.asb.org.uk, 15.

11. Gee Publishing, Ltd. (1992), *Report of the committee on the financial aspects of corporate governance,* 52.

12. Gee Publishing, Ltd. (1995), *Compliance with the code of best practice.*

13. Gee Publishing, Ltd. (1992), *Report of the committee on the financial aspects of corporate governance,* 58.

14. Ibid., 58.

15. Governance Publishing and Information Services (2000, February), *Governance.*

16. Louis D. Brandeis, *Other people's money and how the bankers use it,* London: Bedford Books, St. Martin's Press, 89.

17. Gee Publishing, Ltd. (1992), *Report of the committee on the financial aspects of corporate governance,* 52.

18. Jonathan Charkham (1994), *Keeping good company,* Oxford: Oxford University Press.

19. Ibid., 182.

20. OECD (1998), *Corporate Governance,* Paris.

21. Ibid., 9.

22. Hermes Investment Management Ltd. (1997), *Statement on corporate governance and voting policy,* 1.

23. OECD (1999), *OECD principles of corporate governance,* Paris.

24. Commonwealth Association for Corporate Governance (1999), CACG Guidelines, inside front cover, www.cbc.to

25. Ibid.

26. Stijn Claessens (2003), *Corporate governance and development,* Global Corporate Governance Forum.

27. Hermes Investment Management, Ltd. (1997), *Statement on corporate governance and voting policy,* 1.

28. TIAA-CREF (1997), *Policy statement on corporate governance,* 13.

29. CalPERS (1998), *U.S. corporate governance core principles and guidelines.*

30. *Occupational pension schemes (investment) regulations,* (1996), Regulation 11A.

31. Department of Trade and Industry: Company Law Review Steering Group (2001), *Modern company law: Final report* (vol 1), 49.

32. Ira. M. Millstein (2004), interview in *Directors Monthly, 28* (8), 22.

_____ 3 _____

The History of Corporate Governance in the United States

MICHAEL BRADLEY and STEPHEN M. WALLENSTEIN

The collapse of the equity markets in 2002 resulted in a surge of interest in corporate governance. Much of this interest has focused on the immediate events leading up to the highly publicized governance failures at companies such as Enron, WorldCom, and Tyco. An understanding of today's governance failures and proposed solutions would be incomplete without an examination of their historical background. Although that task could easily take up the entire volume, this chapter attempts to put U.S. corporate governance in a historical perspective.

Throughout this review we draw a distinction between corporate governance on the one hand and the regulation of corporations on the other. While the two are intricately related, they represent two very different forces that ultimately determine the nature and very existence of the public corporation and its internal governance mechanisms.

The regulation of corporations deals with the constraints imposed by governments regarding corporate activity within the economy. In contrast, corporate governance deals with the relations between and among the various stakeholders within corporations. Thus, regulations deal with the external activities of corporations, whereas corporate governance deals with the internal operations of corporations. While the regulation of corporations dates from the inception of this organizational form, corporate governance is a relatively recent phenomenon, becoming relevant only after the emergence of the large-scale public corporation in the 1920s, with its defining characteristic of a separation of ownership and control. Prior to this time, most corporations were owned and controlled by a major stockholder or a small stockholder group. In a closely held corporation, corporate governance is not a major issue. However, when there is a separation between those who control the corporation (its managers and board of directors) from those who own the corporation (its security holders), corporate governance becomes the linchpin that holds the organization together. From this perspective, corporate governance deals with the critical problem of assuring that corporate managers will not expropriate the wealth of those who finance its operations. Corporate governance thus defines the procedures and constraints imposed on corporate managers so that outside investors (security holders) will receive the appropriate return on their invested funds.

COLONIAL ORIGINS

The earliest corporations in the United States operated in an environment of suspicion and distrust, no doubt attributable to the fact that they were chartered by the British government. Firms such as the British East India Company and the Massachusetts Bay Company exerted enormous economic and political power within the early U.S. economy. Many prerevolutionary colonists viewed these firms as instruments of the British monarchy, whose purpose was to control the affairs of the colonists and extract commercial wealth for the benefit of the British citizenry.

In the wake of the Revolutionary War, Americans remained wary of the concentration of wealth and power in large economic enterprises, especially corporations. Reflecting the importance of states' rights at the time, the federal Constitution left the authority to grant corporate charters to state legislatures. Initially, corporate charters were granted only for narrowly defined public purposes such as construction projects and included restrictions on corporate structure and duration. Corporations that exceeded their defined purposes frequently had their charters revoked. Further, in order to limit their power and influence, corporations were forbidden from owning shares in other corporations.

THE EMERGENCE OF THE LARGE-SCALE
PUBLIC CORPORATION

The growth in the number and size of corporations in the United States coincides with the growth of the nation in the latter part of the nineteenth century. Spawned by the Industrial Revolution, Reconstruction after the Civil War, western expansion, and vast improvements in transportation and communication, the optimal size of American firms grew, and the corporation, with its limited liability and access to outside capital, was the ideal organizational form to accommodate this increase in the scale and scope of business activity.

As these firms grew, so did the suspicions and fears of the American people toward them. Reflected in the philosophy of the Populist Party in the late 1800s, most Americans believed that big business was bad business. The preamble to the Populist Party's platform at the time captures the suspicions that early Americans had of large concentrations of economic power: "The Populist Party was established to represent the common folk—especially farmers—against the entrenched interests of railroads, bankers, processors, corporations, and the politicians in league with such interests."

Consequently, severe constraints were placed on corporations, including limits on their size, activities, involvement in political activities, and the right to hold shares in other corporations. These constraints were greatly reduced, if not eliminated completely, when in 1886 the U.S. Supreme Court deemed that a public corporation was a "natural person" under the law and enjoyed all of the rights and protections afforded individuals by the U.S. Constitution and the Bill of Rights. This newfound freedom led to a virtual explosion in the number and size of public corporations. In 1787, fewer than 40 corporations operated in the United States. By 1800 that number had grown to 334, and by 1919 corporations employed more than 80 percent of the U.S. workforce and generated most of America's wealth.

In this laissez-faire environment, corporations thrived, resulting in the creation of giant trusts in the oil, steel, railroad, and mining industries, which dominated both the economic and political agendas of the country. Although the Sherman Antitrust Act, which prohibits contracts in restraint of trade and commerce, was passed in 1880, it was not until the passage of the Clayton Act in 1914 and the creation of the Federal Trade Commission in 1915 that the federal government intervened to curb the further expansion of corporate entities. Although this series of legislative reforms significantly affected the operations of corporations with regard to collusion, price discrimination, fair trade practices, and interstate commerce, they had little if any effect on the internal governance of these enterprises.

There were no serious governance issues in these corporations at the time, since the owners were also the individuals in control of the allocation of their resources. The charters of most of the early corporations contained a unanimity rule, which required the approval of all stockholders for any major changes in the operations of the firm. In essence, there was no separation between ownership and control, which, as discussed above, is the sine qua non of corporate governance.

Corporations in this era faced innumerable regulations dealing with a whole range of activities in both the labor and product markets. However, the internal governance of corporations was left relatively untouched by the first major wave of government regulations of corporate activity. The reluctance of the federal government to involve itself with corporate governance issues reflected the widely held belief that corporations were to be treated as creatures of the various states. Moreover, there was no clamor for major governance reform, since very few Americans held the securities of these firms. At the time, if individuals held any public securities at all, they held either government or railroad bonds—fixed-claim instruments, with stated payoffs. If "outside" financing was needed, it was obtained by issuing bonds, mostly to banks and other financial institutions. The notion of outside equity at the time was somewhat of an oxymoron.

As the American economy continued to grow, firms, exploiting available economies of scale and scope, continued to grow as well, which created a demand for outside capital. Three forces drove the demand for external funds: individual wealth constraints, individual risk aversion, and the advent of the entrepreneur. As firms became larger, it became impossible for any one individual to provide the necessary capital to finance their operations. Large sums of capital were required to purchase the firm-specific assets needed to exploit the economies of scale of a rapidly expanding economy. In addition, the risk aversion of the owners of these growing firms led them to seek outside capital in order to diversify their wealth as more and more it became concentrated in the firms they managed. And finally, the pro-competitive legislation enacted at the turn of the century introduced a new character into the American corporate environment—the entrepreneur, an individual who could raise funds from "outside" investors to finance the creation of large-scale commercial enterprises.

The obvious source for the newly needed capital was the existing financial institutions. However, as Professor Roe has observed, governmental restrictions based on American Populists' inherent distrust of financial institutions hampered their ability to grow and meet this increased demand for additional capital. The next best alternative was outside equity, and the most efficient organizational form to attract outside equity was the public corporation.

There have been volumes written on the advantages of the public corporation relative to a sole proprietorship. These benefits include: limited liability (stockholders can lose only up to their initial investment in the firm); the unfettered alienability of shares (stockholders can sell their shares to anyone at any time without obtaining permission from the issuing firm); the ability to secure significant funds to buy firm-specific capital and bond commitments to fixed-claim holders; the ability to obtain a lower cost of capital by selling equity to well-diversified stockholders; and the fact that the corporation has an indefinite life and therefore has an infinite planning horizon in evaluating projects.

Constitutionally protected by the Commerce Clause and loosely regulated by state governments, corporations enjoyed a laissez-faire period through 1929. The legislatures of many states, most notably New Jersey and Delaware, enacted a number pro-management statutes in order to attract corporations to their jurisdictions. These statutory relaxations included a corporation's right to be formed for any legal purpose (opening the door for conglomerate corporations to run many unrelated businesses) and timeless charters allowing a corporation to exist into perpetuity (enabling corporations to increase their size and scope). Furthermore, even though corporations were considered persons in the eyes of the law and therefore could be sued, managers and shareholders enjoyed the protections of limited liability and were thus protected from personal liability resulting from corporate activities.

BUILDUP TO THE 1929 CRASH

The demand for capital to fuel the growing U.S. economy was met by an increase in investments in corporate securities by U.S. citizens. As a result, the ownership structure of U.S. corporations began to change dramatically. Corporations were increasingly being financed by shareholders, who were separate from management. Under this emerging scheme, a substantial influx of new investors/shareholders entered the market. Between 1900 and 1928 the number of U.S. stockholders increased from 4.4 million to 18 million. The distinguishing characteristic of this new organizational form—the public corporation—was the separation of ownership and control. These emerging corporations were run by groups of professional managers, who in theory, were supervised by a board of directors who owed fiduciary duties to the corporation and its shareholders. Yet, in practice, boards of directors were often appointed by management. In many cases, directors were either current or former officers of the firm. As a result, directors were more often concerned with pleasing the firm's management rather than its stockholders. A lack of transparency developed between management and shareholders, who had little access to information regarding a corporation's internal affairs. This situation created severe conflicts of interest within early U.S. public corporations.

Shareholders were generally widely dispersed and had difficulty binding together to exert power over managerial affairs. Typically, a shareholder's stake in any one company was not large enough to justify the cost and effort necessary to monitor and control managers. Unable to affect any changes in management's operation of the firm, unhappy shareholders were left with only one alternative—to "vote with their feet" and sell the shares of firms they believed to be mismanaged.

In the early stages of the development of U.S. equity markets there were few regulations governing the issuance and sale of securities, which provided a fertile ground for all types of fraud and manipulation. Nonetheless, the United States enjoyed a bull market in corporate equities throughout the decade of the 1920s, which lulled investors into a false sense of security regarding corporate governance. Moreover, at the time, investors were able to purchase stocks on as little as 10 percent margin, that is, by borrowing 90 percent of the purchase price. Underprotected, misinformed, and overextended, investors were ripe for ruin at the end of the decade of the Roaring Twenties.

GOVERNMENT REGULATION IN THE WAKE
OF THE MARKET CRASH OF 1929

The stock market crash of 1929 and the Great Depression that followed ushered in a whole host of government regulations, collectively known as the New Deal, aimed at curbing the perceived abuses of large corporations. These new regulations included the Glass-Steagall Act, which separated investment and commercial banking; the creation of the FDIC, which provided government insurance of deposits in commercial banks; the Social Security Act, which provided direct payments to the unemployed; the National Labor Relations Act, which granted the rights of unions to exist and mandated collective bargaining procedures; the Robinson-Patman Act, which prohibited price discrimination; and the Fair Labor Standards Act, which established a maximum normal workweek and a minimum wage, and prohibited child labor. Needless to say, this wave of regulations had a profound effect on corporate America. However, they had little effect on corporation governance. The two pieces of legislation that did have an effect on corporate governance were the Securities Act of 1933 and the Securities and Exchange Act of 1934, although the effects were indirect, since the legislation dealt mostly with disclosure issues rather than actual governance practices.

FEDERAL REFORM THROUGH THE SECURITIES
ACTS OF 1933 AND 1934

The economic depression in the wake of the market crash of 1929 pushed the nation toward the brink of financial collapse. In order to stimulate new investment and spur economic growth, federal authorities saw the need to protect investors and restore confidence in the securities markets. To address these concerns, Congress passed the Securities Act of 1933 (the 1933 Act), establishing a federal law regulating the initial issuance of securities. Due in part to concerns over the constitutionality of federal legislation, Congress left the existing state securities laws in place. State securities regulations—often called blue-sky laws—exist to this day and continue to safeguard the integrity of the U.S. capital markets.

The major theme throughout the 1933 Act was to provide investors with the information necessary to make educated decisions about securities offered for sale. As such, the 1933 Act required that companies issuing securities disclose significant amounts of information about themselves and the securities being issued. The defining characteristic and philosophy of the 1933 Act was aptly captured by Supreme Court justice Louis Brandeis in his now-famous phrase "Sunlight is the best disinfectant."

Disclosure by companies issuing securities was accomplished through registration of the securities with the Federal Trade Commission (the FTC), and later the Securities and Exchange Commission (the SEC). In general, registration was designed to require companies issuing securities to provide investors with material information while minimizing the financial burden on the company. Four types of disclosures were mandated by the 1933 Act: (1) description of the company's assets and business; (2) description of the securities to be offered for sale; (3) disclosure about the company's management; and (4) audited financial statements certified by public accountants. The FTC (and later the SEC) retained the right to examine the filings for compliance with disclosure requirements, but did not judge the actual merits of the securities being issued.

In addition to the overarching themes of openness and transparency, the 1933 Act explicitly prohibited deceit, misrepresentation, and other fraud in the sale of securities and established a private right of action for securities holders. The private right of action allowed securities holders to bring a suit against any person who signed the registration statement, any person who was a director or partner of the issuer, any person named in the registration statement as being or about to become a director or partner, accountants, engineers, or appraisers, other signatories whose professional expertise presumably gives authority to the statement, and finally, every underwriter with respect to the security in question. To bring suit, the plaintiff must have bought the securities during the initial issuance.

In order to allow for capital formation, the 1933 Act exempted a few types of offerings from the registration requirement. Thus, small (in dollar amount or in number of investors) and intrastate offerings of securities as well as securities issued by municipal, state, and federal governments required no registration statement to be filed under the 1933 Act. Importantly, the 1933 Act did not govern continued disclosures after the initial public offering; that was left to the legislation passed in the following year.

To regulate the much larger secondary market for securities, Congress passed the Securities Exchange Act of 1934 (the 1934 Act). The 1934 Act accomplished four objectives: it (1) created the SEC to regulate stock exchange rules and to prevent fraud and manipulation by brokers and dealers; (2) established a system for regulating the markets and their participants; (3) required the continuing periodic disclosure of information by the issuers of securities; and (4) contained antifraud provisions.

The 1934 Act removed administrative authority from the FTC and granted the newly created SEC broad authority over all aspects of the securities industry and markets. The SEC is charged with many duties, including articulating national policy over U.S. markets, adopting opt-out rules and regulations for implementing federal securities laws, and bringing civil enforcement actions against violators. The SEC also frequently cooperates with the U.S. Department of Justice, which brings criminal actions, and with state regulatory agencies. Between 1934 and 1935 the SEC opened regional offices in New York, Boston, Chicago, and San Francisco in order to establish a visible local presence. The SEC currently has twelve offices across the country.

Among the entities regulated by the SEC are brokerage firms, transfer agents, clearing agencies, and the securities industry's self-regulatory organizations (SROs), such as stock exchanges. The 1934 Act required that these entities register with the SEC, which involves filing and regularly updating disclosure documents. The SROs are further required by the 1934 Act to promulgate rules for disciplining their members as well as measures to ensure investor protection and market integrity. These rules are subject to SEC review and approval.

The 1934 Act further mandated all publicly owned corporations with more than five hundred shareholders and $10 million in assets to file annual and other periodic reports. The SEC makes these reports available to the public. In addition to these disclosures, issuers are required to file all proxy solicitation materials, disclosing material information regarding matters on which shareholders are asked to vote. Furthermore, anyone seeking to acquire 5 percent or more of the company by direct purchase or through a tender offer must disclose such information. These rules were designed to allow shareholders to make informed decisions about crucial corporate events.

Finally, the 1934 Act governed the use of "insider information" in securities trading by company management, directors, and principal stockholders. In addition to the 1934 Act, SEC rules also prohibit activities that defraud an individual by any means. The 1934 Act permits a private action to be brought under many of its provisions.

THE CONTINUING PROBLEM OF SEPARATION
OF OWNERSHIP AND CONTROL

In their seminal 1932 book *The Modern Corporation and Private Property*, Adolf Berle and Gardiner Means reexamined the problem of the separation of management and ownership, identified over a century and a half earlier by Adam Smith. Berle and Means analyzed the state of corporate America, in which economic power was increasingly being concentrated in a small number of large corporations whose managements were clearly disconnected from their owners. They were pessimistic about the viability of a system in which ownership was separated from management, warning that managers had both incentives and opportunities to serve their own interests rather than those of the firm's investors.

Berle and Means further concluded that, as a practical matter, the power of shareholders to select directors was almost nonexistent. With management firmly in charge and ownership structures involving masses of individual shareholders, collective action problems abounded. Discontented shareholders who sold their stock enhanced management's power by leaving a self-selected population of shareholders with a pro-management bias. With such a composition of friendly shareholders, management proposals were virtually assured of shareholder approval.

Shareholders also faced a "free rider" problem, since in the large-scale public corporation no one shareholder held sufficient shares to warrant expending funds on monitoring managers or becoming actively involved in the governance of the company. Although individual shareholders may have supported activists' efforts to reform the governance of a particular firm, their own stakes were generally too small to justify financial support. Consequently, any activist shareholder effectively shouldered the burden of numerous free riders. As Berle and Means stated, the passivity of these millions of shareholders had frozen "absolute power in the hands of corporate managements."

Although the 1933 and 1934 Acts regulated the issuance and trading of securities, they had little or no effect on the governance of the corporations that issued these securities. The typical board of directors acted as a supplemental source of ideas to management rather than a check on management power. CEOs generally determined both the size and composition of the board of directors, and each director was beholden to the CEO for his board membership. The CEO generally acted as chairman of the board and largely dominated the board's decision-making and evaluative processes. Objective reviews of CEO performance were practically impossible, as the boards never met without the CEO present. Berle and Means argued that government regulation was necessary to solve the conflicts of interests inherent in the public corporation.

The fundamental problem with the separation of ownership and control in the "modern" corporation—the fact that boards of directors lacked the proper incentives to oversee management and protect the interests of the firm's shareholders—was left unaddressed by the 1933 and 1934 Acts. The provisions of the 1933 and 1934 Acts forced corporate managers to disclose important information regarding their firms' financial situations and internal operations. The legislation, however, did not address the governance of public corporations, since it was believed that this was the province of the states in which the firms were incorporated.

Even state regulations, however, left the particulars of corporate governance to the corporations themselves, relying instead on the common law notion of fiduciary duties. Thus, under most state laws, corporate boards and managers owe fiduciary duties of care, loyalty, and candor to the corporations they manage, with stockholders having the exclusive standing to sue under these doctrines. The "duty of care" requires that boards exercise "due care" or due diligence in making corporate decisions. This requires boards to conduct reasonable inquiry into matters regarding major corporate decisions. Boards are permitted, and are often required, to seek outside experts regarding important corporate matters. The duty of care is tempered by the "business judgment rule," which holds that courts will not second guess management decisions as long as they were made on an informed basis. The "duty of loyalty" prevents self-dealing transactions and precludes officers and directors from exploiting corporate opportunities to their own advantage. Finally, the "duty of candor" precludes managers from making false or misleading statements regarding the firm's current or future financial status or any major transaction that it has decided to pursue.

THE POST–WORLD WAR II PERIOD AND THE RISE
OF CONGLOMERATES

The post–World War II period, spanning the late 1940s and the 1950s, brought widespread prosperity to America. Increasingly, individuals had disposable income available for investment, and the securities of public corporations were viewed as a good way to save for the future and hedge against inflation. Mutual funds were first introduced in the mid-1950s and permitted individuals to pool their savings and enjoy the benefits of diversification. The concept of "the organization, or company, man" came into vogue during this time period, referring to the loyal relationship between a corporation and its employees who, for the most part, spent their entire careers working for the same corporation.

The 1960s saw the explosive growth of diverse conglomerates such as Litton Industries and Gulf and Western. These conglomerates developed quickly through the acquisition of divisions and subsidiaries as well as entire firms. Many managers believed that they could increase their stock price by diversifying into unrelated industries, much like mutual fund managers do today. The belief was that stockholders would pay a premium for the shares of a diversified firm because, at the time, it was prohibitively expensive for all but the wealthiest investors to create a diversified portfolio through their own investments. For example, Gulf and Western's portfolio of business divisions ranged from sugar refining to the production and distribution of motion pictures. The desire to grow through acquisition was enhanced by the fact that management compensation was more closely correlated with the size and rate of growth of the corporation rather than with its profitability and stock appreciation. As an indication of the trend toward conglomeration, by 1973, fifteen of the largest 200 American nonfinancial companies were diverse conglomerates.

Over the decade of the 1960s, shares of public corporations proved to be a good investment, which induced more Americans to invest in the market. Leading the growth in the market for public equity were conglomerates like Gulf and Western and Litton Industries, computer companies like Sperry Rand and Electronic Data Systems, and noncomputer technology companies such as Polaroid and Xerox. There were also spectacular initial public offerings, such as National Student Marketing Corporation (NSM), which had an initial public offering at $6 per share in April 1968. NSM shares enjoyed a spectacular price increase to a high of $140 in December 1969, trading at a price-to-earnings ratio (P/E ratio) of 100. In fueling its growth during that time period, NSM had solicited approval from the shareholders of Interstate National Corporation (Interstate) to merge the two companies. NSM's auditors subsequently discovered that the company's earnings had been overstated, and thus the proxy statements used to solicit merger approval from Interstate's shareholders were misleading. NSM's attorneys allowed the merger to go forward anyway and allowed some of Interstate's principal shareholders to sell their newly acquired NSM stock without disclosing the material errors in NSM's financial statements to the buyers. By July 1970, NSM's stock was trading at $3.50.

The SEC brought an action against NSM's attorneys in federal district court. The court found the attorneys guilty of aiding and abetting fraud, but was not clear on whether the lawyers had a duty to publicly disclose the fraud. This decision fueled debate about the conflict between attorney-client confidentiality and the gatekeeper responsibility of attorneys. Clearly there is a social interest in allowing clients to freely disclose confidential information to their attorneys. These disclosures often make attorneys the best-positioned parties to protect shareholders. However, clients who are afraid their attorneys will disclose confidential information, even in the name of shareholder protection, may stop disclosing such information. The responsibilities of inside council and other gatekeepers, and the recent regulatory responses to their perceived failures, are discussed in a subsequent section.

THE 1970s AND THE TARNISHED CORPORATE IMAGE

Harvard Business School professor Myles Mace authored an influential study in 1971 examining the statutory legal duty of the board of directors to oversee management. After performing extensive research, Mace concluded that the board of directors in most large and medium-sized corporations did not function as a meaningful check on the CEO. The main explanation for this malfunction was that corporate CEOs usually controlled the selection of board members. Furthermore, few boards met frequently enough to perform meaningful oversight.

The infrequency of board meetings, lack of effective questioning and monitoring by directors, and lack of information available to directors often resulted in boards not being aware of adverse events until a crisis had become unavoidable. Perhaps the best-known example of this phenomenon was the decision by the management of Penn Central Railroad to file for bankruptcy in June 1970. In the two years before Penn Central's collapse, its directors had approved dividend payments of over $100 million while the railroad's debts soared and its working capital deteriorated. Members of the board of directors had not been informed of the company's true financial situation prior to the bankruptcy filing and learned of the bankruptcy filing from the newspapers. Subsequent financial press releases and the academic literature emphasized that the lax oversight of the board of directors of the company was typical of most boards of large corporations. The SEC subsequently launched an investigation of the company and criticized the Penn Central board for failing to oversee the company's operations, for lacking independence from management, and for being unable to identify the company's financial problems.

Despite the existence of SEC regulations and state laws, the 1970s saw a substantial increase in fraud and falsification of corporate records. One of the biggest corporate scandals was the 1973 discovery that some corporations had made illegal campaign contributions to the Nixon election. Bribes and illegal contributions to political figures in foreign countries were also discovered. Following these astonishing revelations, the SEC announced a period during which voluntary disclosures of corporate wrongdoing would not be prosecuted. Hundreds of publicly held corporations investigated their own prior conduct and publicly disclosed instances of illegal conduct. Never before had so many highly respected publicly held corporations announced that they had engaged in improper, illegal, and even criminal conduct.

The effect of these disclosures was to tarnish the image of the large, public corporation as a law-abiding corporate citizen and eliminate much of the residual goodwill enjoyed by corporations since World War II. These disclosures led to a strong surge of interest in revising corporate governance rules. Legislative hearings raised the question of whether Congress, the stock exchanges, or the SEC should mandate more stringent rules of corporate governance.

As a consequence of the illegal payment disclosures, Congress passed the Foreign Corrupt Practices Act in 1977 to bar the payment of bribes to foreign officials in exchange for business. Several other proposals to reform corporate governance were widely debated. In 1974, SEC Chairman William Carey proposed federal minimum standards for state corporate law. Cary proposed enactment of a federal statute that would establish standards of officer and director conduct for all firms above a specified minimum size. The previous year, Harvey Goldschmid (who subsequently became general counsel, and then a commissioner, of the SEC) offered a proposal to restructure boards of directors so that each could provide "a meaningful, independent" review of corporate management. Goldschmid proposed that boards be composed entirely of outside directors who would be sufficiently well compensated to spend significant time reviewing and approving executive decisions.

Following the Penn Central investigation, the SEC focused on financial reporting and board oversight of management. The SEC supported a proposal that boards form committees, composed entirely of independent directors, designed to monitor compliance with SEC regulations on financial reporting. In 1977 the SEC approved a New York Stock Exchange (NYSE) rule requiring all listed U.S. companies to form audit committees comprised of a majority of independent directors. The new listing rule marked the emergence of independent directors as a key element of corporate governance reform.

CORPORATE TAKEOVERS AND FIDUCIARY DUTIES

The 1970s and 1980s brought an unprecedented rise in corporate takeover activity. Many of these transactions were motivated by an attempt to exploit synergies by combining the operations of the target and acquiring firms.

However, the economies of scale and scope promised by the conglomerates created in the 1960s never materialized. As a result, many of these firms became targets of unsolicited tender offers by so-called corporate raiders with the intent of buying the firm's shares in the open market, gaining control of the firm, and selling off (divesting) unprofitable units. These so-called "bust-up" takeovers became more popular with the development of the "junk bond" market in the early 1980s. Known euphemistically as "high-yield debt," this source of funding allowed corporate raiders to raise literally billions of dollars in a matter of days to finance their takeover activities and, as a result, made even the largest firms vulnerable to a hostile takeover.

The rash of hostile takeovers in the 1980s led to two responses. First, corporations began to develop defensive tactics to ward off hostile bidders. Second, states began to enact antitakeover legislation that favored the management of firms incorporated in their state.

The most notorious and effective defensive tactic developed at this time was the poison pill. A poison pill is a security that is issued to stockholders. Although there are many variants of the poison pill, they typically are issued in the form of a preferred stock that is virtually worthless unless the firm become the target of a hostile takeover. The effectiveness of the poison pill stems from its conversion feature, which is "triggered" by an individual or entity buying a specified fraction (typically 15 percent) of the firm's common stock. If a triggering event occurs, then all stockholders *except the entity that triggered the pill* could redeem or convert the preferred stock into two or more shares of newly issued common stock at a substantial discount from its current market price. The obvious effect of this conversion would be to dilute the holdings of the individual or entity that triggered the pill.

After the poison pill had been determined "legal" by the Delaware Chancery Court (*Moran v. Household,* 1985), its use became widespread. The effectiveness of the poison pill is evidenced by the fact that no public corporation has ever been taken over with a poison pill in place. Indeed, after its development and widespread adoption, hostile bidders were forced to condition their bids on the target managers rescinding the outstanding pill. If the target management refused to rescind the pill, hostile bidders would refuse to purchase the target shares, no matter how many shares were tendered by the target stockholders.

The poison pill was justified by corporate officers and the Delaware courts as a mechanism to ensure that target stockholders would receive a fair price for their shares. If a target management felt that a particular bid was "inadequate," it would not rescind the pill, which would result in the bidding firm retracting its bid.

While theoretically the poison pill could be used as bargaining chip in negotiating a deal with a hostile bidder, it quickly became clear that the defense could also be used to entrench the management of a company, making it impossible for a hostile bidder to take control of the firm. Thus, from a corporate governance perspective, the issue was whether the pill would be used by corporate boards to secure a fair price for their stockholders or use the pill to defeat all offers, even those that would be in the interests of their firm's stockholders. The debate concerning the uses and abuses of the poison pill came to a head in 1989 with the Delaware Court's ruling in *Interco*. In that case, the court ruled that a poison pill could be used as a negotiating tool in dealing with a hostile bidder. However, if the bidder were to offer a "fully funded, all cash deal, for all outstanding shares at a 'significant' premium," then the board of directors would be required to rescind the pill or face charges of breaching their fiduciary duty to shareholders. This decision sent a shock wave throughout corporate America and prompted one famous Wall Street attorney, Martin Lipton, who, by the way, "invented" the poison pill, to advise his clients that if the *Interco* decision became the rule of law in Delaware, they should seriously consider reincorporating in another state.

No doubt in response to this threat and the outrage expressed by the managements of the numerous firms incorporated in Delaware, the Delaware bar, and the state's legislators, the court made a 180-degree turn less than two years later in its watershed decision in *Paramount v. Time*. The central issue in this case was whether or not corporate directors were required, under Delaware law, to maximize the (immediate) value of their firm's outstanding stock. The plaintiff in the case, Paramount, Inc., filed suit in the Delaware court alleging that the board of directors of Time, Inc. were breaching their fiduciary duty to their stockholders by refusing to rescind its poison pill and accept an all-cash offer for all of Time's shares at a substantial premium. The offer was made by Paramount just as Time, Inc. and Warner Bros. Studios were finalizing a friendly merger agreement. At the time of bid, the shares of Time were trading at $100. Before the merger between Time and Warner had been consummated, Paramount made a cash tender offer of $200 per share for all of Time's outstanding shares. The offer was conditioned on Time abandoning its merger with Warner and rescinding its poison pill. The Time board refused the Paramount offer and proceeded with its merger with Warner. Paramount sued, alleging that by refusing to accept a 100 percent premium cash bid, the Time board was breaching its fiduciary duty to its stockholders. In a shocking reversal of its earlier position, the court ruled that, under Delaware law, Time was permitted to exercise its "business judgment" in determining the preferred course of action. The court said that Time's board had the freedom to choose which alternative better served the long-run interests of its stockholders. The court went on to state that the directors of a corporation are in a better position than its stockholders to determine the firm's optimal long-range operating strategy. Essentially, the court said that corporate managers (boards) "had the right to be wrong" and could just say "no" to an outstanding bid, provided the firm had an alternative business plan in place.

The clear implication of the Time decision is that in Delaware, stockholders do not have the right to micromanage the firm's operating strategy. If they are displeased with the way a firm is being run, stockholders can replace the firm's board (management) via the proxy process.

In addition to the development of the poison pill, the second major response to the wave of hostile takeovers in the late 1980s was the proliferation of state antitakeover laws. Many of these statutes were enacted within a few days of a hostile bid being made for a "hometown" corporation. The state of Washington passed a law in just three days that prevented a hostile takeover of the state's largest corporation at the time—Boeing. Pennsylvania passed a statute within the same time frame that thwarted a hostile bid for control of Gulf Oil, which is headquartered in Pittsburgh.

CORPORATE GOVERNANCE AND THE PROXY PROCESS

The advent and proliferation of the poison pill together with pro-incumbent-management antitakeover statutes enacted by the various states virtually eliminated the possibility of effecting a hostile takeover through the acquisition of the shares of a target firm in the open market. The poison pill makes it uneconomical to acquire the shares of a target via a tender offer, and the state statutes and judicial rulings protect target managers from stockholder suits alleging a breach of fiduciary duty if the pill is not rescinded. Thus, as of 1990, the only mechanism available to replace inefficient corporate managers was the proxy contest. However, at the time, SEC rules made it very difficult for stockholders to use the proxy process to nominate a slate of new directors or put forth a proposal to change any aspects of the operations of a firm.

The rules governing the proxy process were first established by the SEC in 1935 under the authority granted by the Exchange Act of 1934. Consistent with the spirit of the Exchange Act in general, the initial proxy rules focused primarily on the veracity and completeness of the information being disclosed to stockholders prior to the annual or a specially called meeting. The intent of the SEC was to insure that investors were fully and accurately informed about voting issues, and that voting was fair, honest, and immune from manipulation by soliciting parties. Importantly, the initial rules did not preclude communication among stockholders or statements and announcements made by soliciting agents in the media or through direct stockholder contact. The rules did not preclude third parties (arbitrageurs) from soliciting proxies. They only required that any communications with stockholders adhere to the same antifraud provisions governing solicitations by the incumbent.

The SEC made dramatic changes in the proxy rules in 1956, when it extended its registration and review requirements to include all communications among and between the stockholders of a public corporation by changing the definition of a proxy solicitation. Under the new definition, a solicitation consisted of *any* communication to security-holders under circumstances reasonably calculated to result in the procurement, withholding, or revocation of a proxy. In particular, the new definition allowed the SEC to assert control over any communications between a soliciting party and shareholders; public statements made by dissidents and third parties allied with dissidents; and any impromptu communications made through television, speeches, or on the radio.

Another major component of the 1956 amendments was the requirement of extensive disclosure about the identity, intentions, and associations of dissidents attempting to elect a competing slate of directors. Under the new rule, every person connected with a dissident campaign had to notify the SEC at least five days *before* attempting any communications—even informal word-of-mouth discussions—with security-holders about a potential proxy campaign.

The major effect of these rule changes was to greatly expand the definition of a solicitation to include essentially *any* communication with shareholders regarding *any* issues involving the operations of the firm or issues that were to be decided at a pending stockholders meeting. Clearly, the rules had a stifling effect on stockholder communication.

In October 1992 the SEC enacted major revisions to the proxy rules in order to increase shareholder communication with management and with fellow shareholders. The amendments specifically addressed the regulation of communications with and among shareholders regarding management's performance, elections and nonelection issues, prefiling requirements for both registrants and shareholders, the presentation of management's proposals, insurgent slate nominations, and election contest reporting and filing requirements.

The new rules did away with the proxy-filing requirement for shareholders communicating with each other when not seeking proxy authority. Prior to the 1992 amendments, communication between more than ten shareholders, even through newspaper interviews or other public forums, required that a proxy statement be filed with the SEC. However, since 1992, all oral communications have been excluded from proxy regulation, and written solicitations are exempted unless the shareholder holds over $5 million of a company's securities.

The 1992 amendments also specifically excluded shareholders' public statements of their voting intentions and/or voting rationale from the definition of a solicitation. The exemption also applied to unsolicited communications in response to information requested by another shareholder and any communications by a fiduciary to its beneficiaries explaining how it intends to vote its proxies. Officers and directors who are shareholders are permitted to take advantage of this public statement exemption as well.

In 1998 the SEC enacted new rules that made it easier for shareholders to include a broader range of proposals in companies' proxy materials. Prior to 1998, SEC rules permitted managements to exclude any stockholder proposal from the proxy statement that dealt with the "ordinary business operations" of the firm. Historically, this had been the most used provision of the proxy rules as a basis for excluding shareholder proposals, and has probably engendered more controversy than any other provision of the shareholder proposal rules. The SEC designed the ordinary business operations exclusion to prevent the introduction of shareholder proposals that, if adopted, would present the impractical result of shareholder involvement in the minutiae of day-to-day operations of a company's business. However, companies often relied on the provision to exclude proposals that raised questions of considerable importance to companies and their shareholders.

Under the new regulations, a "qualifying shareholder" may require a listed corporation to include a "shareholder proposal" and an accompanying supporting statement in the company's proxy materials. A "shareholder proposal" is a recommendation or requirement that the company and/or its board of directors take action, which the shareholder intends to present at a meeting of the company's shareholders. In effect, the qualifying shareholder is making a motion at the shareholders' meeting, but is using the company's proxy material as the medium of effectively communicating her proposal to the other shareholders.

A proponent is a "qualifying shareholder" if, at the time she submits her proposal, she has owned at least $2,000 in market value, or 1 percent of the company's stock for at least one year, and if she continuously owns such stock through the date of the meeting. A qualifying shareholder may make only one proposal per meeting, and the shareholder or her representative must attend the meeting in order to present the proposal. The proposal may not exceed five hundred words, including any accompanying supporting statement.

Importantly, the 1992 reform expressly permits companies to omit shareholder proposals that relate to the election of directors. Therefore, if a shareholder wishes to nominate a slate of directors, she must do so through a proxy contest, which involves a dissident presenting her own proxy statement and voting card to shareholders. This process involves legal, printing, mailing, and often solicitation costs and is therefore much more expensive than the shareholder proposal process described above.

In 2000 the SEC further relaxed its rules governing the communication among and between stockholders. The revised rules allow essentially unlimited telephonic or other oral communications, without any filing requirement or other restriction, except of course, antifraud provisions. The Internet is increasingly used as a cheap and quick medium to conduct proxy fights. Typically, insurgents use the Internet by launching websites just before commencing a proxy contest. They then file a copy of the information on the website with the SEC. Under the SEC's framework, dissidents only need to deliver definitive proxy statements to each person to whom a proxy is ultimately furnished—not each person who visits the site or who is solicited to visit the site. Companies often launch their own websites in response to the insurgents'. Companies and insurgents gain attention for their websites through mailings and media ads promoting the site, word of mouth on message boards (insurgents may post messages urging shareholders to visit their site), or e-mail alerts.

On October 2, 2003, the SEC announced that it would consider rules designed to give dissident stockholders easier access to the proxy process. Although the details were not disclosed, the SEC suggested that the process would allow majority bloc holders direct access to the proxy process requiring the incumbent management to include dissident nominees on the ballot. The proposed rules contemplate a two-step procedure in which stockholders voice their disapproval of management by means of a proposal. If a majority of the stockholders endorse such a vote of no-confidence, the dissidents would be able to nominate their own directors and the current management would be required to include the dissidents' nominees on the same ballot as those proposed by management. Because the proposed rules would require dissidents to have a majority bloc of a firm's shares, it is believed that institutional investors would play the lead role in such an action. In fact, it is the recent pressure put on the SEC by the major pension funds that have prompted the SEC to take any action regarding the access of stockholders to the proxy process. As alluded to above, since the courts have all but eliminated the tender offer as a viable takeover mechanism, the institutions have been forced to involve themselves in the only alternative left to remove ineffective corporate managers—the proxy contest. However, in a number of press releases and public statements made in the spring of 2005, the SEC made it clear that due to the avalanche of negative commentary from corporate managers and their general counsels, it is taking a "go-slow" policy regarding reforms that would allow stockholders direct access to the proxy process.

In sum, while the proxy reforms undertaken by the SEC have given shareholders greater participation in the proxy process, they have not gone so far as to make the proxy process an effective means for affecting corporate governance practices and procedures.

THE ADVENT OF STOCK-BASED
MANAGEMENT COMPENSATION

The inability to effect a hostile takeover through the direct purchase of a corporation's stock and the difficulty in waging a successful proxy battle created a demand for alternative mechanisms to better align the interests of corporate managers with those of their stockholders. In this new environment, managers often rejected takeover attempts that would have been beneficial to shareholders in order to preserve their jobs, salaries, and corporate perks. The situation was exacerbated by the fact that managers received very little equity-based compensation in the form of restricted stock or stock options. Some argued that incentive-based equity compensation would better align the interests of management and shareholders and give management a stake in long-term corporate performance. This alignment of interests was thought to be especially important in the takeover context, since managers having large equity stakes would have greater incentives to accept reasonable takeover offers.

Consequently, stock options came to prominence as a form of compensation. Unlike other forms of compensation, stock options, which give managers the right to acquire stock of the company at a fixed price, were not immediately reflected in the company's bottom line. Because stock options were viewed as being a redistribution of ownership from the shareholders to management, they were not expensed and thus did not decrease net income. Stock options also allowed corporations to do an end run around the $1 million cap on compensation deduction to top executives, which Congress inserted into the tax code in 1993.

Given these benefits, the use of stock options as compensation quickly proliferated throughout the corporate world. In 1984, equity made up less than 1 percent of the average CEO's compensation package. By 1990, 8 percent of CEO compensation was equity based. By 2001 this percentage had exploded to 67 percent. Between 1990 and 2001, stock options rose from 5 percent of shares outstanding at the largest two thousand firms to 15 percent. The dollar value of options at these firms increased from $50 billion in 1997 to $162 billion in 2000.

However, stock option compensation produced its own set of misaligned incentives for management. Prior to 1991, Rule 16(b) of the 1934 Act had required managers to hold stock for six months following acquisition. Any gain from the sale of the underlying stock during the six-month holding period would be surrendered back to the corporation as a prohibited "short-swing profit." Rule 16(b) was intended to prevent insiders from trading on information unknown to the investing public. In 1991 the SEC amended the holding period for stock acquired through exercise of a stock option to include the time since the option was granted, without regard to whether the options had vested. Under the amended rule, if the stock option had been held for six months or longer, an executive could sell shares immediately upon exercise of the option. Since most stock options typically vest over a four-year period before they may be exercised, this revision allowed senior executives to sell shares immediately after exercising the stock option and exploit temporary spikes in their firm's stock price. Inadvertently, the SEC's amendment led some corporate managers to focus on short-term stock price performance rather than to manage for long-term value creation.

BREAKDOWN OF GATEKEEPER RESPONSIBILITIES

Gatekeepers such as outside auditors, investment bankers, and lawyers were given a prominent role in corporate governance with the passage of the 1933 and 1934 Acts and their emphasis on disclosure of material information about the corporation's business. Gatekeepers were once assumed to pledge their reputational capital to protect the interests of dispersed investors, and it was assumed that they had little to gain from the perpetuation of fraud by corporate management. However, as a result of conflicts of interest, outside auditors, investment bankers, and lawyers often failed in their gatekeeper duties to act as meaningful checks on a firm's management. Over the past twenty-five years, each of these gatekeeper entities has been induced into breaching its duty to provide oversight responsibilities and pursuing the gatekeeper's self-interests to the detriment of shareholders.

During the 1990s the risks of gatekeeper liability decreased substantially. The Supreme Court decision in *Lampf v. Gilbertson* (1991) reduced the statute of limitations applicable to securities fraud. In 1994 the Supreme Court held in *Central Bank of Denver v. First Interstate Bank* that professional advisers such as accountants, bankers, and lawyers were not liable for civil damages in cases brought for aiding or abetting corporate fraud under Rule 10(b) of the 1934 Act. In so ruling, the Supreme Court intended to decrease the cost of doing business for professional advisers, who were considered only peripherally involved in the alleged fraud but whose deep pockets made them prime targets for legal action. The legacy of this ruling, however, has served to decrease the incentives for vigilance by professional advisers.

During the 1990s a coalition of public companies was formed to lobby against the increasing number of "frivolous" class action shareholder lawsuits. In 1995, Congress responded to this heavy lobbying by passing the Private Securities Litigation Reform Act (the PSLRA), overriding President Clinton's veto. The PSLRA raised pleading standards for securities class actions and created a "safe harbor" for forward-looking information. In so doing, the PSLRA was intended to decrease the number of "nonmeritorious" securities class action lawsuits filed. The number of audit-related suits filed against the Big Six accounting firms was 192 in 1990 and 172 in 1991. By 1996, only six of the 105 securities class action lawsuits named auditors.

THE ACCOUNTING INDUSTRY AND THE ROLE
OF AUDIT COMMITTEES

In the accounting industry, the increased freedom from civil liability led to an erosion in the quality of financial reporting, as evidenced by the soaring number of restatements filed in the late 1990s. Of these restatements, 39 percent involved revenue recognition issues, particularly premature income recognition. Another inherent conflict of interest arose because most accounting firms bundled auditing and consulting services to their clients. Consulting revenues were, on average, three times larger than auditing revenues. As a result, auditing services were viewed as simply an entry point into the business of lucrative clients. This disparity in revenues created internal pressure on auditors to go to great lengths to maintain friendly relationships with a client's management in order to cross-sell consulting services and led to lax oversight in the auditing function.

In the late 1990s, at the behest of the SEC chairman, Arthur Levitt, SROs undertook an attempt to shore up the corporate governance process. In a joint effort in September 1998 the NYSE and the National Association of Securities

Dealers (the NASD) established a Blue Ribbon Committee on Improving the Effectiveness of Corporate Audit Committees (the Blue Ribbon Committee). The Blue Ribbon Committee was cochaired by experts from the government, investment banking, and legal sectors, and its recommendations focused on the role of the audit committee of the board of directors. The Blue Ribbon Committee's ten recommendations included requiring an independent audit committee, implementing a more rigorous definition of independence, and mandating financial literacy for audit committee members.

In response to these recommendations, the SEC adopted a series of rules in 1999 regarding disclosure of the composition of audit committees. Simultaneously, the NASD, the NYSE, and the American Stock Exchange each required all domestic-listed companies to have at least three directors on the audit committee, all of whom were to be independent and "financially literate," and to create written charters setting forth audit committee responsibilities.

EQUITY RESEARCH ANALYSTS AS GATEKEEPERS

Equity research analysts traditionally played a gatekeeper role because their job was to carefully analyze corporations and make informed recommendations to clients about investment decisions. Prior to 1975, brokerage firms charged fixed commission rates that paid for the equity research that analysts provided. On May 1, 1975, these fixed commission rates were eliminated. Without fixed commission rates to fund equity research, equity research analysts migrated to the investment banking side of the business. This migration produced a conflict of interest in the banking industry. Investment banks that sought underwriting business from a corporation now controlled the research analysts who made "buy" or "sell" recommendations on the corporation's securities, resulting in a systematic bias toward optimism. The ratio of "buy" to "sell" recommendations increased from 6 to 1 in 1991 to 100 to 1 by 2000, and banks were rewarded with new or continued underwriting and trading business with the corporations their analysts covered.

This situation was exacerbated in the late 1990s by the influx of discount brokers into the marketplace, offering substantially lower commission rates. These discount brokers gave unprecedented electronic market access to small investors. Particularly in the bubble years of the late 1990s, millions of novice traders—referred to as "day traders"—invested in the stock market for the first time, and often these unsuspecting investors relied on equity research tainted by conflicts of interest.

ENVIRONMENT RIPE FOR SCANDAL: THE PERFECT
STORM AND ENRON

The cumulative effect of these failures among gatekeepers was a recipe for the corporate scandals at the turn of the millennium. Immense stock option compensation packages combined with the ability to sell the underlying stock immediately upon exercise gave corporate executives a dual financial incentive to manipulate earnings to meet short-term performance targets and artificially peak the stock price above a sustainable level when their options vested. Boards of directors were too closely tied to management to conduct objective independent reviews. Exacerbating the situation was the fact that board members received compensation in the form of stock options as well. In the accounting industry, the revenue inequity of the dual auditing and consulting functions gave accounting firms incentive to placate management on auditing issues to gain consulting business, particularly in a legal system in which accountants were not liable for aiding and abetting corporate fraud. Stock prices were driven higher by optimistic recommendations from equity research analysts, who were employed by investment banks eager to underwrite IPOs. These banks and their preferred clients benefited from increased stock prices for the firms they underwrote. Stock prices were soaring by the late 1990s. No one, including investors themselves, had much incentive to investigate the weaknesses of the corporate governance system.

The conflicts in the system and the failures of gatekeepers at end of the twentieth century created the perfect storm for scandal. This storm crashed through many formerly respected corporations and professional service firms. Enron, in particular, clearly illustrates the devastating effects of this storm on shareholders, business partners, and other stakeholders.

Prior to its collapse, Enron was one of the world's largest energy companies. Based in Houston, Texas, Enron was created from the 1985 merger of Houston Natural Gas and InterNorth of Omaha, Nebraska. Originally an oil pipeline company, Enron rapidly developed into a diverse conglomerate. Its expanded businesses included energy futures, electricity delivery, financial risk management services, and e-commerce around the world.

In December 2000, Enron's shares hit a fifty-two-week high of $84.87. Just eleven months later, Enron set a Wall Street record with the heaviest single-volume trading day for a NYSE or NASDAQ listed stock. On that day, Enron's share price fell below $1. Over the course of those eleven months, Enron disclosed hundreds of millions of dollars in hidden losses, filed for bankruptcy, was investigated by the SEC, and attracted unprecedented public attention through daily headlines and ubiquitous media coverage. In the wake of Enron's collapse came that of its auditor, Arthur Andersen, one of the then Big Five (now Big Four) accounting firms.

Enron unraveled to spawn one of the largest investigations ever undertaken by the Department of Justice. Many of Enron's problems could be traced to the failure of its management, board of directors, and auditors. At the end of 2000, Enron still held many expensive high-technology investments that retained little value as the dot-com bubble burst. As the company incurred substantial losses, Enron's management and auditors colluded to insulate Enron's stock from an inevitable downward movement by concealing these losses from shareholders. Off–balance sheet entities were used to hide debt. Structured-finance transactions (specifically prepays) were used to make loans appear to be cash from operating activities. In the end, Enron attempted to hide more than $2.6 billion in debt.

While Enron went to considerable lengths to hide losses, the fact that Enron had the ability to hide those losses for nearly eighteen months is truly remarkable. This could not have happened if its gatekeepers had functioned in a responsible manner.

As Enron's auditors, Arthur Andersen suspected wrongdoing and discovered fraud, but failed to disclose their knowledge of the fraud. With the prospect of cross-selling lucrative consulting services and without the threat of civil liability, Andersen continued to certify Enron's financial statements and even destroyed documents containing evidence of Enron's misdeeds. Eventually, Arthur Andersen was found guilty of obstructing an SEC investigation of Enron, leading to the firm's eventual demise. Enron's board of directors also came under attack, with shareholders alleging that the board did not exercise its fiduciary duties to shareholders in the oversight of management.

RESPONSE TO CORPORATE GOVERNANCE FAILURES

Following the highly publicized Enron and Arthur Andersen collapses, a seemingly endless stream of additional corporate failures and financial scandals came to light. These failures, together with the bursting of the dot-com bubble and the dramatic fall in the value of U.S. securities in their wake, created a public outcry for wide-ranging reforms to restore investor confidence in the U.S. capital markets. After the failure of the communications company WorldCom in 2002, Congress quickly passed the Sarbanes-Oxley Act (Sarbanes-Oxley) by a vote of 97-0, with very little debate. Sarbanes-Oxley is the most significant piece of legislation in the history of federal securities regulations for two reasons. First, the legislation represented a dramatic departure from the traditional view that the regulation of U.S. corporations was the purview of the various states, a view clearly articulated by the U.S. Supreme Court in its 1987 decision in *CTS v. DCA*, upholding the Indiana state anti-takeover statute. The second aspect of the Sarbanes-Oxley Act that made it so remarkable is the fact that it mandated specific requirements as to the internal organization and function of public corporations. Although the federal regulations enacted in 1933 and 1934 affected the operations of public corporations, the effects were indirect in that they primarily dealt with disclosure and antifraud issues. In contrast, Sarbanes-Oxley dealt specifically with the corporate governance of public corporations.

To address auditor failures, Sarbanes-Oxley created the Public Company Accounting Oversight Board (PCAOB) to set and enforce standards and rules for the audit of public company accounting records. All public company auditors must register with the PCAOB. To eliminate the use of audit services as a loss-leader for consulting and other more lucrative services, Sarbanes-Oxley also prohibits a registered accounting firm from bundling certain services contemporaneously with audit services, including system design, internal audit, investment banking, and legal services. To increase auditor independence, the lead audit partner for any client is limited to five consecutive years; after which time the lead audit partner must relinquish this position to another partner for an additional five years. Anyone in a corporation with a "financial reporting oversight role," such as a CEO, CFO, treasurer, or controller may not have been employed by the external auditor or have participated on the audit within one year preceding the start of a new audit engagement. These and other requirements are intended to foster auditor independence and produce higher quality public reporting.

Sarbanes-Oxley greatly increased corporate responsibilities from the top down. The CEO and CFO of every public company are now required to certify that each periodic report containing financial statements filed by the company as the issuer of securities with the SEC "fully complies" with the 1934 Act and fairly presents, in all material respects, the financial condition and operating results of the company. CEOs and CFOs are subject to criminal liability if they knowingly make a false certification with regard to this requirement. To facilitate this certification, many companies have established compliance committees to review the quarterly and annual reports prior to such certification and have required line managers to certify the financial statements of each business unit.

In response to the off–balance sheet transactions that allowed Enron and others to conceal debt, Sarbanes-Oxley now requires enhanced financial disclosures. Issuers of securities must now disclose all material off–balance sheet transactions, obligations, and other relationships with consolidated entities or other persons. Most types of corporate loans to directors and executive officers are no longer permissible. Corporate insiders are now required to report transactions in their company's securities within two business days instead of one month. Periodic reports as well as reports of material changes in financial condition and results of operation must now be filed on an accelerated basis. Sarbanes-Oxley also expands penalties for wrongdoing. It increases maximum penalties for preexisting crimes and creates new criminal offenses for obstructing justice or impeding an investigation. Federal sentencing guidelines for financial fraud have been lengthened.

Much more emphasis is now being put on the oversight responsibilities of the board of directors. Audit committee responsibilities, in particular, have increased greatly. Sarbanes-Oxley requires all listed companies to have an audit committee composed entirely of independent, outside directors who receive no fees from the company other than board or committee fees, and to disclose whether one or more of the members is a "financial expert" (and if not, why not). The audit committee is required to have the authority to engage its own independent advisers and establish procedures for receiving complaints about auditing-related matters. The NYSE listing standards have also increased audit committee authority and responsibility. These listing standards give audit committees the authority to appoint and terminate external auditors and require audit committee members to review reports from external auditors at least annually.

One of the most controversial provisions of Sarbanes-Oxley extends the SEC's jurisdiction to attorneys who practice before it. Under Sarbanes-Oxley, outside lawyers are now required to play a greater role in corporate governance. They must report knowledge of any material violations of securities laws or breaches of fiduciary duties "up the ladder," all the way to the company's chief legal counsel or CEO. If these senior executives do not respond appropriately, outside lawyers are required to then make a report to the company's audit committee or even to the full board of directors. If "up the ladder" reports are disregarded by each of these company representatives, the lawyers may make a "noisy withdrawal" by filing the reasons for their withdrawal with the SEC. Although such a noisy withdrawal is still voluntary, its mere existence may weaken the attorney-client relationship as clients fear an erosion of attorney-client confidentiality.

Eliot Spitzer, attorney general for New York, drove the effort to address the failures arising from the conflicts inherent in relationships between equity research analysts and investment banks. Acting under the authority of a 1921 New York statute allowing the attorney general's office to conduct broad investigations of securities companies, Spitzer found e-mail evidence indicating that Merrill Lynch research analysts promoted companies underwritten by Merrill investment bankers. Numerous internal e-mails privately disparaged companies that were hailed in released reports. E-mails also showed that at least one company's securities had been downgraded by Merrill analysts when it did not give Merrill its investment banking business. Furthermore, analysts were compensated according to the amount of investment banking business they brought in. In May 2002, Spitzer reached an unprecedented agreement with Merrill to reform its research analyst practices by severing the link between analyst compensation and investment banking. Merrill was required to begin disclosing in its research reports whether the corporation being rated was also an investment banking client. This settlement led to investigations of, and settlements with, twelve other investment banks.

Analysts are now prohibited from participating in investment banking presentations. Investment banking departments are restricted from controlling or approving research reports prior to publication and cannot provide incentive compensation to analysts based on investment banking business. These prohibitions, however, leave open the questions of who will pay analysts, since brokerage commissions do not cover the costs of equity research, and whether more stocks will be covered by each analyst.

CONCLUDING THOUGHTS

The corporate governance pendulum has swung back toward distrust and a tighter rein over corporations and senior management. Sarbanes-Oxley and revised NYSE and NASD listing standards have placed great emphasis on the role of an independent board of directors in management oversight, risk management, and strategic planning. Some of the new requirements are expensive to implement, and the burden may fall disproportionately on smaller companies that have little revenue. The time requirements and costs of implementing increased reporting requirements, internal controls, and executive certifications of financial statements, and the substantial increase in directors' and officers' liability insurance premiums, have greatly increased the number of public companies expressing interest in going private. Investor confidence, however, seems to be returning, with the stock market rebounding substantially from its 2002 lows.

Many top executives, on the other hand, assert that no corporate governance system will be effective, no matter how stringent, unless appropriate values are communicated from the top down. They argue that without strong leaders who embrace the fiduciary duties to shareholders that they are entrusted with, corporations and their managements will rationally continue to exploit loopholes and inadvertent incentives inherent in any one-size-fits-all corporate governance system.

It is too early to assess the full impact of Sarbanes-Oxley. Many of its key provisions, like expanded internal controls under Section 404, are only being implemented as this volume goes to press. There is no question, however, that Sarbanes-Oxley is a serious legislative effort to address the conflict of interests inherent in the separation of ownership and control in the large-scale public corporation and make management more accountable to shareholders by increasing and strengthening the oversight role of the board of directors.

REFERENCES

Ackman, D. (2002, January 18). The scapegoating of Arthur Andersen. Forbes.com. Accessed on November 12, 2004, at http://www.forbes.com/2002/01/18/0118topnews.html

Baviera, G. J., and Walther, L. M. Stock option accounting: Defying the usual answers. Accessed on November 12, 2004, at http://www.nysscpa.org/cpajournal/2004/504/essentials/p36.htm

Berle, A. A., and Means, G. C. [1932] (1968). *The modern corporation and private property*. New York: Harcourt Brace and World.

Busbee, D. Symposium: Corporate governance symposium: Corporate governance: A perspective. *NAFTA L. and Bus. Rev. Am. 9*, 5.

Calio, J. E., and Zahralddin, R. X. (1994). The Securities and Exchange Commission's 1992 proxy amendments: Questions of accountability. *Pace L. Rev., 14*, 495, 486–488.

Coffee, J. C. Jr. (2004). What caused Enron? A capsule social and economic history of the 1990s. *Cornell L. Rev., 89*, 269.

Concannon, C. J. (1995). *Central Bank of Denver v. First Interstate Bank*: The end of aiding and abetting liability under Section 10(b) of the Securities Exchange Act of 1934. *St. Louis U. Pub. L. Rev., 14*, 679.

Cowell, E. F. (2001, October). Internet technology permits new proxy contest techniques. *Insights.*

CRS Report for Congress. (2003, January 30). The Enron collapse: An overview of financial issues.

Day, K. (2003, July 16). SEC chief supports plan to aid investors. *The Washington Post*, p. A1.

DeMott, D. A. Down the rabbit-hole and into the nineties: Issues of accountability in the wake of eighties-style transactions in control. *Geo. Wash. L. Rev.*, *61*, 1130.

Enron and Andersen: The story so far. Time.com article posted on New York State Society of CPAs website. Accessed on November 12, 2004, at http://www.nysscpa.org/enron/overview.htm

The financial collapse of Enron, part I. Hearing before the Subcommittee on Oversight and Investigations of the Committee of Energy and Commerce, House of Representatives, 107th Cong., 2d Sess. (February 5, 2002). Serial Number 107-86.

Goforth, C. (1994). Proxy reform as a means of increasing shareholder participation in corporate governance: Too little, but not toolate. *Am. U.L. Rev.*, *43*, 379, 400.

Haines, M. J. The elevated headnote. Law.com. Accessed on November 12, 2004, at http://www.law.com/jsp/article.jsp?id=1050369429283

Ignatius, A. Wall Street's top cop. Accessed on November 12, 2004, at http://www.time.com/time/personoftheyear/2002/poyspitzer.html

Kobler, G. P. (1998). Shareholder voting over the Internet: A proposal for increasing shareholder participation in corporate governance. *Ala. L. Rev.*, *49*, 673, 682–683.

MacAvoy, P. W., and Millstein, I. M. (2003). *The recurrent crisis in corporate governance.* New York: Palgrave MacMillan.

NASD Press Release. (1999, February 8). Blue ribbon committee on improving the effectiveness of corporate audit committees. Accessed on November 18, 2004, at http://www.nasd.com/stellent/idcplg?IdcService=SS_GET_PAGE&ssDocName=NASDW_010132&ssSourceNodeId=1108

NYSE History. Timeline at http://www.nyse.com/about/history/timeline_1980_1999_index.html

Painter, R. W. (2000). Case studies in legal ethics: Irrationality and cognitive bias at a closing in Arthur Solmssen's *The Comfort Letter. Fordham Law Review, 69.*

Pound, J. (1988). Proxy contests and the efficiency of shareholder oversight. *Journal of Financial Economics, 20, 237–265.*

Pound, J. (1991). Proxy voting and the SEC: Investor protection versus market efficiency. *Journal of Financial Economics, 29,* 241–286.

Roe, M. J. (1994). *Strong managers, weak owners: The political roots of American corporate finance.* Princeton University Press.

Roth, B. (1998, Fall). Proactive corporate-shareholder relations: Filling the communications void," *Cath. U.L. Rev.*, *48*, 101.

SEC adopts new rules concerning audit committees. Accessed on November 18, 2004, at http://www.murthalaw.com/_documents/Publication%5CPublication15.pdf

Securities Industry Association. Basic laws, Securities Exchange Act of 1934. Accessed on November 15, 2004, at http://www.sia.com/capitol_hill/html/sec_exchange_act_of_1934.html

Sharara, N. M., and Hoke-Witherspoon, A. E. (1993, November). The evolution of the 1992 shareholder communication proxy rules and their impact on corporate governance. *Bus. Law, 49,* 327.

Stabile, S. J. (1999). Motivating executives: Does performance-based compensation positively affect managerial performance? *U. Pa. J. Lab. and Emp. L., 2,* 227.

U.S. Securities and Exchange Commission. *Laws that govern the industry.* Accessed on November 15, 2004, at http://www.sec.gov/about/whatwedo.shtml#laws

Wexler, B. History of the Securities Exchange Commission. Accessed on November 11, 2004, at http://www.sechistorical.org/museum/Museum_Papers/Archive_Paper_PDFs/Wexler_History_SEC_1975.pdf

Worthy, J. C., and Neuschel, R. P. (1984). *Emerging issues in corporate governance.* Northwestern University, J. L. Kellogg School of Management.

II
ROLES AND RESPONSIBILITIES OF CORPORATE DIRECTORS

4

Promoting Good Corporate Governance

A SPEECH BY WILLIAM H. DONALDSON

On February 18, 2003, William H. Donaldson became the twenty-seventh chairman of the U.S. Securities and Exchange Commission, which is charged with overseeing the regulation of U.S. securities markets, ensuring compliance with the enforcement of securities laws, and ensuring the protection of investors' interests. Donaldson, former CEO of Donaldson, Lufkin and Jenrette, of Aetna, and of the New York Stock Exchange, was pressed into service in the wake of severe criticism of the SEC's watchfulness during the previous decade. The collapse of blue-chip firms such as Enron and great concern over conflicts of interest in the securities industry led to the resignation of Donaldson's predecessor, Harvey Pitt.

In this presentation to the Directors' College at the Stanford Law School, Donaldson describes the SEC's key steps that were taken to restore trust after the recent troubles. His remarks constitute a snapshot of the concerns and initiatives that drove securities regulation in the early years of the new century.

When I became SEC chairman, I put forth five goals: restore investor confidence, hold accountable those who have violated the public trust, make the securities markets more efficient and transparent, implement structural changes to the commission that would help it become more anticipatory, and promote responsible corporate governance. These objectives are fundamental to the foundation of our securities markets. It was clear that the work to advance them would be challenging, not to mention urgent. The corporate landscape was littered with high-profile failures, scandals had come to dominate the business news, and equity markets had plunged. Beyond that, there were compelling signs that shortcomings in the performance of corporate leaders were more pervasive—making the numbers, managing earnings in "good" ways, and other troublesome practices seemed too common, and, even worse, there were signs that this sort of unacceptable behavior was on the verge of becoming accepted practice.

The cumulative effect of all this produced a crisis of investor confidence, which in turn led to a demand for corrective action. The enactment of Sarbanes-Oxley marked the beginning of a new era for American business. The SEC staff has skillfully implemented the many different provisions of the landmark law. The process has been marked by the commission's focused rulemaking in a number of areas, augmented by efforts aimed at cleaning up after corporate scandals and tackling the wrongdoing in the mutual fund industry. At the same time we are seeking to adopt regulations for governing the functioning of our securities markets, which are becoming more technical, active, and global. While the job is not complete, I believe we have made real and lasting progress toward reform and, in so doing, toward restoration of investor confidence.

Let me begin by talking about some of these initiatives and accomplishments since I was here a year ago, and then move on to a few comments on the vital issues of corporate governance that have brought you all together for this conference.

INTERNAL REFORMS AT THE COMMISSION

Upon becoming chairman, internal reform of the structure at the commission has been one of my top priorities. It was clear to me that we needed to devote more time and energy to anticipating potential problems across the corporate and financial industries before they occur. While I have referred to this effort as "looking over the hill and around the corner" for the next emerging problem, what we're really referring to is a systematic and philosophical approach to risk assessment embraced by the commission. It is an effort to anticipate "red flags" and address upcoming problems before they happen—instead of arriving at the scene of the accident after it has occurred.

To do this has required a complete reevaluation of how the SEC should function—to foster an unprecedented level of communication, coordination, and cooperation between staff in the divisions and offices. Thanks to significant budgetary help from Congress and the president, we have been able to hire over 840 professionals for the commission's staff.

We have initiated a new program of risk assessment, with multidiscipline teams drawn from inside the agency, designed to be integrated with our new Office of Risk Assessment and Strategic Planning, the first of its kind at the commission. The goal is twofold: to become better equipped to anticipate potential problems, and then to seek to prevent these problems from infecting our markets.

Our first priority has been to infuse the agency's various divisions and offices with a commitment to risk assessment in their own spheres of responsibility. We have organized internal risk teams for each major program area. This framework allows for a bottom-up approach to assessing risk in each of our divisions. A good example of this approach can be found in our Office of Compliance Inspections and Examinations, where our frontline examiners across the country produced a complete "risk map" of potential problems— new or resurgent forms of fraud and illegal or questionable activities—in the mutual fund and broker-dealer industries.

I believe the risk assessment initiative will influence all of our work in the agency—from enforcement, to examinations, to rule-makings, to our review of required filings. It will arm senior managers at the commission with the information they need to make better decisions and to proactively adjust operations, resources, and methods of oversight to address new challenges and prevent new problems. The initiative will also help foster better communication, coordination, and even cross-fertilization between the divisions and offices within the commission.

TASK FORCES

A different illustration of our effort to encourage this communication, coordination, and cross-fertilization is the creation of policy task forces. These task forces bring together staff from various divisions and offices to brainstorm, evaluate, and create policy options that will help us undertake issues of emerging concern in protecting our securities markets. Currently there are six such task forces tackling a number of important issues: soft-dollar arrangements, bond market transparency, college savings plans, or the so-called "529 plans," self-reporting regime for mutual funds and self-regulatory organizations (SROs or markets), and, over the longer haul, our entire disclosure regime. The task forces are meeting with relevant, interested parties such as individual investors, industry representatives, and fellow regulators to gather critical intelligence and data, and then they will produce policy options designed to address problems over the long haul.

ENFORCING AMERICA'S SECURITIES LAWS

Critical to the commission's work, of course, is the enforcement of America's securities laws. In the past year alone, the Enforcement Division has brought charges of misconduct against twelve of the twenty-five largest mutual fund complexes. The division also filed more enforcement actions in the previous fiscal year than in any other year on record (679), and this year it has already obtained orders for more than $2.2 billion in penalties and disgorgements.

I cite all of these numbers only as measures of just how pervasive malfeasance has been in recent years, and of the impact of the expanded enforcement powers vested with the SEC thanks to Sarbanes-Oxley. Those expanded powers are not only helping us to pursue wrongdoers, but also to return to investors a portion of the penalties we impose against firms, through the Fair Fund provisions. While aggressively pursuing wrongdoing, the division's core code is to execute its mission in a manner that is both forceful and fair. I believe we are delivering on this imperative.

MARKET STRUCTURE REFORM

The Division of Market Regulation is tackling a number of critical issues—none more important than addressing changes in the structure of America's equity markets. As our financial markets continue evolving due to new technologies, new market entrants, and changing investment patterns, the commission must monitor these changes and ensure that the regulation of the market structure remains up to date.

In February the commission proposed Regulation NMS—National Market System—which is a comprehensive package of rule proposals aimed at modernizing the national market system that Congress mandated in 1975. In brief, the proposed regulation would modernize trading rules, establish greater consistency in access fees, ban the display of sub-penny quotes in most stocks, and alter the rules concerning how market data is disseminated and priced.

REFORM THE MUTUAL FUND INDUSTRY

A particularly urgent priority for the commission has been our efforts to reform the mutual fund industry. Over the years we have all seen isolated cases of wrongdoing here and there. But I think everyone was shocked to discover the complicity of certain elements of the industry in condoning widespread unethical and illegal practices. The commission has moved swiftly and forcefully in this area, considering twelve new mutual fund rule-making proposals—all of which, taken together, seek to strengthen the governance structure of mutual funds, address conflicts of interests, enhance disclosure to mutual fund shareholders, and foster an atmosphere of high ethical standards and compliance within the industry.

On Wednesday the commission will consider for final approval a rule to bolster the effectiveness of independent directors and to solidify the role of the fund board as the primary advocate for fund shareholders. The rule includes a requirement for an independent board chairman and a board on which at least 75 percent of the directors are independent. The proposal also solidifies the role of the fund board as the primary advocate for fund shareholders.

Conflicts of interest are inherent in the mutual fund context, where the interests of fund shareholders are not always aligned with the interests of the adviser or the adviser's shareholders. The commission recognizes that there are interested fund chairmen who strive to represent the interests of fund investors in the boardroom while also serving as executives of the fund's adviser. But no matter how hard they try, they cannot eliminate the inherent conflicts of interest. When the chairman or CEO of a mutual fund's adviser is simultaneously serving as the chairman of the mutual fund itself, this individual is put in the untenable position of having to serve two masters. On the one hand, he or she owes a state-law-imposed duty of loyalty and care to the mutual fund, augmented by the Investment Company Act requirement that the fund must be operated solely for the benefit of the fund's shareholders. On the other hand, he or she owes a separate duty of loyalty and care to the shareholders of the fund's investment adviser. It is easy to see that these two duties are often in conflict; for example, consider the conflict that necessarily arises when it comes to setting the level of fees the fund will pay the adviser.

REGISTRATION OF HEDGE FUND ADVISERS

It has been hard to miss the media coverage concerning the SEC's attention to hedge funds, and the role several prominent hedge funds played in recent mutual fund scandals. Given the rapid rate of growth in hedge funds, the size of their assets—about $800 billion and rapidly approach $1 trillion—and the involvement of some hedge fund managers in illegal behavior, the commission staff is evaluating a form of registration and an oversight regime for hedge fund managers.

The goal is simple: to enable the commission to collect more accurate information about this important industry and better target our inquiries to those hedge fund managers where there is some reasonable concern that they may be violating the federal securities laws. There is no desire to regulate how hedge funds make their investments, to require disclosure of their methods, or to choke off their expansion, as hedge funds have an important role to play in our equity markets.

IMPROVING GOVERNANCE GENERALLY

I want to turn to the commission's rule-making on governance issues, but first I'd like to say a few words about how we should all think about SEC rules versus our own responsibilities.

It is important to remember that the commission's rules have never been enough, are not enough today, and will never be enough in the future to ensure that our markets and our corporations are clean and ethical. What's really needed is a change in mind-set—a company-wide culture that fosters ethical behavior and decision-making. Creating that culture means doing more than developing good policies and procedures, doing more than installing a

competent legal and accounting staff, and doing more than giving them resources and up-to-date technology. It means instilling an ethic—a company-
wide commitment to do the right thing, this time and every time—so much so
that it becomes the core of what I call the essential "DNA" of the company.

Companies, management, their gatekeepers, and above all their directors
must look beyond just conforming to the letter of the new laws and regulations. They must redefine corporate governance with practices that go beyond
mere adherence to new rules and demonstrate ethics, integrity, honesty, and
transparency. The recent shifting of primary corporate governance responsibilities to corporate boards demands that directors be the true stewards of
corporate governance, and their actions must demonstrate their dedication to
this stewardship without undue interference from the CEO and other members
of management.

One litmus test for this new board stewardship of corporate governance
involves executive compensation. In making compensation decisions, boards
and compensation committees must focus above all on long-term performance. And directors should examine their dependence on management and
compensation consultants when making decisions about compensation for the
chief executive and other senior management. The conventional wisdom of
many corporate boards these days has become that in order to remain competitive, executive compensation must be in the top quarter of companies in
their industry. But we don't live in Lake Wobegon, where, as Garrison Keillor
says, "All the women are strong, all the men are good-looking, and all the
children are above average." Rather, it is the job of the board to set appropriate
compensation that is related to the goals and performance of top management,
not the pressure to meet an artificial standard informed by outside consultants
who do not share the responsibility of being board members.

Some have said government should rein in the high pay of CEOs. I don't
believe that the government should intervene to set compensation levels, but I
do believe that company boards must show greater discipline and judgment in
awarding pay packages that are linked to long-term performance. I would
like to see a much broader definition of performance—performing an evaluation that goes well beyond earnings-per-share (EPS) and other financial
measures, to identify what management excellence, and hence reward, is all
about.

Of course, we can in fact support your stewardship efforts through focused
and fair rule-making by the commission. We have labored hard to meet this
standard at the SEC—all against the backdrop of a decade in which corporate
governance was often grossly inadequate, and sometimes failed completely.
Sarbanes-Oxley and all the rules we have adopted to implement Sarbanes-
Oxley have helped to correct these failures, and have forced a reassessment
of the role of the board of directors in particular. At bottom, all these legislative and rule changes have reinforced the notion that the responsibilities of
directors must be partially redefined, with the objective that directors should

finally emerge from the long shadow of the imperial CEO and should assert their oversight authority in corporate decision-making.

And when we looked at how directors should be elected to these refocused and reenergized corporate boards, we realized that the proxy process needed some critical attention. In the pre-Sarbanes-Oxley world, overly compliant boards of directors often allowed management almost unfettered control over many critical governance issues, including over the proxy process related to nominating and electing directors. As a result, some company boards and management would completely ignore dissatisfied shareholders in the proxy process. Immediately after the annual meeting, shareholder resolutions passed by a large plurality or a majority of votes cast were just disregarded and never implemented. And when significant numbers of company shareholders expressed their disapproval of management's director nominees by withholding their votes, management and the incumbent board ignored the withheld votes, too. Management and boards refused to respond in any demonstrable way to a clear expression of dissatisfaction of large numbers of shareholders.

The commission took the first step to address this issue head-on last fall, when we adopted new standards to address the breakdown in shareholder communications by improving corporate disclosure in two areas. First, improved disclosure regarding the process by which nominating committees consider director candidates, including those recommended by shareholders. And second, improved disclosure about the processes by which security holders could communicate directly with members of the board. We hope that the transparency created by these standards will help produce more communication among management, directors, and shareholders generally, but especially with respect to the nomination of candidates for boards of directors.

A second step the commission took to address the issue is a proposed rule that would require the inclusion of shareholder nominees in the company's proxy materials, under limited circumstances and only upon the occurrence of certain triggering events.

Consider the situation faced by a sizable group of shareholders who are committed to the long-term prospects for a certain company but who confront a company management that refuses to respond to, or even communicate about, the shareholder group's concerns. The dilemma is that the shareholders have only two practical choices. First, they can choose to cease being committed to the long-term health of the company; in other words, they can sell their stock. Under this choice, they would be forced to give up their belief that, with some modest changes in company direction, the company could be more successful in its markets and therefore be an extremely productive investment over the longer term.

Their second—and only other—choice is to wage an extremely expensive proxy fight. This contest could be for the entire board of directors or for only some seats on the board—a so-called "short slate." In either case, the proxy fight takes on the trappings of a contest for control. Under this choice, too, therefore, the shareholders would be forced to give up their belief that modest changes in company direction could produce the long-term benefits they seek. Instead, they are forced to divert the company's resources away from the business they're building, to the proxy fight they're waging—the last thing the shareholders really want for the company's future.

The proxy access proposal under consideration by the SEC is an attempt to find a middle ground between the extreme choices of forcing shareholders to give up their long-term interest in the company and sell their stock on the one hand and forcing them to wage a wasteful proxy fight on the other. It is an attempt to find a middle ground that would, under certain restrictions and limitations, provide shareholders having a true interest in the long-term health of the company with a more effective proxy process that gives them a better voice in this nomination and election of the board of directors. In essence, it is an attempt to encourage management and long-term shareholders to communicate more effectively with each other about the company's future.

The current proposal is important, but complex and controversial. Unfortunately, the controversial aspect threatens to overshadow the importance of what the commission is trying to accomplish. There are strongly held views on all sides of this issue. While we welcome the expression of all views—that is the essence of our notice-and-comment rule-making process—the escalating, shrill, and fearful rhetoric on all sides of this issue has drowned out thoughtful discourse and comment. Those who believe that our proposal is a serious and unwarranted threat to the operation of boards and those who believe that our proposal does not go far enough in giving shareholders a more effective proxy process have gone well beyond the bounds of thoughtful and sensible comment.

For example, some proposed offering the company a chance to "cure" the shareholder communication problem on its own—that is, if a majority of shareholders withheld their vote for an incumbent director, the board nominating committee would be empowered to replace the "withheld" director with a new director more acceptable to the shareholders. In response, a prominent publication quoted someone summarizing the proposal like this: "If Bozo A gets voted down, the nominating committee can substitute him for Bozo B." Similarly, a corporate governance activist has derided this idea as doing no more than replacing "Tweedledum with Tweedledee."

On the other side, the Business Roundtable has said that this one modest change in the proxy rule would, and I quote, "put companies, shareholders, and the economic recovery at risk." The U.S. Chamber of Commerce has said that the proposal "could seriously impair the competitiveness of America's best companies [and] put proprietary business information at risk."

That this is an election year doesn't help. Reports that this is a partisan political issue miss the point entirely. Republicans and Democrats alike are on all sides of this issue. Politics must not be allowed to drive the public debate or the commission's deliberations on this matter, or any other. The imperative here is to approach this issue—like all others—in a thoughtful, measured way and to try to do the right thing for the corporations and shareholders who own them.

I remain committed to responsible and constructive change in this area, and will proceed thoughtfully and carefully. Our goal is the right course rather than a hasty, less thoughtful course. We will not be forced to act in the face of an artificial deadline. However, after sixty years of repeated commission consideration of this topic, the time has come for sensible, balanced, and constructive debate leading to action designed to improve our proxy process for the nomination of directors.

So I would encourage you—and the companies you serve—to avoid unproductive rhetoric and focus rather on the central problem the proposed rule addresses—how to find a middle ground between the extreme choices of forcing shareholders to give up their long-term interest in the company and sell their stock on the one hand, and forcing them to wage a wasteful proxy fight on the other. Let's not mock those who struggle to find this middle ground. And let's not proclaim the end of American economic competitiveness if any such middle ground were found. Instead, I would ask you and your companies to provide thoughtful, meaningful input that will help the commission arrive at an effective, workable solution that will benefit investors, our companies, and our markets. Frankly, they deserve nothing less.

CONCLUSION

I am encouraged by the work the commission staff has set in motion, on a range of issues, as well as the work it has completed. And I know this has been a difficult period for everyone working in or around American business. The past five years or so have had more peaks and valleys, and general tumult, than any other equivalent time period in recent memory. Extraordinary wealth has been created, and destroyed, during this period. Regaining the confidence of all investors will still take time, but I believe the pendulum is swinging in the right direction, and by working together we will win back this confidence.

5

Shareholder Primacy Is a Choice, Not a Legal Mandate

CONSTANCE E. BAGLEY

A basic misconception, captured succinctly in a recent *New Yorker* cartoon, pervades corporate America. In the cartoon, a group of men, presumably corporate directors, are sitting around a table as one laments, "I, too, hate being a greedy bastard, but we have a responsibility to our shareholders." Notwithstanding the frequent incantation that directors must do everything within the law to maximize shareholder value,[1] there is no statutory or common law fiduciary duty on the part of a director to put on blinders and look solely at the impact of a proposed action on the company's stock price. Individual directors may *choose* to put the interests of shareholders first, to do anything in their name as long as it is not illegal, without regard for the effects on others, but they are not *required* to do so. The law has come a long way in the past two decades to reassure directors that they need not check their sense of ethics at the boardroom door.

DUTY OF DIRECTORS TO ACT IN THE BEST INTERESTS OF THE CORPORATION

In Delaware (and most other jurisdictions) the corporation statute provides that the corporation shall be managed by or under the direction of the board of directors. The directors are elected by the shareholders, the providers of capital, and ultimately they are subject to replacement if the shareholders are displeased with their actions. Nonetheless, while in office, it is the directors, not the shareholders, who are responsible for governing the corporation. As Delaware chancellor William T. Allen explained in a case that ultimately upheld the right of the directors of Time, Inc. to rebuff an offer by Paramount and instead complete a leveraged buyout of Warner Communications that a majority of the Time shareholders opposed, "It has not been and is not now the law that the directors must act in accordance with the wishes of a majority of its shareholders."[2]

Instead, directors are required to manage the corporation in the best interests of the corporation. Moreover, under the judicially created standard of review known as the *business judgment rule,* courts will generally presume "that in making a business decision the directors of a corporation acted on an informed basis, in good faith and in the honest belief that the action taken was in the best interests of the company."[3] The presumption "can be overturned only if a plaintiff can show that a majority of the directors expected to derive personal financial benefit from the transaction, that they lacked independence, that they were grossly negligent in failing to inform themselves, or that the decision of the Board was so irrational that it could not have been the reasonable exercise of the business judgment of the Board."[4]

Constituency Statutes

More than thirty states have adopted so-called constituency statutes, which expressly authorize the board to take into account the interests of all constituencies (such as shareholders, employees, customers, suppliers, the community, and the environment) when deciding how to act.[5] Although most of these statutes do not require directors to take all constituencies into account, they reflect a consensus that corporations can best maximize their long-term wealth-producing capabilities by fairly taking into account the interests of all those responsible for the corporation's success.[6]

For example, in an effort to thwart a hostile takeover bid by the Belzbergs of Canada for Armstrong, a major Pennsylvania employer, the Pennsylvania legislature amended the Pennsylvania Business Corporation Law in 1990 to, inter alia, permit directors to consider the "effects of any action upon any or all groups affected by such action, including shareholders, employees, suppliers, customers and creditors of the corporation, and upon communities in which offices or other establishments of the corporation are located."[7] The board is not required to regard any corporate interest or the interests of any particular groups as a dominant or controlling interest or factor.[8]

Delaware Boards Have the Right to Take All Constituencies into Account

Delaware, where a majority of the *Fortune* 500 companies are incorporated, does not have a constituency statute, but the Delaware Supreme Court has made it clear through case law that in discharging their obligation to manage the corporation in the corporation's best interest, directors may consider the effects of their decision not just on shareholders but on other constituencies. As discussed further below, it is only after the board has decided that a change-of-control transaction (such as a merger or dissolution) is in the best interest of the corporation, after having considered the impact on these constituencies, that the directors must seek to achieve the highest possible value for the shareholders.

In an extreme case, the Delaware Court of Chancery approved a non-monetary settlement of shareholder derivative and class action lawsuits challenging the Occidental Petroleum board's decision to spend more than $85 million of Occidental's money to build and fund an art museum to house the art collected by founder and chairman of the board Armand Hammer, who had acquired much of it with Occidental's funds.[9] The court rejected claims that the gift was a waste of Occidental's assets, holding that given the net worth of Occidental, its annual net income before taxes ($574 million), and the tax benefits to Occidental, the gift was within the range of reasonableness.[10] The court held that the decision was protected by the business judgment rule even though, in the court's view, the shareholders would be warranted in electing different directors.[11] The court also approved the settlement's generous provisions limiting future contributions to Hammer-affiliated charities to an amount equal to the dividends paid to shareholders.

Example: Ford Motor Company

One of the earliest proponents of corporate policies designed to benefit employees and customers was Henry Ford, founder of the Ford Motor Company. Originally, Ford's Model T sold for more than $900. The price was lowered from time to time notwithstanding improvements made to the car, and by 1916 the car cost only $360.[12] In 1914, Ford built the first fully automated assembly line and cut the production time from twelve hours in 1908 to an hour-and-a-half.[13] When the new manufacturing facility opened, "Ford announced unprecedented wage increases—from an average of $2.40 for a 9-hour day to a minimum of $5.00 for an 8-hour day."[14] Even though Ford's cars were produced by the highest-paid industrial workforce in the United States, they cost only half as much as the cars sold by Ford's nearest competitor.[15] Rather than follow suit, many manufacturers denounced Ford for driving up wage scales.[16]

Ford's policies of selling improved cars at lower prices and paying workers well was driven by his business philosophy: "My ambition . . . is to employ still more men to spread the benefits of this industrial system to the greatest possible number, to help them build up their lives and their homes."[17]

Ford was able to do this while still paying its founders cash dividends in the first thirteen years of the company's existence that were fifty times the original paid-in capital.[18] For the year ended July 31, 1916, Ford's strategies of reducing price and increasing output resulted in profits of $59,994,118 and capital surplus (assets minus liabilities and stated capital) of $111,960,907.[19]

The Michigan Supreme Court upheld the decision of the Ford directors to pay above prevailing salary levels and to charge less for its cars than the market would bear.[20] Minority Ford shareholders had sued to block board-approved expansion plans and to demand that more special dividends be paid out of Ford's capital surplus of almost $112 million. In his answer to the complaint, Henry Ford (then the majority stockholder) argued that retaining large cash reserves to fund expansion and to prevent massive layoffs in bad times "ultimately redound to the best financial interests of the company and its stockholders."[21] The Michigan Supreme Court upheld the Ford directors' discretion to set employee wages and working conditions and car prices and to spend more than $24 million to expand the business to include the smelting of iron ore for use in the manufacture of Ford automobiles.

The court held, however, that at the outer limit "it is not within the lawful powers of a board of directors to shape and conduct the affairs of a corporation for the merely incidental benefit of shareholders and for the primary purpose of benefiting others...."[22] In light of Ford's exceedingly strong cash position and the regularity and size of its cash flow going forward, the court ordered Ford to declare a special dividend of one-half of accumulated cash surplus less the amount of special dividends ($2,000,000) paid after the suit was filed, for a total special dividend of $19,275,386. This still left Ford with a cash surplus of more than $30 million and a total surplus of more than $90 million.[23]

DECONSTRUCTING CORPORATE LAW

This paradigm of directors' duties is consistent with the history behind corporations in the United States. The first corporations were established in the late eighteenth and early nineteenth centuries to complete projects (such as new roads and bridges) or to perform services (such as supplying water or banking facilities) for the public good. Limited liability, normally a privilege accorded only governmental entities, was extended by the state legislatures to these quasi-public entities chartered to serve the public interest.

Explicit in these quasi-public rights was the quid pro quo of social, not simply legal and economic, responsibility to interests broader than shareholders' profits.[24] Ronald Seavoy makes it clear that corporate charters "assumed that corporations were legally privileged organizations that had to be closely scrutinized by the legislature because their purposes had to be made consistent with public welfare."[25] Louis Hartz notes, for example, that in 1833 there was vigorous legislative opposition to Pennsylvania's grant of a coal company charter on the grounds that the industry had become sufficiently developed that it could attract private capital and thus had no need for a charter.[26] Joseph Davis similarly describes the rigorous debates in which legislatures engaged on the subject of incorporation.[27] John Davis confirms that "[e]arly in the [nineteenth] century, it was not considered justifiable to create corporations for any purpose not clearly public in nature."[28]

The public purpose tradition of the corporation retained much of its legitimacy throughout the twentieth century. President Theodore Roosevelt commented to Congress early in the century: "Business success, whether for the individual or for the Nation, is a good thing only so far as it is accompanied by and develops a high standard of—honor, integrity, civic courage.... This Government stands for manhood first and for business only as an adjunct of manhood."[29] President Woodrow Wilson stated, "I hate that old maxim 'Business is business,' for I understand by it that business is not moral. The man who says, 'I am not in business for my health,' means that he is not in business for his moral health, and I am an enemy of every business of this kind. But if business is regarded as an object for serving and obtaining private profit by means of service, then I am with that business."[30]

Leaders of industry echoed these sentiments. Frank Abrams, speaking in 1951 as the chair of Standard Oil Company, stated that the responsibility of management is "to maintain an equitable working balance among the claims of the various directly interested groups—stockholders, employees, customers, and the public at large."[31] In testimony quoted in *A. P. Smith Mfg. Co. v. Barlow*,[32] Abrams testified that corporations are expected to acknowledge their public responsibilities in support of the essential elements of the U.S. free enterprise system. He indicated that it was not "good business" to disappoint "this reasonable and justified public expectation," nor was it good business for corporations "to take substantial benefits from their membership in the economic community while avoiding the normally accepted obligations of citizenship in the social community."

But there are other philosophical antecedents to the notion that corporate governance should take more into account than just the company's stock price. Adam Smith, the proponent of giving free rein to the market's "invisible hand," predicated the "society of perfect liberty" that he advocated in *The Wealth of Nations* on the notions of self-control and adherence to social rules and codes of behavior articulated in his first major work, *The Theory of Moral Sentiments*.

Most, if not all, stock corporations are formed with the expectation that they will earn a profit for those who put up the necessary capital—the shareholders. Yet, as the history of corporations makes clear, the government initially granted corporations entity status, limited liability for shareholders, and perpetual life because the corporations of that day served important social purposes by supporting public works. Thus, the compact between the corporation and its shareholders, which entails providing a mechanism for shareholders to obtain attractive returns to meet their own needs, is only part of the picture. There is also at least the residue of another compact, that between society (represented by the government that authorizes the formation of the corporation) and the corporation. As Dennis W. Bakke, president and chief executive officer of AES Corporation, remarked, earning profits for share-holders is like having oxygen to breathe; you need oxygen to survive, but it's not your purpose for living. Instead, he asserts in the September 1998 issue of *Director's Monthly,* the "ultimate purpose" for which corporations do and should exist "is to steward resources to meet the needs of the world."

ECONOMIC RATIONALES FOR DIRECTORS' DISCRETION

The discretion the law gives directors to look beyond the shareholders to all constituencies affected by their actions is also consistent with the need to address the market inefficiencies that result from the exploitation of negative externalities, that is, actions by one party that adversely affect the welfare of another. For example, toxic discharge from a nearby factory, which spoils the neighbors' environment and threatens their health, is an externality because it affects people and firms other than those making the decisions. Market inefficiencies occur to the extent that decision-makers do not take these externally imposed costs into account in their decision-making.

As Stanford economists Paul Milgrom and D. John Roberts explain:

A firm's decisions about the design and placement of its factories can affect community housing values, traffic, and environmental quality; its choices of suppliers can affect the distribution of wages and profits among the potential suppliers; and its pricing policy affects both competitors and customers. . . .

With incomplete markets and imperfect bargaining, the way various interests are weighed in decisions can have consequences for the efficiency of the economic system that cannot be ignored. For example, in the plant closing decisions, investments by workers and others in houses near the factory may lose much of their value if the factory were to close. Such investments are cospecialized with the plant. Efficiency requires that the homeowners' interests be given some weight in this decision. Similarly, the workers may have invested in firm-specific human capital that is, by its very nature, cospecialized with the plant. Closing the plant destroys the value of these investments. The township as a whole may have invested in roads, sewage-treatment facilities, schools, and other assets whose value depends on the plant's continued operation.[33]

A myopic focus on shareholder value can result not only in the unfair treatment of nonshareholder constituencies, but also in economic harm to the shareholders. In the age of the Internet and 24/7 cable networks dedicated exclusively to news, misdeeds in faraway places are often featured on the evening news at home the same day. Nongovernmental organizations (NGOs) and other interest groups track and report on the working conditions in overseas factories, the dumping of hazardous waste and spoliation of forests and rivers, the exploitation of indigenous peoples, and the sale of shoddy and dangerous products. Maintaining a reputation for integrity and honesty is more important than ever as customers vote with their feet and boycott clothing made in sweatshops in the Mauritius Islands or gasoline made from oil transported in pipelines built with slave labor in Myanmar.

Joseph Neubauer, CEO of Aramark Worldwide Corporation, walked away from two well-priced and fully negotiated overseas acquisitions that were perfectly suited to Aramark's goal of international expansion after a closer look at their operations and books revealed unsavory business practices. He justified the loss of time and money, stating, "It takes a lifetime to build a reputation, and only a short time to lose it all."[34]

Professors Henry Mintzberg, Robert Simons, and Kunal Basu characterized the assertion that corporations exist solely to maximize shareholder value as a "half-truth" that contributed significantly to the "syndrome of selfishness" that took hold of our corporations and society in the late twentieth and early twenty-first centuries.[35] They argued that focusing on shareholder value without taking account of other stakeholders' interests "reflects a fallacious separation of the economic and social consequences of decisionmaking."[36]

Even economist Michael C. Jensen, a staunch believer in shareholder primacy, acknowledged in a 2001 article the importance of focusing on long-term not short-term shareholder value: "Short-term profit maximization at the expense of long-term value creation is a sure way to destroy value."[37] Jensen explained, "In order to maximize value, corporate managers must not only satisfy, but enlist the support of, all corporate stakeholders—customers, employees, managers, suppliers, local communities."[38] He cautioned that "we cannot maximize the long term market value of an organization if we ignore or mistreat any important constituency."[39]

DIRECTORS' FIDUCIARY DUTIES IN THE TWENTY-FIRST CENTURY

Fast forward to the twenty-first century. No special government permission is required to incorporate in many jurisdictions. All that's required is a check for the filing fee plus a bare-bones document setting forth the corporation's name, the classes of authorized stock, a boilerplate statement of purpose, and the name of an agent for service of process. Corporations can be formed for virtually any lawful purpose with no special governmental permissions required.

The American Bar Association's *Corporate Director's Guidebook* summarizes a corporate director's responsibilities as follows:

> Stated broadly, the principal responsibility of a corporate director is to promote the best interests of the corporation and its shareholders in directing the corporation's business and affairs.

> In so doing, the director should give primary consideration to long-term economic objectives. However, a director should also be concerned that the

corporation conducts its affairs with due appreciation of public expectations, taking into consideration trends in the law and ethical standards. Furthermore, pursuit of the corporation's economic objectives may include consideration of the effect of corporate policies and operations upon the corporation's employees, the public, and the environment.[40]

The American Law Institute's Project on Principles of Corporate Governance echoes these standards. It states as a general rule that "a corporation . . . should have as its objective the conduct of business activities with a view to enhancing corporate profit and shareholder gain."[41] Nevertheless, "[e]ven if corporate profit and shareholder gain are not thereby enhanced, the corporation, in the conduct of its business: . . . [m]ay devote a reasonable amount of resources to public welfare, humanitarian, educational, and philanthropic purposes."[42] The comment to the ALI principle elaborates:

> It is now widely accepted that the corporation should at least consider the social impact of its activities, so as to be aware of the social costs those activities entail. By implication, the corporation should be permitted to take such costs into account, within reason. For example, the corporation may take into account, within reason, public-welfare concerns relevant to groups with whom the corporation has a legitimate concern, such as employees, customers, suppliers, and members of the communities within which the corporation operates.[43]

Directors have a "triad" of fiduciary duties owed to the corporation they serve: the duty of loyalty, the duty to act in good faith, and the duty of due care.[44]

Duty of Loyalty

The duty of loyalty requires directors to act in the best interests of the corporation. They must disclose any possible conflicts of interest to their fellow board members and may not secretly benefit at the corporation's expense. If they become aware of corporate opportunities in the company's line of business, directors must offer those opportunities to the company before pursuing them on their own.

Duty to Act in Good Faith

The duty to act in good faith is often subsumed within the duty of loyalty, but recent cases in Delaware and elsewhere have broken it out as a separate duty.[45] This is most likely being done to parallel the language the Delaware legislature used when it amended Section 102(b)(7) of the Delaware General Corporation Law to permit corporations to amend their corporate charters to limit or eliminate directors' personal liability for breaches of the duty of care but not for breaches of the duty of loyalty or failure to act in good faith.

At a minimum, good faith means showing up and honestly trying to fulfill the duties of a director. Directors who become aware of potential risks to the corporation but adopt a passive "come what may" attitude have not acted in good faith. Thus, the directors of Abbott Laboratories did not act in good faith when they allegedly failed to act after being put on notice that one of Abbott's facilities, which contributed 20 percent of its earnings, had been repeatedly cited by the Food and Drug Administration for not complying with the FDA's manufacturing standards.[46] As a result, they were potentially personally liable for the $100 million fine Abbott paid and the millions of dollars of inventory it had to destroy because of quality control problems.

Similarly, the directors may not give unfettered discretion to the chief executive officer to hire or fire key officers or to enter into expensive multiyear employment contracts or other severance arrangements. The Delaware Court of Chancery refused to dismiss a shareholder directive suit brought against the Walt Disney Company's directors for alleged breaches of fiduciary duty in connection with the hiring and firing of Michael Ovitz and the payment of $140 million in severance when he was fired without cause fifteen months later.[47] The plaintiffs alleged that the board had not independently evaluated the compensation package Disney CEO Michael Eisner had negotiated with his longtime friend Ovitz. They also alleged that the board failed to consider whether Ovitz could be terminated for cause, which would have made him ineligible to receive the $140 million in severance pay. The court held that the facts alleged "belie any assertion that [the Disney directors] exercised *any* business judgment or made *any* good faith attempt to fulfill the fiduciary duties they owed to Disney and its stockholders."

Duty of Care

The duty of care requires directors to act with the same degree of care a reasonably prudent director would use under similar circumstances. It includes a duty to be informed before making a decision. The directors of Trans Union breached this duty when they agreed to sell the company without first determining the intrinsic value of the company.[48]

Directors are entitled to rely on the reports of officers and certain outside experts, but that reliance must be in good faith. No statement is entitled to blind reliance. The directors have a duty to pursue reasonable inquiry, which becomes particularly important when an expert's conclusion is questionable in light of other information known to the directors. The directors of SCM breached this duty when they blindly relied on an oral assertion by a partner at Goldman Sachs that two divisions were being sold at option prices that were "within the range of fair value." The directors did not inquire what the range of fair value was or how it was calculated. Nor did they ask why two divisions that they knew generated more than two-thirds of SCM's earnings were being sold for less than half the purchase price of the entire company.[49]

The duty of care includes a responsibility to be reasonably informed concerning the corporation's affairs.[50] To satisfy this duty of oversight, directors must take reasonable steps to ensure that there are information and reporting systems in place that in concept and design are adequate to assure the board that appropriate information concerning the corporation and its compliance with law will come to its attention in a timely manner as a matter of ordinary operations. Failure to ensure that adequate systems and procedures are in place may render the directors personally liable for losses caused by non-compliance with applicable legal standards.

DUTIES IN CONNECTION WITH POSSIBLE SALES
OF THE CORPORATION

The short-term interests of the shareholders and other constituencies are most likely to diverge when an unsolicited offer is made by an outside bidder to acquire a company at a premium over the current trading price.

For directors in corporations incorporated in any of the many states that have adopted the corporate constituency paradigm, it is clear that they have no obligation to sell the company to the highest bidder if, after giving due consideration to the likely effect of the proposed sale on all of the corporation's constituencies, they conclude that a sale would not be in the best interests of the corporation and all of its constituencies. Even if the board decides to sell the company in a transaction that would result in a change in control, directors may agree to a lower sale price in exchange for more favorable treatment of employees, the community where the company does business, or other constituencies.

Even in Delaware, which does not have an express constituency statute, the duty to maximize shareholder value arises only when the breakup of the corporation or a change-in-control has become inevitable. It is only then that the role of the directors shifts from "defenders of the corporate bastion to auctioneers charged with getting the best price for the stockholders at a sale of the company."[51]

Negotiating with Potential Bidders

A board is not required to negotiate with potential bidders even if they offer a price per share substantially higher than the company's current trading price or to sell the corporation if the board makes a good faith, informed decision that it would be in the corporation's best interests to reject the offer.[52] In fact, directors have a fiduciary duty to oppose offers that in their good faith judgment are not in the best interests of the corporation and its constituencies.[53]

Thus, the Delaware Court of Chancery dismissed a complaint in which shareholders of MSB Bancorp claimed that the board had violated its fiduciary duties when it rejected an unsolicited bid after having considered its

investment banker's analysis of the offer. The court concluded that the decision was protected by the business judgment rule because the plaintiffs had
failed to show that the directors were self-interested or that they were motivated to entrench themselves in office or that the board's behavior amounted to
gross negligence.

Similarly, the U.S. Court of Appeals for the Second Circuit ruled that there
was no statutory or case law in New York requiring the board of a New York
corporation to consider merger offers and negotiate with the bidder. Indeed,
the court explained, "there are New York statutes that allow management
considerable leeway in defending against hostile takeovers. . . ."[54]

Adopting Antitakeover Defenses

In Delaware, because of the "omnipresent spectre" that a board adopting a
defensive measure designed to thwart a hostile bid may be acting to entrench
itself in office, the Delaware Supreme Court imposes a two-tier proportionality
test.[55] Before being entitled to the protections of the business judgment rule, the
directors first must show that they had reasonable grounds for believing that
there was a threat to corporate policy and effectiveness. Then they must demonstrate that the defensive measures adopted in response to the threat were
reasonable in relation to the threat.

In making these determinations, the board must analyze "the nature of the
takeover bid and its effect on the corporate enterprise." In doing so, the directors may consider, among other things, "the impact on 'constituencies'
other than shareholders (i.e., creditors, customers, employees, and perhaps
even the community generally)."[56] Directors are further authorized "to make
decisions that are expected to promote corporate (and shareholder) long-run
interests, even if short-run share value can be expected to be negatively affected, and thus directors in pursuit of long-run corporate value may be sensitive to the claims of other 'corporate constituencies.'"[57] As a result, even if
the board takes active steps to thwart a takeover bid, by instituting a poison pill
antitakeover device,[58] for example, the business judgment rule will apply if the
directors can show that they had reasonable grounds for believing that the
unwelcome suitor posed a threat to corporate policy and effectiveness and that
the defense was reasonable in response to that threat.[59]

If the directors succeed in making this initial showing, then: "[U]nless it is
shown by a preponderance of the evidence that the directors' decisions were
primarily based on perpetuating themselves in office, or some other breach of
fiduciary duty such as fraud, overreaching, lack of good faith, or being unin-
formed, a court will not substitute its judgment for that of the board."[60]

There are limits to this discretion, however. In *Revlon, Inc. v. MacAndrews and
Forbes Holdings, Inc.*,[61] the Delaware Supreme Court held that "[a] board may
have regard for various constituencies in discharging its responsibilities, provided there are rationally related benefits accruing to the stockholders."

Consideration of nonstockholder interests becomes inappropriate when break-up of the corporation is "inevitable"[62] or there is a change in control because, from the shareholders' perspective, at that point "there is no long run."[63] Once the board decides to break up the company or sell control, the directors' role changes from being "defenders of the corporate bastion to auctioneers charged with getting the best price for the stockholders at a sale of the company."[64] As auctioneers, the directors "have an obligation of acting reasonably to seek the transaction offering the best value reasonably available to stockholders."[65]

In evaluating a bid, directors of a firm in *Revlon* mode are not required to seek out "the hypothetically ideal transaction."[66] Their duty is to seek the best price and other terms reasonably available under the circumstances. Thus, the board must evaluate all aspects of a bid, including its likelihood of consummation and anticipated timetable.[67]

This exception to the ability to consider other constituencies is very narrow and has been applied in only the following three situations:

> (1) "when a corporation initiates an active bidding process seeking to sell itself or to effect a business reorganization involving a clear break-up of the company";
> (2) "where, in response to a bidder's offer, a target abandons its long-term strategy and seeks an alternative transaction involving the break-up of the company"; or
> (3) when approval of a transaction results in a "sale or change of control." In the latter situation, there is no "sale or change in control" when "control of both [companies] remains in a large, fluid, changeable and changing market."[68]

In cases where a breakup or sale of control is not inevitable, the business judgment rule applies, and "[c]ircumstances may dictate that an offer be rebuffed, given the nature and timing of the offer; its legality, feasibility and effect on the corporation and the stockholders; the alternatives available and their effect on the various constituencies, particularly the stockholders; the company's long term strategic plans; and any special factors bearing on stockholder and public interests."[69]

Paramount Communications, Inc. v. Time Inc.[70] provides a graphic example of the broad discretion Delaware law gives directors. In that case the Delaware Supreme Court held that the Time Inc. board had not put Time up for sale when it agreed to a stock-for-stock merger with Warner Communications whereby the former shareholders of Warner would control 62 percent of the new combined entity. Because both corporations were owned by a "fluid aggregation of unaffiliated public shareholders," dissolution of the Time corporate entity was not inevitable. As a result, the Time directors were not required to "abandon deliberately conceived corporate plans for a short-term shareholder profit" and could rebuff a hostile takeover offer by Paramount to preserve Time's "culture" of "editorial integrity." The court upheld the Time directors' exercise of business judgment even though the holders of a majority of the Time stock preferred the Paramount offer.

In contrast, in a subsequent case, the Delaware Supreme Court ruled that Paramount's agreement to merge with Viacom did constitute a change of control because more than 90 percent of Viacom's stock was held by a single person, Sumner Redstone.[71] Because Redstone would control the combined entity, there would be no other opportunity for Paramount's public shareholders to secure a control premium. As a result, the Paramount board had a duty to negotiate with hostile bidder QVC to get the best price available for its shareholders.

Disenfranchising Shareholders

If the directors take actions to purposefully disenfranchise its shareholders, to interfere with their right to elect the directors, then that action is strongly suspect and cannot be sustained without a compelling justification.[72] Thus the Delaware Court of Chancery struck down a poison-pill plan that could be removed only by the current directors.[73] The plan made a takeover of the company not approved by the current directors prohibitively expensive. As a result, even if the bidder commenced a proxy contest and elected its own slate of directors, the new directors would not have the power to remove the pill and authorize the sale of the company. The court concluded that the so-called dead-hand pill impermissibility interfered with the ultimate right of the shareholders to elect a fully empowered board of their own choosing.

Application of the Business Judgment Rule

Figure 5.1 presents a decision tree summarizing the fiduciary duties of directors in a Delaware corporation in a variety of situations and the application of the business judgment rule.

STEWARDS NOT MERCENARIES

By freeing directors from a myopic preoccupation with current stock price, the law empowers those directors whose sense of personal ethics calls on them to consider the effects of their actions upon all who may be affected to make corporate decisions within that broader frame of reference. Thus, directors are more akin to stewards of the assets under their control than mercenaries hired to win at all costs.

Before expecting directors to assume a stewardship role, it is important to explain what that does and does not entail. A steward of a for-profit corporation would not give all, or even most, of the corporation's profits to charity. It would clearly be a breach of the directors' fiduciary duties to do so. A corporate steward would instead distinguish between two types of harm—harm flowing directly from the corporation's action or failure to act, and harm not of the corporation's making. In evaluating a course of action that involved

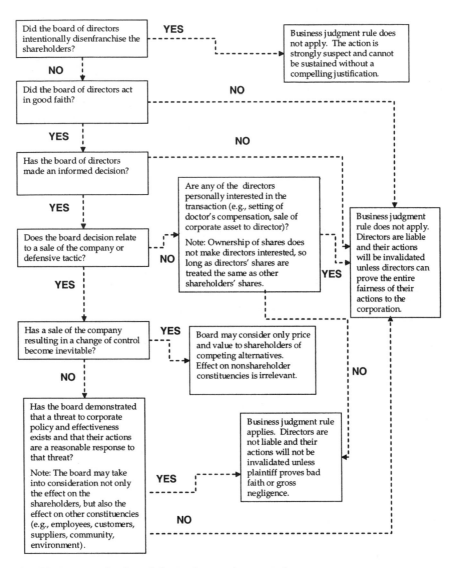

FIGURE 5.1. Application of the Business Judgment Rule

the potential for harm of the first type, corporate stewards would first inform themselves as to the potential harm, then seek to minimize it and ensure that it falls on those best able to bear it.

For example, the corporate stewards of a company building a manufacturing facility in a country without stringent environmental laws would first evaluate the effect their waste disposal would have on the area and its inhabitants. If the plant is to be built near a river, the directors should instruct management to consider the effect of discharging waste into a river used for drinking water by people living downstream. They should then consider the likelihood that the firm might be liable under existing tort law, which may treat the discharge of hazardous waste as a public nuisance or trespass.

In 2004, eight states (including California, New Jersey, and New York) and New York City commenced a lawsuit against five of the largest U.S. power producers, alleging that their discharge of carbon monoxide and other greenhouse gases is causing global warming and therefore constitutes a public nuisance.[74] This is the first time government officials in the United States have sued private power companies to reduce greenhouse gases. Thus, even if the proposed action would not violate existing law, the board should consider the likelihood that the law will be changed retroactively or applied more broadly in the future.

The potential for liability under existing or future laws may make it prudent to install state-of-the-art pollution control equipment to protect the share-holders from potentially ruinous damage awards. Even if the board concludes that the chances of future liability are low, it might still install the equipment because it's the "right thing to do."

Those same directors might decide not to clean up a river contaminated by someone else, in the same way that an individual might responsibly decide not to wage a one-person war on hunger. But in the same way that an individual might contribute a small percentage of his or her income to a food bank, directors of a drug company might responsibly donate a small percentage of its antibiotics, at cost or for free, to people in impoverished countries who would die without them. Indeed, corporate donations can best be justified when the corporation is acting to remedy ills it is particularly well suited to cure (for example, UPS helping design logistics for delivering relief) and therefore can generate the greatest bang for its buck.

THE ETHICAL BUSINESS LEADER'S DECISION TREE

The accompanying Ethical Business Leader's Decision Tree is a decision-making tool directors can use when deciding how to act in a legal and socially responsible manner.

Is the Action Legal?

Managers should first ask themselves whether the proposed action is legal. Legality is addressed first to reinforce the notion that legal compliance is the baseline standard. If an action is not in accordance with the letter and the spirit of the law then, regardless of the likely effect on shareholder value, the action should not be taken.

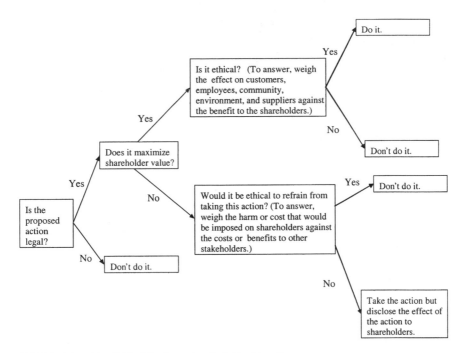

FIGURE 5.2. The Ethical Business Leader's Decision Tree

Would It Maximize Shareholder Value?

The filter for shareholder value is intended to require consideration early on of whether the interests of the shareholders—the group given the ultimate legal authority to change management—are or are not being served by the proposed action. Yet the inquiry need not stop there.

Is the Action Ethical?

The next question to consider is whether the proposed action would be ethical.

Ideal courses of action are ethically sound and maximize shareholder value. Great managers reframe issues and work hard to create such solutions. Ralph Larsen, CEO of Johnson and Johnson, rejected what he termed the "tyranny of the 'or'" and refused to treat social responsibility and profit maximization as mutually exclusive. When asked whether he would rather be a good corporate citizen or maximize profits, Larsen replied, "Yes."[75]

Some actions might maximize at least short-term shareholder value, but are nonetheless unethical. Because there is generally no legal obligation to undertake actions solely because they maximize shareholder value, an ethical business leader will not take such actions.

If an action does not maximize shareholder value and the firm has no ethical reason to act, the action should not be taken. Indeed, taking actions that will not maximize shareholder value without any other justification might result in liability for waste of corporate assets.

Is the Action Ethically Required?

Sometimes firms will have an ethical reason to act, even though acting will not maximize shareholder value (at least not in the short term). This situation can present the most difficult issues for ethical decision-makers. Because the firm is under no legal duty to maximize shareholder value at the expense of all other stakeholders, when shareholder value and ethics are truly at odds, directors should follow the ethical high road and disclose the reasons for taking the action to the shareholders. Disclosure is important to prevent directors from using social responsibility as a fig leaf to cover up mediocre performance or self-dealing.

CONCLUSION

Edward Simon, president of Herman Miller, asked, "Why can't we do good works at work?"[76] He went on to state, "Business is the only institution that has a chance, as far as I can see, to fundamentally improve the injustice that exists in the world."[77] In an award-winning *Harvard Business Review* article, Professor Stuart Hart expressed a similar sentiment: "Like it or not, the responsibility for insuring a sustainable world falls largely on the shoulders of the world's enterprises, the economic engines of the future."[78]

Riots at the World Trade Organization meeting in Seattle in 1998 and other public displays of concern and, in some areas of the world, rage about what many perceive as unchecked capitalism practiced by powerful and seemingly autonomous global corporations graphically demonstrate the high stakes involved. Corporations will not live up to their historic legacy and take their rightful place as leaders in making the world a better place for all until directors take up the mantle of stewardship and refuse to do anything in the name of a corporation that they would consider unethical if they were acting solely for themselves.

NOTES

Certain arguments presented in this article were first articulated in Constance E. Bagley and Karen L. Page (1999), The devil made me do it: Replacing corporate directors' veil of secrecy with the mantle of stewardship, *San Diego L. Rev.*, 36, 897 (hereinafter referred to as The devil made me do it).

1. See, for example, James C. Van Horne (1998), *Financial management and policy 3* (11th ed.). ("The objective of a company must be to create value for its shareholders.")

2. *Paramount Communications, Inc. v. Time, Inc.*, Fed. Sec. L. Rep. (CCH), para. 94, 514 (Del. Ch. July 13, 1989), *aff'd,* 571 A.2d 1140 (Del. 1990).

3. *Aronson v. Lewis*, 473 A.2d 805, 812 (Del. 1984).

4. *Sullivan v. Hammer*, 1990 Del. Ch. LEXIS 119, *15, Fed. Sec. L. Rep. (CCH), para. 95, 415 (August 7, 1990).

5. See Richard A. Booth (1998, February) Stockholders, stakeholders, and bag-holders (or how investor diversification affects fiduciary duty), *Bus. Law, 53,* 429–478. See also The devil made me do it, at 921–22, nn. 118–120.

6. See Steven M. H. Wallman (1991), The proper interpretation of corporate con-stituency statutes and formulations of director duties, *Stetson L. Rev., 21,* 1.

7. 15 Pa. Cons. Stat. Ann. sec. 1715(a).

8. 15 Pa. Cons. Stat. Ann. sec. 1715(b). See AMP Inc. v. Allied Signal Inc., 1998 U.S. Dist. LEXIS 15617 (E.D. Pa. Oct. 8, 1998) (directors of a Pennsylvania cor-poration owe a fiduciary duty solely to the corporation and have no specific duty to shareholders above or beyond those owed to other constituencies).

9. *Sullivan v. Hammer*, 1990 Del Ch. LEXIS 119, Fed. Sec. L. Rep. (CCH) para. 95, 415 (Del. Ch. August 7, 1990), *aff'd sub nom.* Kahn v. Sullivan, 594 A. 2d 48 (Del. 1991). The settlement agreement provided, inter alia, that the museum name be changed from the Armand Hammer Museum of Art and Cultural Center to the Occidental Petroleum Cultural Center Building.

10. *Kahn v. Sullivan*, 594 A. 2d 48 (Del. 1991). The Delaware Corporation Code, 8 Del. C., sec. 122(9), expressly authorizes charitable donations by Delaware corpora-tions. Although Section 122(9) places no limitations on the size of a charitable cor-porate gift, the Delaware Court of Chancery has construed the section "to authorize any reasonable corporate gift of a charitable or educational nature." Theodora Holding Corp. v. Henderson, 257 A. 2d 398, 405 (Del. Ch. 1969).

11. *Sullivan v. Hammer*, 1990 Del Ch. LEXIS 119, Fed. Sec. L. Rep. (CCH), para. 95, 415 (Del. Ch. August 7, 1990). The court characterized the settlement as "leav[ing] much to be desired" but stated that its role in reviewing it was quite restricted. Idem. The court went on to add: "If the Court was a stockholder of Occidental it might vote for new directors, if it was on the Board it might vote for new management and if it was a member of the Special Committee it might vote against the Museum project." Idem at *12.

12. *Dodge v. Ford Motor Co.*, 170 N.W. 668 (Mich. 1919).

13. *A delicate experiment: The Harvard Business School from 1908–1945* (1987), 68.

14. Ibid.

15. Ibid.

16. Ibid., 69.

17. Quoted in *Dodge v. Ford Motor Co.,* 170 N.W. 668 (Mich. 1919).

18. Ibid. In 1908, Ford amended its articles to increase the capital stock from the original paid-in capital of $100,000 to $2,000,000. Idem. The difference of $1,900,000 represented shareholders' waiver of the right to previously declared dividends. Idem. Thereafter, Ford paid regular dividends each year equal to 60 percent of the capital stock of $2,000,000 ($1,200,000) or twelve times the original paid in capital of $100,000. Idem. In addition, Ford paid $41,000,000 in special dividends in the period from 1911 to 1915. Idem.

19. Ibid.

20. Ibid.

21. Quoted at ibid.

22. Ibid., 684.

23. Ibid.

24. Harry J. Van Buren III (1995, spring) Business ethics for the new millennium, *Bus. and Society Rev., 93,* 51, 54.

25. Ronald Seavoy (1982), *The Origins of the American business corporation, 1784–1855: Broadening the concept of public service during the industrialization,* 5.

26. Louis Hartz (1968), *Economic policy and democratic thought, 1776–1860.*

27. Joseph S. Davis (1965), *Essays in the earlier history of American corporations,* 26.

28. John P. Davis (1961), *Corporations: A study of the origin and development of great business combinations and of their relation to the authority of the state,* II:269.

29. Message to Congress, December 5, 1905, quoted in *The Wiley book of business quotations,* 142.

30. *New York Times* (April 25, 1911).

31. Quoted in Robert L. Heilbroner (1972), *In the name of profit,* 241.

32. 98 A.2d 581 (N.J. 1953).

33. Paul Milgrom and John Roberts (1998), *Economics, organization, and management,* 318.

34. Nannette Byrnes et al. (2002, September 23), The good CEO, *BusinessWeek,* 80.

35. Henry Mintzberg et al. (2002, fall), Beyond selfishness, *MIT Sloan Mgmt. Rev.,* 67.

36. Ibid., 69.

37. Michael C. Jensen (2001) (Value maximization, stakeholder theory, and the corporate objective function, *J. Applied Corp. Fin., 14,* 8, 16.

38. Ibid., 8, 9.

39. Ibid., (emphasis in original).

40. *American Bar Association corporate director's guidebook* (2d ed.) (1994).

41. *American Law Institute principles of corporate government* 2.01(a) (1994). The comment notes that "reasonableness" is to be determined by considering factors such as: "the customary level at which resources are devoted to such purposes among comparable corporations in proportion to earnings and assets, and the strength of the nexus between the use of corporate resources and the corporation's business. In general, the greater the amount of corporate resources that are expended, the stronger should be the nexus."

42. Ibid., 2.01(b)(3).

43. Ibid., cmt. i.

44. *Emerald Partners v. Berlin,* 726 A.2d 1215, 1221 (Del. 1999).

45. But see William T. Allen, Jack B. Jacobs, and Leo E. Strine Jr. (2001, August), Function over form: A reassessment of standards of review in Delaware corporation law, *Bus. Law, 56,* 1287, 1305 n.69. (questioning whether good faith should be treated as "a compartmentally distinct fiduciary duty of equal dignity with the two bedrock fiduciary duties of loyalty and due care").

46. In re Abbott Laboratories Derivative Shareholders Litigation, 325 F.3d 795 (7th Cir. 2003).

47. In re The Walt Disney Company Derivative Litigation, C.A. No. 15452 (Del. Ch. May 28, 2003).

48. *Smith v. Van Gorkom*, 488 A.2d 858 (Del. 1985).

49. *Hanson Trust PLC v. ML SCM Acquisition, Inc.*, 781 F.2d. 264 (2d Cir. 1986).

50. In re Caremark International Derivative Litigation, 698 A.2d 959 (Del. Ch. 1996).

51. *Revlon, Inc. v. MacAndrews and Forbes Holidays, Inc.*, 506 A.2d 173 (Del. 1986).

52. See, for example, *Unitrin Inc. v. American General Corp.*, 651 A.2d 1361 (Del. 1995).

53. *Gilbert v. The El Paso Co.*, 575 A.2d 1131 (Del. 1990).

54. *Minzer v. Keegan*, 218 F. 3d 144 (2d Cir. 2000), *cert. denied*, 531 U.S. 1192 (2001).

55. *Unocal Corp. v. Mesa Petroleum Co.*, 493 A.2d 946 (Del. 1985).

56. Ibid.

57. TW Services, Inc. Shareholders Litig., [1989 Transfer Binder] Fed. Sec. L. Rep. (CCH) P 94,334, at 92,179 (Del. Ch. March 2, 1989).

58. *Moran v. Household Int'l, Inc.*, 500 A.2d 1346 (Del. 1985).

59. *Unocal Corp. v. Mesa Petroleum Co.*, 493 A.2d 946 (Del. 1985).

60. Ibid.

61. 506 A.2d 173 (Del. 1986).

62. Ibid.

63. In re Lukens, Inc. Shareholders Litigation, 757 A.2d 720 (Del. Ch. 1999), *aff'd*, 757 A.2d 1278 (Del. 2000) (holding that a merger of Lukens with Bethlehem Steel triggered *Revlon* duties because 62 percent of the consideration was cash).

64. Ibid., 182.

65. *Paramount Comm., Inc. v. QVC Network*, 637 A.2d 34, 49. See *Equity-Linked Investors, L.P. v. Adams*, 705 A.2d 1040, 1055 (Del. Ch. 1997) (in a change-of-control situation, the board is required "to act reasonably to maximize current, not future, value").

66. *Cede and Co. v. Technicolor, Inc.*, 634 A.2d 345 (Del. 1993), *after remand*, Cinerama, Inc. v. Technicolor Inc., 663 A.2d 1156 (Del. 1995).

67. *Mills Acquisition Co. v. Macmillan, Inc.*, 559 A.2d 1261 (Del. 1989).

68. *Arnold v. Society for Sav. Bancorp.*, 650 A.2d 1270, 1290, *aff'd*, 678 A.2d 533 (Del. 1996), citing *Paramount Comm., Inc. v. QVC Network*, 637 A.2d at 42–43; *Paramount Comm. v. Time Inc.*, 571 A.2d at 1150.

69. *Mills Acquisition Co. v. Macmillan, Inc.*, 559 A.2d 1261, 1285, n.35 (Del. 1989).

70. *Paramount Comm. v. Time Inc.*, 571 A.2d 1140 (Del. 1990).

71. *Paramount Comm. v. QVC Network, Inc.*, 637 A.2d 34 (Del. 1994).

72. See *Stroud v. Grace*, 606 A.2d 75 (Del. 1992); *Unitin, Inc. v. American Gen. Corp.*, 651 A.2d 1361 (Del. 1995); *Blasius Indus v. Atlas Corp.*, 564 A.2d 651 (Del. Ch. 1988).

73. *Carmody v. Toll Bros., Inc.*, 723 A.2d 1180 (Del. ch. 1998). See also *Quickturn Design Systems, Inc. v. Shapiro*, 721 A.2d 1281 (Del. 1998) (invalidating "delayed-hand" plan could not be removed by new directors for six months after taking office).

74. *Connecticut v. American Power Co.*, No. 1: 04-cv-05669-LAP (S.D.N.Y. July 21, 2004), 73 U.S.L.W. 2056 (August 3, 2004).

75. Alden Lank (1998), The ethical criterion in business decision-making: operational or imperative? In Touche Ross and Co., *Ethics in american business: a special report*, 28 (the Touche Report).

76. Quoted in Peter M. Senge, *The fifth discipline: the art and practice of the learning organization*, 5.

77. Stuart L. Hart (1997), Beyond greening: Strategies for a sustainable world, *Harv. Bus. Rev.*

78. Ibid.

6

Institutional Investors and Corporate Governance

JAMES E. HEARD

Institutional investors play a critical role in corporate governance in the United States today. This was not always the case, for only in the past two decades have institutional investors begun to define a new, and more active, role for themselves in the corporate governance process. This article reviews the traditional role of institutional investors as shareholders and how that role has changed. It also considers reforms that have been made in the corporate governance system in response to recent scandals. In evaluating recent reforms, the article focuses on additional changes that institutional investors might support to improve the corporate governance system. The article reflects the experiences of one who has worked for more than twenty-five years to strengthen the role of institutional investors in corporate governance and who believes that active involvement by institutional investors in corporate governance benefits investors and society at large.

TRADITIONAL ROLE OF INSTITUTIONAL INVESTORS

The role of institutional investors in corporate governance has changed significantly over the past two decades. Traditionally, institutions such as banks, insurance companies, and mutual funds were passive owners of public companies in which they invested. These institutions followed a practice known as "the Wall Street rule" in regard to ownership: They either supported the management of the companies in which they invested or they sold their shares.

This rule applied to investment performance, corporate strategy, and corporate governance.

The logic to this position was reflected in the ownership structure of public corporations. For much of the twentieth century, individuals, not institutions, were the largest owners of shares, and ownership was widely dispersed. As Adolf Berle and Gardiner Means pointed out in *The Modern Corporation and Private Property* (1932), the dispersion of ownership that accompanied the development of twentieth-century public corporations in the United States greatly enhanced the power of management at the expense of shareholders. The latter, in fact, were largely disenfranchised, reduced to ratifying the selection of directors often controlled by management itself. Unhappy shareholders had few choices but to sell, or suffer their disappointments in silence.

The ownership structure of public corporations began to change following the enactment of the Employee Retirement Income Security Act in 1974. ERISA, as it is widely known, created statutory duties of care and loyalty for pension funds and their managers while also requiring pension funds to diversify their portfolios.

Increasingly, pension funds and their managers found themselves owning larger and larger portfolios of stock, and by the late 1980s their holdings had grown dramatically. This reaggregation of ownership caused some institutional investors to question the Wall Street rule. For one thing, selling became more expensive and more difficult if holdings were very large. And some began to ask whether there might not be another option: to exercise voice rather than to exit.

Also in the 1980s, indexing began to grow in popularity as many large institutions decided to abandon active management in favor of the practice of buying, and holding, a broadly representative portfolio of securities. By definition, indexing ruled out the sell option, except to rebalance portfolios. The larger the portfolio, the more attractive indexing became as a lower-cost alternative to active buying and selling.

NEW LEGAL REQUIREMENTS

By the late 1980s the U.S. Department of Labor, which administers ERISA, had begun to articulate ownership responsibilities for pension funds and their investment managers. In a series of pronouncements beginning in 1988, the Labor Department outlined the view that the voting of proxies is a fiduciary duty, subject to ERISA, to which statutory duties of loyalty and care apply. The Labor Department formalized this position in a 1994 regulation. Pension funds and their investment managers were now required to exercise oversight through voting, long thought by many to be an empty formality. (The regulation is set forth in 29 CFR Part 2509, Interpretive Bulletin 94-2, July 29, 1994.)

The 1990s also witnessed a growth in mutual fund assets similar to what had occurred among pension funds in the 1980s. By the end of the 1990s, mutual funds were comparable in size to pension funds, and they faced many of the same issues associated with portfolio size that had confronted pension funds in the 1980s. To be sure, portfolio turnover of the average mutual fund is high, and the many active traders hardly consider themselves to be owners. But averages can be deceiving: The largest mutual funds are either indexed, or they have much lower portfolio turnover than average (and smaller) funds. These funds buy and hold substantial positions in public corporations, and they, like large pension funds and pension fund managers, have reassessed the Wall Street rule.

Following the Labor Departments of a decade before, the U.S. Securities and Exchange Commission, which regulates mutual funds and registered investment advisers, ruled in 2003 that voting involved the exercise of fiduciary duties. Like the Labor Department, the SEC took the position that proxy voting by both mutual funds and registered investment advisers is subject to fiduciary standards of loyalty and care. It directed registered investment advisers and mutual funds to disclose to their clients their voting policies. And, in the case of mutual funds, it required them to disclose publicly not only their policies but their actual votes. (The regulations can be found at 17 CFR Parts 239, 249, 270, and 274, January 31, 2003; and 17 CFR Part 275, January 31, 2003.)

At the same time that pension funds and mutual funds were growing in size, and when they were also being told that voting their shares was a fiduciary duty, takeover battles of the 1980s underscored just how valuable the vote might be. Large companies began to restrict the rights of shareholders (ironically, with shareholder consent) to tender their shares to hostile bidders who offered control premiums; very often these bidders, or "raiders" as they were called, sought to oust incumbent management. First corporate charters and then state statutes were altered to strengthen the ability of management to resist unsolicited takeover bids.

Some institutional investors resisted this trend, and thus was born the modern phenomenon of institutional investor activism. Ironically, the public pension funds leading the opposition to shareholder disenfranchisement are not subject to ERISA, which applies only to private sector pension funds and their investment managers. But they were quick to grasp that asking shareholders to transfer rights and responsibilities from owners to managers so that the former could be protected from value-enhancing transactions that might displace the latter was a poor bargain. Public pension funds from California, New York, Pennsylvania, Wisconsin, and other states spoke out in opposition to this trend. Unfortunately, few other institutions paid much attention to what was happening at the time. By the mid-1990s most large companies had adopted a host of so-called antitakeover devices, including staggered boards, supermajority voting requirements, poison pills, and the like. This tilted an already slanted playing field further in management's direction, either by restricting the rights of shareholders to tender their shares to hostile bidders, or by making it more difficult to vote to change control.

By the end of the 1990s, then, two important changes had taken place in the ownership of public corporations in the United States. Institutional investors, especially pension funds and mutual funds, had become the dominant owners of public companies. Collectively, institutional investors owned more than half of the shares of publicly traded companies, and often as much as 70 to 80 percent of the largest companies. At the same time, ownership responsibilities of these fiduciaries were modernized and given specific applicability with regard to exercise of the shareholder franchise.

INSTITUTIONAL INVESTORS AS SHAREHOLDERS

Two decades after it began, institutional investor involvement in corporate governance has come of age. A relatively small number of institutions, most of them public pension funds and labor union pension funds, have become shareholder activists. These institutions evaluate the governance of portfolio companies, sponsor shareholder resolutions, and engage in other types of activism. They provide the direction and much of the energy for shareholder involvement in corporate governance. Other institutions, including mutual funds and portfolio managers, are now voting their shares according to fiduciary standards set by federal regulations. These institutions tend to be followers, not leaders, but their votes do have an impact.

Much of the energy surrounding shareholder activism is devoted to sponsoring shareholder resolutions. Most of these resolutions are nonbinding, but they provide a means for shareholders to express their opinions on a variety of corporate governance issues. In the most recent year, 2004, activist institutions sponsored proposals on a variety of topics, including proposals to elect all directors annually, to require boards to have a majority of independent directors, to repeal so-called poison pill takeover defenses, to require companies to take an accounting charge for the cost of stock options, and to limit excessive executive compensation. (See generally Institutional Shareholder Services 2004.)

In years past, many companies ignored shareholder sentiment, even when proposals received a majority vote. Recently, companies have responded more favorably. For example, in 2004, more than fifty companies offered their own shareholder proposals to declassify their boards and elect all directors annually. This included a number of companies that had ignored shareholder votes in the past. More than forty companies took actions to redeem or revise their poison pill takeover defenses, and a number of others agreed to begin treating the granting of stock options as an expense on their income statements.

Institutional investors have also made creative use of what has become known as "vote no" campaigns. These involve coordinated efforts to withhold votes for directors. The campaigns are largely symbolic: There are no alternative candidates, and in most instances so-called no votes have no binding effect because most U.S. companies elect their directors by plurality and not majority. In practice this means that so long as a quorum is present, directors will be elected, even if a majority of votes are withheld, so long as the directors receive even a single "for" vote.

The most significant withhold campaign ever occurred in 2004 at Walt Disney, where 45 percent of the shares were withheld from Chairman and Chief Executive Officer Michael Eisner in a campaign to strip Mr. Eisner of his title as chairman. Within days the board removed Eisner as chairman, allowing him to remain as CEO and as a director. At Federated Department Stores, Inc., more than 50 percent of the shares were withheld from directors who had ignored previous majority votes, and at MBNA, a withhold campaign urging the removal of directors who were not independent of management garnered more than 40 percent of the vote. At all three companies there was widespread sentiment that boards had engaged in governance practices inimical to the interests of shareholders. In contrast, vote no campaigns at two other high-profile companies—Safeway and Comcast—received tepid support because the labor union pension funds sponsoring the proposals were widely believed to be using vote no campaigns not to fix governance problems but to support labor union collective bargaining objectives (see 2004 Postseason Report, pp. 3–5, 24–25).

Among U.S. institutional investors, few have devoted more resources to corporate governance than the Teachers Insurance and Annuity Association–College Retirement Equities Fund (TIAA-CREF). TIAA-CREF, as it is known, is the largest private retirement fund in the United States and one of the largest institutional investors in the world. TIAA-CREF maintains a full-time staff of governance experts, who consult regularly with its portfolio managers. It also conducts "quiet diplomacy" with portfolio firms to discuss corporate governance concerns. It makes its concerns about individual companies public only if such quiet diplomacy fails. And in a number of cases, such as the withhold vote campaign at MBNA in 2004, it has been willing to commit its resources and its prestige to pressure companies publicly to improve their corporate governance (see TIAA-CREF Policy Statement on Corporate Governance, January 2004, and 2004 Postseason Report, p. 6).

Most other private sector institutions, including mutual funds and other professional money managers, have been even more circumspect than TIAA-CREF. They have tended to play a behind-the-scenes supportive role on governance reform. Most eschew publicity and confrontation, partly out of fear that they may offend potential clients to whom they wish to market their investment products, and partly because many have been unsure of the relationship between shareholder activism and investment performance. The bull market of the 1990s provided little evidence that weak governance impacted shareholder returns; in fact, many drew the conclusion that governance mattered not at all. The scandals that followed the bull market and the destruction of shareholder wealth that accompanied the scandals have led many institutional investors to reconsider their previous assumptions about the relationship between corporate governance and shareholder returns.

SCANDALS AND REFORM

The corporate scandals that began to unfold in 2002 highlighted unseemly practices that were initially thought to involve only a handful of bad actors. But the scandals actually revealed a number of systemic weaknesses in the corporate governance system. At hundreds of companies, auditors failed to audit properly, analysts failed to analyze, and directors failed to exercise proper oversight. The checks and balances that are at the heart of any good governance system were found to be weak throughout corporate America. Many billions of dollars in shareholder wealth was destroyed as a result of the greatest failure of corporate accountability in modern times, and public confidence in the integrity of corporate America sustained a major blow.

It is probably too much to say that weak corporate governance caused the scandals, but weak governance certainly was a factor. Behind every overly aggressive accounting scheme were individuals, usually including top executives, who believed that the potential rewards outweighed the risks of detection. There were many contributing factors to this environment, including distracted auditors and undermanned regulators. But the failure of boards of directors to monitor management's behavior must be seen as a fundamental flaw in our corporate governance system that led to the scandals of the 1990s and early twenty-first century.

Legislative and regulatory reforms were quick in coming. Enron and WorldCom were soon followed by Sarbanes-Oxley—federal legislation that established a new regulatory framework for auditors, prohibited corporate loans to officers and directors, required top executives to certify personally the accuracy of financial statements, and imposed new internal control reporting requirements. Sarbanes-Oxley became the most far-reaching extension of federal authority over corporate governance since the Great Depression of the 1930s. The New York Stock Exchange and other listing bodies revised their corporate governance listing standards to require more independent directors and new board committees composed of independent directors. And the Securities and Exchange Commission, which did little in the 1990s to check widespread abuses, was given more resources and became a tougher cop on the beat.

The scandals were also a wake-up call for institutional investors. Many had previously viewed corporate governance generally, and voting in particular, as little more than a compliance requirement. The scandals demonstrated a clear link between governance and performance. Like many others affected by the scandals, institutional investors are now more focused on improving the system of corporate governance. And like so many others, they, too, are focused on stronger, more independent boards of directors and on the role that they as shareholders can play in the selection of directors.

The scandals have also ushered in a new appreciation of the relationship between corporate governance and risk. Institutional investors have embraced

new corporate governance rating systems developed by Institutional Shareholder Services and other organizations that evaluate the strengths and weaknesses of public company corporate governance structures. The ISS rating
system, for example, focuses on board structure and board composition,
charters and bylaws, state of incorporation, director and executive compensation, and a number of other practices. (See www.isscgq.com for a detailed
explanation of the ISS corporate governance rating system.) It and other rating
systems apply best practice standards to individual companies and grade them
against both peers and broad market indices. Institutional investors are using
these rating systems to select portfolio companies, assess portfolio risk, and
target portfolio companies for review and inquiry. It is probably premature to
say that institutions are selecting companies on the basis of good corporate
governance, but it can be said that a number have decided to avoid companies
that have bad governance ratings.

HOW TO SELECT DIRECTORS

As institutional investors examine ways to strengthen the independence and
performance of boards of directors, new attention is being focused on how
directors are selected. In theory, directors are chosen by shareholders to
monitor management and replace management when necessary. In practice,
shareholders have little or no control over the selection of directors. Management and the incumbent board control the nomination and election process. It is extremely difficult, and expensive, for shareholders to nominate and
solicit proxies for their own director candidates. Shareholders may withhold
their votes for directors, a symbolic act at best, but unless they want to pay the
considerable costs involved in being in a proxy contest, they are stuck with
management's slate of directors as their only option.

The fact that shareholders have little choice in the selection of directors
must be seen as a fundamental flaw in the current system of corporate governance. Giving shareholders a real voice in the selection of directors should be
high on the reform agenda for institutional investors interested in promoting
better corporate governance.

The Securities and Exchange Commission offered a solution in 2003 when
it proposed that shareholders be allowed to include up to three of their own
nominees in a company's proxy statement. The SEC's proposal contained
many hurdles to guard against abuses. Even so, business organizations such as
the Business Roundtable and the U.S. Chamber of Commerce went all out to
block the proposal, with the latter threatening to sue the SEC if it adopted
the rule.

Supporters of the proposal view it as a pragmatic proposal to give some real
meaning to the rights of shareholders to choose directors. As one supporter
observed: "The recent corporate governance crisis highlighted the importance
of good board performance. Reforming corporate elections would improve the

selection of directors and the incentives they face." The same commentator noted:

> Although shareholder power to replace directors is supposed to be an important element of our corporate governance system, it is largely a myth. Attempts to replace directors are extremely rare, even in firms that systematically underperform over a long period of time. By and large, directors nominated by the company run unopposed and their election is thus guaranteed. The key for a director's re-election is remaining on the firm's slate. Whether the nomination committee is controlled by the chief executive officer (CEO) or by independent directors, incentives to serve the interests of those making nominations are not necessarily identical with incentives to maximize shareholder value. (Bebchuck 2003, 43–66)

Opponents have argued that the Sarbanes-Oxley legislation, new stock exchange listing standards, and other reforms are sufficient. They warn, too, that giving shareholders the right to include their own nominees for director in a company's proxy would weaken the current corporate governance system. The following comment summarizes the views of many opponents in the business community:

> Allowing shareholders to run an election contest through the company's proxy statement, however, would be a serious mistake. Increasing the ease and frequency of election contests would have a negative impact on public companies and their boards, with no clear benefit. A number of issues are immediately apparent: the risk of an influx of special interest directors; the disruption and diversion of resources that could accompany annual election contests; the risk of balkanized and dysfunctional boards; the risk of deterring the most skilled men and women from serving on public company boards. (Lipton and Rosenblum, 2003, 67–94)

The same commentators cautioned not to give institutional investors a voice in selection of directors:

> In addition, there is serious doubt as to whether institutional shareholders, public pension funds, and labor unions—the parties most likely to qualify for the right to include director nominees in a company's proxy statement under most proposals—are well suited to the role of nominating directors. Each has duties to its own constituencies; each has its own agenda; but none has legal duties or obligations to the public company or other shareholders. (Lipton and Rosenblum, 2003)

An alternative to the SEC's proposal would require the New York Stock Exchange and other markets, including the NASDAQ stock market, to adopt new listing standards that would require each director to be elected by a majority of shares voted on his or her election. Any director who failed to receive a majority vote cast would be deemed not to have been elected. If one or more directors failed to receive a majority vote, the board would be required to replace them, either by appointment or by nominating new candidates for election. If a majority of directors failed to receive the required majority vote, the board would be required to call a new election within 120 days. In effect, the proposal would count "withhold" votes as "no" votes and would permit shareholders to veto board nominations. It would still be the incumbent board's responsibility, however, to nominate replacements. (See letter of March 3, 2004, from Ira M. Millstein to Alan L. Beller of the Securities and Exchange Commission, together with attached memorandum.)

Yet another alternative would be to amend state business incorporation statutes, or the charters or bylaws of individual companies, to require that directors receive a majority of votes cast rather than a plurality. Chief Justice Norman Veasey of the Delaware Supreme Court endorsed this approach in a letter to the SEC, in what he characterized as his personal views:

> A requirement that a director must receive a majority of the votes cast could be imposed by the certificate of incorporation of the issuer or by state statute. Another possibility might be a bylaw, provided that such a bylaw is validly adopted under state law. . . .
>
> This change in the way directors are elected would give stockholders a stronger voice in the election process. This concept would seem to be consistent with the goals of the Commission and is more consistent with principles of federalism than the imposition of the proposed rule would be without such a reference to state law. . . . (Chief Justice Norman Veasey of the Delaware Supreme Court, letter to Alan L. Beller of the Securities and Exchange Commission, March 11, 2004)

A fourth proposal, suggested by Stanford Law School professor and former SEC commissioner Joseph A. Grundfest, urges the SEC to adopt a new rule that would define as "unratified" any director who is elected pursuant to state law but who fails to obtain a majority of the votes cast. Boards that permit unratified directors to continue to serve would be required to make extensive disclosures regarding the deliberations and decisions of such boards to permit unratified directors to remain on the board. The clear intent of the proposal is to use the SEC's unquestionable authority to require companies to disclose information about board nomination procedures to create disincentive for unratifed directors to continue to serve, even if lawfully elected. Like all the other alternatives to the SEC's proposal, this proposal, too, would leave selection of new nominees in the hands of the incumbent board. (Professor Joseph A. Grundfest, letter to Jonathan G. Katz of the Securities and Exchange Commission, April 7, 2004.)

At this writing, almost a year and a half has passed since the SEC proposed to give shareholders the right to have their nominees for director included in company proxy statements. Statements by individual SEC commissioners and press reports suggest that the SEC is badly split on whether to adopt the proposal. The longer the SEC waits, the less likely it is to act. But because the SEC had announced no formal decision, the alternative proposals have yet to receive serious attention.

Whether or not it adopts the original proposal, the SEC has certainly provoked a much-needed discussion on how directors are selected. And if it drops the idea of giving shareholders the right to have their nominations for director included in proxy statements, alternatives should be considered. The time has come to move from myth to reality in making sure that shareholders have a real voice in the selection of directors.

THE CHAIRMAN AND THE CHIEF EXECUTIVE OFFICER

No examination of ways to strengthen boards can fail to take note of how the concentration of power in the hands of chief executive officers who also serve as board chairmen has affected board independence and board performance.

In a highly regarded report in 2003, the Conference Board's Commission on Public Trust and Private Enterprise noted the dominant role of CEOs at many companies recently beset by scandal:

> The Commission is profoundly troubled by the corporate scandals of the recent past. The primary concern in many of these situations is that strong CEOs appear to have exerted a dominant influence over their boards, often stifling the efforts of directors to play the central oversight role needed to ensure a healthy system of corporate governance. In such circumstances, boards have often either lacked the structure and information to perform their roles properly, or they have simply abdicated their responsibilities to provide the oversight required of them. In such circumstances, the board cannot properly oversee the CEO's performance. (The Conference Board, 2003, p. 18)

The Conference Board stopped short of recommending the separation of the offices of chairman and chief executive officer in all cases. Instead, it offered three alternatives: separate chairman and CEO, with the chairman chosen from among the independent directors; separate chairman and CEO, with a lead independent director if the chairman is not an independent director; combined chairman and CEO, with a presiding director who serves as lead independent director. Titles aside, all three approaches are intended to provide, in the commission's words, "an appropriate balance between the powers of the CEO and those of the independent directors in which the ability of the independent directors to be informed, to discuss and debate issues they deem important, and to act objectively on an informed basis is not compromised" (Conference Board, p. 19).

Even at companies not tainted by scandal, the concentration of power in the hands of a single individual who serves as both CEO and chairman of the board undermines the board's independence. If the board's chief responsibility is to evaluate and oversee management's performance, its ability to perform this function effectively is compromised if the chairman also serves as chief executive officer.

After reviewing many of the reforms of the past decade, including the Sarbanes-Oxley legislation, new stock exchange listing standards, and more vigorous SEC enforcement, Paul W. MacAvoy and Ira M. Millstein in their most recent book, *The Recurrent Crisis in Corporate Governance,* reach the following conclusion:

> We cannot expect the CEO, in his other role as chairman, to prepare the board to evaluate lapses and failures on his part, or on the part of his chosen management. Nothing short of separating the roles of board leadership and management leadership will suffice. Ideally, the board's chairman should be an independent director, thus separating the roles in form as well as substance. That chairman would ensure that focused information on key issues reaches the board. That chairman could create meaningful agendas and call for management presentations around issues, not just around current problems that need resolution. He or she could chair meetings with content rather than routine, based on position papers rather than reports. That chairman, having this "job," could spend the time and energy, with a separate staff when necessary, which is essential to fill the information void. Then, and only then, will the governance reform structures, now a decade in place, enable substantive assessments by the board, leading to gains in performance. (MacAvoy and Millstein, 2003, p. 4)

To be sure, requiring the CEO to share power with an independent chairman would diminish the CEO's power. That is, in fact, the principal purpose and the desired effect of the proposal. Not surprisingly, CEOs have been less than enthusiastic about the proposal to share power with an independent chairman. Very few companies have chosen to separate the two positions, and many that have done so recently, including Microsoft, Dell, and Citicorp, have appointed their former CEOs as chairmen instead of selecting new chairmen from among their independent directors.

However, a number of boards have been willing to take the interim step toward independent leadership by appointing a lead independent director. The lead director works with the chairman/CEO or the chairman (if he is not an independent director) to set an agenda for board meetings and to make sure that all directors receive timely information. While creation of the lead director position acknowledges the need for independence, it stops short of being the most effective solution.

The closest thing to a requirement that companies have independent board leadership is the New York Stock Exchange's requirement that listed companies designate a presiding director to chair meetings when independent directors meet privately. However, no other duties are required.

Even though many companies seem hesitant to act, institutional investors are in a strong position to push for change on this issue. This can be accomplished in a variety of ways, from "quiet diplomacy" to support for shareholder proposals to "vote no" campaigns targeting individual companies. In the process, institutional investors may discover a secret source of support: outside directors anxious for independent board leadership.

CONCLUSION

This paper has suggested that the role of institutional investor as shareholder has changed considerably in recent years. Many institutions have abandoned the passive role once assigned to them as owners, as they find themselves today in a position to exert considerable influence on corporate governance. Some institutions—most notably public pension funds and labor union pension funds—have welcomed the chance to play a more active role as owners, embracing shareholder activism with great enthusiasm. Many others, including most mutual funds and institutional fund managers, have been more hesitant, but they, too, are now involved in oversight in ways that few would have imagined until quite recently.

As they assume a more active role in the governance process, institutional investors should be careful not to overreach. It is not their job to manage the businesses of portfolio companies. Rather, they should focus on making sure that portfolio companies are well governed by their boards. Where boards are failing to meet their responsibilities to shareholders, institutional investors are justified in intervening, either to encourage boards to change their behavior or to bring about change in board composition.

Institutional investors must also be mindful of concerns that they will abuse the power they now exercise. Such concerns underlie some of the strongest opposition to proposals to give shareholders a greater voice in the selection of directors. The best way to respond to such concerns is to stay focused on good governance as a means to improve economic performance. Institutional investors that use their power to pursue other objectives will inevitably invite efforts to curb the power of all institutional investors. At a time when institutional investors are just beginning to get comfortable with more active oversight, this would be an unfortunate step backward.

REFERENCES

Bebchuck, L. A. (2003, November). The case for shareholder access to the ballot. *Business Lawyer, 59,* 43–66.

Berle Jr., A. A., and Means, G. C. (1932). *The modern corporation and private property.* Macmillan.

Institutional Shareholder Services, Inc. (2004, September). *2004 postseason report: A new corporate governance world: From confrontation to constructive dialogue.*

Ira M. Millstein, letter to Alan L. Beller, Securities and Exchange Commission, March 3, 2004.

Joseph A. Grundfest, letter to Jonathan G. Katz, Securities and Exchange Commission, April 7, 2004.

Lipton, M., and Rosenblum, S. A. (2003, November). Election contests in the company's proxy: An idea whose time has not come. *Business Lawyer, 59,* 67–94.

MacAvoy, P. W., and Millstein, I. M. (2003). *The recurrent crisis in corporate governance.* Palgrave Macmillan.

Norman Veasey, letter to Alan L. Beller, Securities and Exchange Commission, March 11, 2004.

Securities and Exchange Commission. (2003, January 31). *Final rule: Disclosure of proxy voting policies and proxy voting records by registered management investment companies.* 17 CFR Parts 239, 249, 270, and 274.

Securities and Exchange Commission. (2003, January 31). *Final rule: Proxy voting by investment advisers.* 17 CFR Part 275.

Teachers Insurance Annuity Association–College Retirement Equities Fund. (2004, January). *TIAA-CREF policy statement on corporate governance.*

The Conference Board. (2003). *Commission on public trust and private enterprise.*

U.S. Department of Labor, Pension and Welfare Benefits Administration. (1994, July 29). *Interpretive bulletin 94-2.* 29 CFR Part 2509.

7

One Practitioner's Random Thoughts on Shareholders' Rights in the Modern Corporation

DAVID J. BERGER

M odern corporate law theory views shareholders as the "owners" of the corporation, which gives them a higher status than other corporate constituencies. This is the so-called "shareholder primacy" model, which holds that directors and managers of the corporation owe a fiduciary obligation to act for the benefit of the shareholders, and failure to give primacy to shareholder interests can give rise to a cause of action by the shareholders against the directors.[1] This view is a relatively recent phenomenon, and while it dominates corporate law in the United States, it is rare in most other countries.[2]

While the shareholder primacy model assumes that shareholders are the owners of the corporation, current corporate law does not give shareholders significant rights in the corporation. Rather, the dominant view of corporate law today is that the business and affairs of the corporation are managed by the company's board of directors.[3] As a practical matter, the board delegates and relies upon management to handle the day-to-day operations of the company, creating a further separation between the shareholders, the supposed owners of the company, and those running it. Shareholders have no right to direct or control the assets of the corporation and generally do not decide (or even have significant input into) such fundamental issues as whether a company should (i) be bought or sold, (ii) issue dividends, or how it should handle other financial issues, or (iii) what businesses it should pursue.[4] Such decisions are typically left to the board and management, who are constrained in their actions by the fiduciary obligations they owe to shareholders. However, shareholders do not have any claim against directors or managers who make poor business decisions so long as those decisions were made following reasonable investigation and in what the board and/or management perceived to be in the interests of the corporation.[5]

In fact, shareholders today have very limited rights with respect to the corporation. As discussed in more detail below, shareholders have the right to vote on certain issues, including the election of directors and certain fundamental economic issues such as a merger or liquidation. They also have the right to receive certain information from the company, and in rare circumstances to take certain actions on behalf of the company. Consistent with these limited rights, shareholders have very limited responsibilities for the company. Indeed, assuming a shareholder is not a majority shareholder or otherwise in control of the corporation, the shareholder owes no duties or responsibility to other shareholders of the company.

This chapter outlines the rights of the shareholder in the modern American corporation. The next section briefly reviews the historical role of the shareholder in the corporation as well as the philosophical debate that led to the current shareholder primacy model. The final section discusses the rights shareholders have today as well as the role of the board under the shareholder primacy model. The chapter concludes by reviewing some alternatives to the shareholder primacy model, including how other corporate constituencies are seeking to participate on corporate actions, as well as briefly reviewing how these issues are resolved in some other countries.

SHAREHOLDER RIGHTS IN THE CORPORATION:
A HISTORICAL PERSPECTIVE

It has long been held that shareholders have very limited rights with respect to the affairs of the corporation.[6] One oft-cited opinion written nearly one hundred years ago described the role of the shareholder as follows:

> As a general rule, stockholders cannot act in relation to the ordinary business of a corporation. The body of stockholders have certain authority conferred by statute which must be exercised to enable the corporation to act in specific cases, but except for certain authority conferred by statute, which is mainly permissive or confirmatory . . . they have no express power given by statute. They are not by any statute in this state given general power of initiative in corporate affairs. Any action by them relating to the details of the corporate business is necessarily in the form of an assent, request, or recommendation. Recommendations by a body of stockholders can only be enforced through the board of directors, and indirectly by the authority of the stockholders to change the personnel of the directors at a meeting for the election of directors.[7]

Yet while courts have long recognized the limited authority of shareholders, the common law did not make directors directly answerable to shareholders.

Rather, the traditional view was that directors owe fiduciary duties to the corporation, not to individual shareholders.[8] This was because directors were acting directly on behalf of the corporation, whereas a special obligation to shareholders arose only when directors undertook special obligations or actions directly on behalf of shareholders.

The responsibility of directors to the corporation as a whole, as opposed to just the shareholders, was part of the general corporate law in most states. For example, the Massachusetts Supreme Judicial Court held that a shareholder did not have a right to bring a claim for insider trading against a director because there was no privity between directors and shareholders.[9] The court cited the "imposing weight of authority in other jurisdictions" in rejecting the proposition that directors are trustees toward individual shareholders.[10]

The view that directors generally do not owe fiduciary duties directly to shareholders began to change as a result of the 1929 stock market crash. The Securities Act of 1933 (Securities Act)[11] and the Securities Exchange Act of 1934 (the Exchange Act),[12] established an obligation on the corporation to provide full disclosure about its financial condition and affairs to shareholders. In addition, the creation of the Securities and Exchange Commission (SEC), with a mandate to protect investors, seemed to emphasize a new role for directors, where they would be held more accountable to shareholders.

The new federal legislation took place against the backdrop of one of the most significant debates in American corporate law history, that between Adolf Berle and E. Merrick Dodd in the *Harvard Law Review*.[13] This debate helped create the intellectual recognition that directors should be viewed as trustees with the responsibility to represent the interests of shareholders, and the corresponding view that shareholders may have a claim against directors acting in their own interests rather than on behalf of the corporation and its shareholders.[14]

While shareholder rights increased during this period, they were only one of many constituencies that had a claim on the corporation. Thus during the middle of the twentieth century it was recognized that directors owed duties to a wide variety of constituents, including the company's employees, customers, and even the general public. For example, in 1946 the chairman of Standard Oil described the goal of the modern corporation as maintaining " 'an equitable and working balance among the claims of the various directly interested groups—stockholders, employees, customers and the public at large.' "[15] The notion that the corporation had a responsibility to nonshareholder constituencies was sufficiently settled by the mid-1950s that even Adolf Berle recognized that "[corporate] powers [are] held in trust for the entire community" and that therefore the debate between him and Dodd "has been settled (at least for the time being) squarely in favor of Professor Dodd's contention."[16]

This view began changing in the 1980s, with the increasing role of institutional investors and the rise of the takeover boom, which increasingly led to the view that American managers who focused on nonshareholder constituencies were too concerned about their own interests at the expense of shareholders.[17] In response to the managerial view of American capitalism, the "shareholder primacy" model took hold and became the dominant view of the role of the shareholder and the director. Under this theory, the primary purpose of the corporation is to maximize shareholder value, and thus the role of directors is to act on behalf of shareholders to increase the corporation's economic value.[18]

This view was articulated in a series of court decisions in the mid-1980s, the most notable of which are perhaps the Delaware Supreme Court's decisions in *Revlon, Inc. v. MacAndrews and Forbes Holdings, Inc.,*[19] and *Unocal Corp. v. Mesa Petroleum Co.*[20] In *Revlon,* the court held that when a sale of the corporation becomes "inevitable," the board's duty changes "from the preservation of [the corporation] as a corporate entity to the maximization of the company's value at a sale for the stockholders' benefit."[21] Under these circumstances, the court held that it was inappropriate for the board to consider nonstockholder constituencies such as the interests of bondholders, employees, or others.[22] In *Unocal,* the court held that before giving the board the protection of the business judgment rule on a decision adopting a defensive measure designed to make a takeover of the company more difficult, the board must meet a two-part test: first, that the directors adopting the defensive measure have "reasonable grounds for believing that a danger to corporate policy and effectiveness existed" prior to the adoption of the challenged defensive measure;[23] and second, that the challenged defensive measure was "reasonable in relation to the threat."[24] Meeting this standard requires "an evaluation of the importance of the corporate objective threatened; alternative methods for protecting that objective; impacts of the 'defensive' action, and other relevant factors."[25]

Revlon and *Unocal* were widely viewed as making clear that shareholders were the primary constituency within the corporation, and that a director's decision (at least in the corporate control context) must be based upon shareholder interests. In response to these decisions a number of states, including Indiana, New Jersey, North Carolina, Ohio, Pennsylvania, and Virginia, adopted so-called "nonshareholder constituency statutes," specifically rejecting the shareholder primacy philosophy and the corresponding additional burdens on directors requiring them to give primacy to shareholder interests. For example, the New Jersey statute states that if "the board of directors determines that any proposal or offer to acquire the corporation is not in the best interest of the corporation, it may reject such proposal or offer," and if the board "determines to reject any such proposal or offer, the board of directors shall have no obligation to facilitate, remove any barriers to, or refrain from impeding the proposal or offer."[26]

The rationale for these statutes was explained by the court in *Norfolk Southern Corp. v. Conrail Inc.,* a case challenging defensive measures adopted under Pennsylvania's statute.[27] The court noted that it "seems clear" that Pennsylvania's statute was enacted with Delaware decisions such as *Revlon* and *Unocal* "clearly in mind" and was adopted specifically to "exclude those." The court then described Delaware's focus upon stockholders rather than the corporation as a whole as "myopic" and expressly rejected the notion under Pennsylvania law that "the sole or at least the primary consideration by a board of directors in considering a competing offer by potential acquirers of the control of a corporation should be which competitor offers the best short-range price or profit for shareholders."[28]

Although this debate has continued, the majority position from both a legal and philosophical view is the shareholder primacy model. In part this reflects the sheer dominance of Delaware in corporate law, as more than half of all U.S. public companies and more than 60 percent of the *Fortune* 500 are incorporated in Delaware.[29] In addition, within the scholarly literature the debate has clearly been decided at present in favor of the shareholder primacy norm.[30]

SHAREHOLDER RIGHTS IN THE CORPORATION: THE MODERN VIEW

The general view today is that shareholders are the "owners" of the corporation, and that they "hire" (or vote) for directors and officers to manage the company's assets on their behalf. This is the so-called "principal-agent" model, where the primary issue in corporate law is to make directors and officers more accountable to the shareholders on whose behalf they act.[31] Yet a more accurate description of the relationship between the various interest groups in the corporation was given by Dean Robert Clark as follows:

> (1) corporate officers like the president and treasurer are agents of the corporation itself; (2) the board of directors is the ultimate decision-making body of the corporation (and in a sense is the group most appropriately identified with "the corporation"); (3) directors are not agents of the corporation but are *sui generis*; (4) neither officers nor directors are agents of the stockholders; but (5) both officers and directors are "fiduciaries" with respect to the corporation and its stockholders.[32]

Professor Clark's model is consistent with the reality of the property interest that shareholders actually have; specifically, this interest is solely in their shares, and not in the corporation's assets. Thus, shareholders have no direct access or claim on a corporation's assets, nor do they have the right to direct or control the disposition of those assets.[33] In addition, shareholders generally do not act like owners of the corporation. For example, their purchase of shares is typically not done to invest capital in the corporation (other than in the private equity or initial public offering contexts), and often the same institutional investors seeking the power and privileges of an owner either engage in active trading of their shares (and thus do not invest in the company for the long-term) or are passive investors holding their stock in index funds that they do not manage.[34]

Despite this, the shareholder primacy model remains in firm control today. Accordingly, this chapter discusses the direct rights of shareholders under current law as well as the current relationship between directors and shareholders, with a particular focus on the duties directors owe shareholders and how those duties are interpreted by the courts.

Shareholders' Voting Rights

Voting for Directors

The most fundamental right shareholders have is to vote on certain specific issues. Of these the most important is the right to vote on the election of directors, which occurs annually except where the company has a "classified" or "staggered" board in which the directors are divided (typically into three groups) such that each group of directors serves a staggered three-year term.[35] The staggered board has become a fairly common feature among public companies, undoubtedly at least in part because directors on a staggered board cannot be removed except for "cause" and because this feature requires two annual elections to change a majority of the board, even if a majority of the shareholders are opposed to the directors.[36]

The courts have been extraordinarily vigilant to protect a shareholder's right to vote, calling it the "ideological underpinning upon which the legitimacy of directorial power rests."[37] In *Blasius Industries, Inc. v. Atlas Corp.*, for example, the court held that when the board takes action "for the sole or primary purpose of thwarting a shareholder vote," the board must overcome the "heavy burden of demonstrating a compelling justification for such action."[38] Blasius owned 9 percent of Atlas's outstanding stock and initiated a consent solicitation to (i) expand the size of the Atlas board from seven to fifteen members and (ii) fill the eight vacancies with its own nominees. In response, the Atlas board adopted a bylaw amendment increasing the size of the board from seven to nine, and filling the two new vacancies. The effect of the bylaw amendment was that even if Atlas succeeded in its consent solicitation, it would still not control a majority of the board. The court found that in taking these actions the Atlas board was "not selfishly motivated simply to retain power" and that it acted in "a good faith effort to protect its incumbency, not selfishly, but in order to thwart implementation of the recapitalization [being proposed by Blasius] that it feared, reasonably, would cause great injury to the [corporation]."[39]

Despite finding that the board acted in good faith and on an informed basis, the court still enjoined the board's adoption of the bylaw as "an unintended breach of the duty of loyalty." The court held that when the board acts for "the sole or primary purpose of thwarting a shareholder vote" it must overcome the "heavy burden of demonstrating a compelling justification for such action." The court found that the Blasius board had failed to meet this burden because "it had time (and understood that it had time) to inform the shareholders of its views on the merit of the proposal subject to stockholder vote."[40] The court ruled that:

> The only justification that can, in such a situation, be offered for the action taken is that the board knows better than do the shareholders what is in the corporation's best interest. While that premise is no doubt true for any number of matters, it is irrelevant (except insofar as the shareholders wish to be guided by the board's recommendation) when the question is who should comprise the board of directors. The theory of our corporation law confers power upon directors as the agents of the shareholders; it does not create Platonic masters.[41]

The court concluded by finding that the power to vote on directors had "transcending significance" within Delaware law, as it was what "legitimates" director power over "vast aggregations of property that they do not own."[42]

Voting in Other Contexts

The other primary areas where shareholders are given the direct right to impact corporate action are instances in which shareholder votes are a necessary step in authorizing a transaction such as a merger, a sale of substantially all of the corporation's assets, or dissolving the enterprise.[43] In the merger context a majority of shareholders of the company(ies) being merged generally must vote in favor of the transaction after the respective boards of each company have approved the proposed transaction.[44]

Yet it is important to note that shareholders in this situation have no substantive rights. For example, other than the right to vote, shareholders do not have the right to take any other action with respect to a merger. Thus if the merger occurs between two publicly traded companies, under Delaware law shareholders may have no right to appraisal (assuming that the consideration to be paid is publicly traded stock).[45] Further, while the documents sent to shareholders contain a tremendous amount of information concerning the merger, including the risks associated with the merger and the background and reasons for the board's recommendation, the merger documents do not contain any debate on the benefits of the proposed merger.[46]

As a result of this, and perhaps not surprisingly, an overwhelming majority of mergers are supported by shareholders. Indeed, one recent study found that of 209 acquiring-firm merger votes occurring between 1990 and 2000, all were approved by shareholders, with an approval rate based on voting rights (i.e., including abstentions and other nonvotes) of approximately 73 percent, and an approval rate based on nonabstention votes cast of nearly 98 percent.[47] Undoubtedly part of this result can be explained by the reality that a board that believes its proposed merger is not going to be approved by shareholders is likely to restructure or withdraw from the deal rather than have shareholders vote the deal down, but the numbers certainly indicate that the voting requirement, while significant (and perhaps most significant for its deterrent effect), has limits as a corporate governance mechanism.

Shareholder Direct Action outside the Voting Contest: The Litigation Alternative

Shareholder lawsuits have become a common way for shareholders to attempt to exercise their rights. Although there are multiple types of lawsuits shareholders can bring against companies, the three most typical are (i) suits under the federal securities laws, (ii) derivative actions, and (iii) class action lawsuits under state law challenging director conduct in mergers and acquisitions.[48] This chapter focuses upon cases under state rather than federal law, consistent with the focus of shareholder rights under state law.

Derivative suits are actions by a shareholder on behalf of the corporation to obtain redress for an injury to the corporation.[49] The potential benefits and risks inherent in derivative suits were explained by the Supreme Court more than a half century ago, in the landmark decision *Cohen v. Beneficial Industrial Loan Corp.*,[50] in which the court upheld a New Jersey statute requiring a derivative plaintiff to post a twenty-five-thousand-dollar bond as security for defendants' legal fees and costs in the event that the litigation was dismissed as being without merit:

> This [derivative] remedy born of stockholder helplessness was long the chief regulator of corporate management and has afforded no small incentive to avoid at least the grosser forms of betrayal of stockholders' interests. It is argued, and not without reason, that without it there would be little practical check on such abuses.
>
> Unfortunately, the remedy itself provided opportunity for abuse which was not neglected. Suits sometimes were brought not to redress wrongs, but to realize upon their nuisance value. They were bought off by secret settlements in which any wrongs to the general body of shareowners were compounded by the suing stockholder, who was mollified by payments from corporate assets.[51]

Following the *Cohen* decision as well as other contemporaneous criticisms of potential abuses with derivative actions,[52] a number of jurisdictions adopted various procedural steps in an attempt to ensure that a plaintiff seeking to act on behalf of the company not bring a frivolous claim. For example, and in addition to the bond requirement, these include making a demand upon the board of directors before proceeding with the litigation as well as being a "contemporaneous owner" of the company's stock throughout the litigation.[53] Whether because these cases are generally without merit (as many argue) or because the procedural and substantive burdens are so high (as plaintiff's counsel claim) or some combination of both, the reality is that derivative suits generally provide little direct benefits to shareholders, with the bulk of any funds paid going primarily to plaintiff's counsel.[54]

Class action lawsuits challenging a director's actions under state law, particularly in the merger and acquisition context, have also become more common in recent years.[55] Like derivative cases, these cases typically involve multiple, identical (or nearly identical) complaints filed within days of an announced acquisition, either in the company's state of incorporation or principal place of business (or both). The claims involved typically concern an alleged breach of the directors' duty of care (typically for not achieving a high enough price or getting a good enough deal) and/or loyalty (for obtaining benefits not equally available to other shareholders). Over 75 percent of the time the cases are filed by a small group of well-defined plaintiffs' law firms, and, unlike cases currently brought under the federal securities laws, these cases typically do not have institutional investors as plaintiffs.[56]

These cases have come under many of the same criticisms that other shareholder actions have faced. In particular, the high costs of defense, generally small returns to shareholders, and relatively high payments to plaintiffs' counsel (particularly in relation to the purported benefit being provided to shareholders) has led many to question whether these actions truly benefit shareholders.[57]

Guardian of the Corporate Bastion on Behalf of the Shareholders: The Board of Directors and the Business Judgment Rule

The Berle-Dodd debate in the 1930s assumed that the corporation was controlled by its managers, leading to the famous question "For whom are corporate managers trustees?"[58] In today's world this question has been settled. Corporations are, at least in theory, controlled by the board of (independent) directors, who have the obligation to run the company on behalf of shareholders.[59] This theory is consistent with both the American Law Institute's Corporate Governance Project[60] and the emphasis in the recently adopted Sarbanes-Oxley Act, which emphasizes the importance of independent directors and their role in monitoring the corporation and its management. The reality, however, is somewhat different. Thus, as Roberta Karmel has noted:

> The modern public corporation is a vast bureaucratic organization of great complexity. Although shareholders have the power to vote for directors and, in theory, the directors appoint the managers, both shareholders and directors are part time participants in the corporation's affairs. The corporate scandals of recent years have demonstrated that corporate managers, and in particular, CEOs, have great power and insufficient accountability. Without such power, they probably could not manage the modern corporation, which is based on a hierarchical structure.[61]

In managing the corporation, both the board and the officers are constrained by the fiduciary obligations they owe the company and its shareholders. These obligations include the fundamental duties of care and loyalty.[62] The duty of care requires that directors act on "an informed basis," which has been given a variety of interpretations, from a requirement that directors "exercise the care that an ordinarily prudent person would exercise under similar circumstances"[63] to a requirement that directors "inform[] themselves ... 'of all material information reasonably available to them.' "[64] In practice the standard of liability has become one of "gross negligence" such that a plaintiff challenging the board's actions under the duty of care standard must allege facts that show the board's conduct is grossly negligent to state a claim. As the Delaware Supreme Court held in *Smith v. Van Gorkum*, "The concept of gross negligence is also the proper standard for determining whether a business judgment reached by a board of directors was an informed one."[65] In addition (and in response to this decision and its definition of "gross negligence") the Delaware legislature adopted a statutory provision to exculpate directors for a violation of the duty of care provided that the action was taken in good faith.[66] This has reinforced the notion that a director cannot be held liable under the duty of care unless the decision was grossly negligent.[67]

The duty of loyalty requires that a director act in good faith, put the interests of the company and its shareholders above his or her own interests, and not take advantage of his or her position as a director to harm the corporation or its stockholders.[68] As described by the Delaware Supreme Court in the seminal case of *Guth v. Loft*:[69]

> Corporate officers and directors are not permitted to use their position of trust and confidence to further their private interests.... A public policy, existing through the years, and derived from a profound knowledge of human characteristics and motives, has established a rule that demands of a corporate officer or director, peremptorily and inexorably, the most scrupulous observance of his duty, not only affirmatively to protect the interest of the corporation committed to his charge, but also to refrain from doing anything that would work injury to the corporation.... [T]he rule that requires an undivided and unselfish loyalty to the corporation demands that there shall be no conflict between duty and self-interest.

A shareholder bringing an action alleging that a director (or board) breached either of these duties must overcome the presumptions of the business judgment rule. The business judgment rule is both a rule of procedure and a substantive rule of law.[70] Procedurally, the rule places the initial burden on the plaintiff to allege facts in the complaint sufficient to show that a director (or board) violated one of these two duties. Thus at the pleading stage the plaintiff must allege in detail how a director acted with gross negligence (to state a claim under the duty of care) or acted in self-interest to the detriment of the corporation (to show a violation of the duty of loyalty).[71] Failing to allege such facts with adequate specificity will result in dismissal of the complaint.[72]

Substantively, if the business judgment standard of review is held to apply to a board's decision, the decision will not face substantive review (or be "second-guessed") by the court. Thus, under this rule a director's decision will not be subject to challenge, review, or liability, even if erroneous, so long as the duties of care and loyalty are satisfied.[73] As the Delaware Supreme Court summarized these protections, "[i]f a shareholder plaintiff fails to meet this evidentiary burden, the business judgment rule operates to provide substantive protection for the directors and the decisions that they have made."[74]

It is important to note that there are situations where the substantive or procedural protections of the business judgment rule do not apply. For example, if it is shown that a director of a company stands on both sides of a particular transaction, then the director (and the board) may be required to show that the transaction was "entirely fair" to the corporation and its shareholders, meaning that both the price and process employed in the transaction were fair to shareholders.[75] In addition, under the so-called *Unocal* standard discussed earlier, Delaware generally shifts the burden of proof whenever a board adopts a defensive measure in response to a threat to the corporation, its policies, or stockholders. Under these circumstances, before a board can receive the protections of the business judgment rule, directors must satisfy a two-part test. This test requires the board to show (i) after reasonable investigation, that a "danger to corporate policy and effectiveness existed"; and, once this finding is made, the board still has the burden of proof to demonstrate (ii) that the specific measure adopted in response was "reasonable in relation to the threat posed."[76]

Yet despite these modifications, the bedrock principles supporting the business judgment rule continue to ensure that directors remain the primary decision-makers in the corporation. When combined with the shareholder primacy theory dominating corporate law today, this means that a board decision that the directors reasonably believed was in the interests of the shareholders and taken in good faith will not be subject to substantive review by a court.

SOME FINAL THOUGHTS ON THE RIGHTS OF SHAREHOLDERS: ARE WE AT THE END OF CORPORATE LAW AND SHOULD WE BE HAPPY?

The primacy of Delaware law in American corporate law jurisprudence, when combined with its emphasis on the business judgment rule and the rights of shareholders, means that the shareholder primacy model dominates today's legal landscape. Yet this domination is rather remarkable, given that a large number of states and many countries have statutory regimes allowing or mandating that directors consider the effects of their actions on other corporate constituencies, including employees, communities, and others. Further, as described above, these statutes are consistent with what, until at least the middle of the twentieth century, was the general legal landscape in the United States.

There are a number of powerful critics of this shareholder primacy model. For example, one school of thought has argued at length for a "stakeholder" model of governance. This model argues that the shareholder primacy model gives shareholders too much of a claim to the rights and benefits of the corporation and argues that some of these privileges and rights should go to other stakeholders in the corporation, such as employees and others.[77] This is consistent with many state statutes, which gained favor in response to the takeover boom in the late 1980s and remain part of the corporate landscape in many states.

A second model focuses on director primacy, looking to the board to act as a mediator between the various corporate constituencies, and explains why the traditional notions of shareholders as owners and the shareholder primacy models are not accurate.[78] Under this model, directors are in the best position to recognize the role of employees, creditors, executives, and even the community in the success of the firm, and balance these competing interests. As one of the principal proponents of this theory describes it, the "board of directors is not an agent of the shareholders; rather, the board is the embodiment of the corporate principal, serving as the nexus of the various contracts making up the corporation."[79]

A third model, which at least historically was common to a number of European jurisdictions, views the corporation as a public entity, which has its first responsibility to the community in which it exists. This model emphasizes the ethical responsibility of the corporation to its community as well as to the stockholders and is grown out of the historical basis view that the corporation was an enterprise of the state.[80]

As a practitioner in today's environment, it is easy to dismiss these alternative models that seem so far from the shareholder primacy norm. Further, there is an argument that in today's environment of corporate scandals, the need for shareholders to act like owners is greater than ever, as failure to establish stronger standards by which shareholders can exercise ownership rights gives management greater ability to act in its own interests and contrary to those of not just shareholders but other corporate constituencies. Yet in the end what is most striking about any of these models is how little direct authority shareholders have in today's corporation. Rather, what all the models discussed above have in common is that each looks to some force other than the shareholders—the presumptive owners of the corporation—to act as the controlling influence on the corporation. Whether this control resides in the hands of managers, directors, or even the state, what is clear is that the separation of stock ownership from control of the corporation, which was the issue raised in the great Berle-Dodd debates, is as great as at any time in history.

NOTES

The author would like to thank Lisa Schwartz Kirby and Leila Ahlstrom Guerrero for their assistance with this article. However, the author is solely responsible for any errors, and the views expressed herein are solely his and not those of his firm.

1. See generally Stephen M. Bainbridge (2003), Director primacy: The means and ends of corporate governance, *N.W. U. L. Rev.*, 97, 547 (discussing the model and its impact).

2. There are also a number of states in which the director primacy model is explicitly rejected. See section II, infra. Professor Constance Bagley discusses this issue from a somewhat different view in her chapter in this book. See Constance Bagley, Shareholder primacy is a choice, not a legal mandate.

3. Del. Code Ann. tit. 8, sec. 141(a).

4. See Roberta S. Karmel (2004, May), *Should a duty to the corporation be imposed on institutional shareholders?* Brooklyn Law School, Public Law Research Paper No. 11, available at http://ssrn.com/abstract=546642

5. This is the so-called business judgment rule. See generally notes 70–76 and corresponding text, infra.

6. There are three general types of corporations in the United States today. The first, and the type that is the focus of this chapter, is the publicly held corporation, which is typically owned by a large number of shareholders. The second is the privately held corporation, which may have any number of shareholders but whose shares are not sold to the public. Finally, there is the close corporation, generally defined as a corporation owned by a limited number of shareholders, most of whom are actively involved in the management of the corporation. Most public corporations in the United States are incorporated in Delaware, and thus generally this chapter looks to Delaware law when discussing the state laws governing corporations.

7. *Continental Sec. Co. v. Belmont*, 99 N.E. 138, 141 (N.Y. 1912).

8. See Karmel, supra p. 6 at n.15 (citing *Percival v. Wright*, 2 Ch. 421 (1902)).

9. *Goodwin v. Agassiz*, 186 N.E. 659 (Mass. 1933). See generally, Karmel, supra.

10. *Goodwin*, 186 N.E. at 660.

11. 15 U.S.C. sec. 77a et seq.

12. 15 U.S.C. sec. 78a et seq.

13. See A. A. Berle Jr. (1931), Corporate powers as powers in trust, *Harv. L. Rev.*, 44, 1049; E. Merrick Dodd Jr. (1932), For whom are corporate managers trustees? *Harv. L. Rev.*, 45, 1145. See also Adolf A. Berle Jr. and Gardiner C. Means (1932), *The modern corporation and private property*.

14. Some commentators have argued that the Michigan Supreme Court's decision in *Dodge v. Ford Motor Co.*, 170 N.W. 668 (Mich. 1919) was the earliest and strongest opinion supporting the shareholder primacy view. However, as a number of scholars have pointed out, Dodge was a highly unusual case, and the real issues in the case may not have been between shareholders and stakeholders but rather between competing groups of shareholders. See, for example, Jesse H. Choper et al. (1989), *Cases and materials on corporation law* (3d ed.,) 994–95; Margaret Blair and Lynn Stout (1999), A team production theory of corporate law, *Va. L. Rev.*, 85, 247, 301–3.

15. See Eugene V. Rostow, To whom and for what ends is corporate management responsible, in *The corporation in modern society*, 46, 60 (Edward S. Mason, ed.). See also Blair and Stout, A team production theory of corporate law, supra at 286.

16. Adolf A. Berle Jr. (1954), *The twentieth-century capitalist revolution,* 169.

17. See, for example, Stephen M. Bainbridge (2003), Director primacy: The means and ends of corporate governance, *Nw. U.L. Rev., 97,* 547; Bernard Black and Reinier Kraackman (1996), A self-enforcing model of corporate law, *Harv. L. Rev., 109,* 1911.

18. See, for example, Black and Kraackman, supra *Harv. L. Rev., 109,* at 1921 (describing the "maximizing [of] the company's value to investors" as the "principal function of corporate law").

19. 506 A.2d 173 (Del. 1986).

20. 493 A.2d 946 (Del. 1985).

21. Revlon, 506 A.2d at 182.

22. For a thorough discussion of *Revlon* and its progeny as well as how the case has been applied over the years, see Dennis J. Block, Nancy E. Barton, and Stephen A. Radin, *The business judgment rule,* (5th ed)., 694–770.

23. Unocal, supra 493 A.2d at 955.

24. Ibid., 955.

25. *Paramount Communications Inc. v. Time Inc.,* 571 A. 2d 1140, 1154 (Del. 1990). See generally Block et al., *The business judgment rule,* supra (discussing the case law interpreting *Revlon* and *Unocal*).

26. N.J. Bus. Corp. Act sec. 14A:6-1(3), cited in Block, supra at 688–689.

27. No. 96-7167, 1996 WL, 33649421 (E.D. Pa. November 19, 1996), *aff'd* mem., 111 F.3d 127 (3d Cir. 1997).

28. Ibid., Tr. at 646–655.

29. In contrast, the state incorporating the second-largest number of *Fortune* 500 companies (New York) has approximately 5 percent. See Kent Greenfield (2004), Democracy and the dominance of Delaware in corporate law, *Law and Contemporary Problems, 67,* 101, 102.

30. See generally Blair and Stout, Team production theory, supra at 324–327 (discussing why the shareholder primacy model gained general acceptance within the academic community during this period); Karmel, supra note 4 (same).

31. The literature using the principal-agent approach has been described as "to voluminous too cite in its entirety." Blair and Stout, A team production, supra at 248, n.1. The leading articles include Victor Brudney (1985), Corporate governance, agency costs, and the rhetoric of contract, *Colum. L. Rev., 85,* 1401, Frank J. Easterbrook and Daniel R. Fischel (1991), *The economic structure of corporate law,* and Frank J. Easterbrook and Daniel R. Fischel, The proper role of a target's management in responding to a tender offer, *Harv. L. Rev.,* 94, 1161.

32. Robert C. Clark (1985), *Agency costs versus fiduciary duties, in principals and agents: The structure of business* (John W. Pratt and Richard J. Zechhauser eds.,), 56.

33. See generally Stephen Bainbridge (2002), The board of directors as nexus of contracts, *Iowa L. Rev., 88,* 1.

34. See generally Karmel, supra at 2.

35. Del. Code Ann. tit. 8, sec. 141(d).

36. See Lucian A. Bebchuk, John C. Coates IV, and Guhan Subramanian (2002), The powerful antitakeover force of staggered boards: Further findings and a reply to symposium participants, *Stan. L. Rev., 55,* 885. Lucian Bebchuk, Alma Cohen, and Allen Farrell, *Discussion paper no. 491* (09/2004, revised 11/2004), available at http://papers.ssrn.com/abstract_id=593423

37. *Blasius Industries, Inc. v. Atlas Corp.*, 564 A.2d 651, 659 (Del. Ch. 1988).

38. Ibid., 661–662. The so-called "*Blasius* doctrine" was subsequently adopted and affirmed by the Delaware Supreme Court. See, for example, *Stroud v. Grace*, 606 A.2d 75 (Del. 1992).

39. Blasius, 564 A.2d at 656–658.

40. Ibid., 661–663.

41. Ibid., 663.

42. Ibid., 659–662.

43. See generally *Williams v. Geier*, 671 A.2d 1368, 1379 (Del. 1996); Del. Code Ann. tit. 8, secs. 271(a), 251(c).

44. See for example, Del. Code Ann. tit. 8, sec. 251.

45. See for example, Del. Code. Ann. tit. 8, sec. 262. See generally Peter V. Letsou (1998), The role of appraisal in corporate law, *B.C. L. Rev., 39,* 1121 (discussing use and theory of appraisal remedy).

46. See generally James A. Fanto (2000, May 22), *Breaking the merger momentum: Reforming corporate law governing mega-mergers.*

47. See Timothy R. Burch, Angela G. Morgan, and Jack G. Wolf (2004, May), *Is acquiring-firm shareholder approval in stock-for-stock mergers perfunctory?*

48. There are numerous articles and studies concerning shareholder lawsuits under the federal securities laws and derivative suits. For a summary of this literature as well as a discussion about how "acquisition-oriented suits are now the dominant form of corporate litigation," see Robert B. Thompson and Randall S. Thomas, *The new look of shareholder litigation: Acquisition-oriented class actions,* Vanderbilt University Law School, Law and Economics, Working Paper No. 03-04, available at http://ssrn.com/abstract_id=401580

49. See generally D. Block et al., *The business judgment rule,* supra at 1379–1385.

50. 337 U.S. 541 (1949).

51. Ibid., 548. For a historical discussion of derivative suits, see Franklin S. Wood (1944), *Survey and report regarding stockholders' derivative suits;* for a more recent analysis, including a discussion of the Wood report and its impact, see Thompson and Thomas, *The new look of shareholder litigation,* supra.

52. See, for example, Wood, supra.

53. The literature on the procedural requirements for bringing a derivative action is voluminous, and the standards continue to develop and change. For an overview and discussion of these requirements see Block et al., supra note 22. For a recent discussion of the changing nature of the derivative action, and in particular what constitutes a derivative claim as opposed to a direct claim, see *Tooley v. Donaldson, Lufkin and Jenrette, Inc.,* 845 A.2d 1031 (Del. 2004) (Delaware Supreme Court redefining the distinction between direct and derivative claims).

54. Again, the studies on the benefits and costs of derivative suits are numerous and voluminous. See generally Thompson and Thomas, *The new look of shareholder litigation* supra (discussing various studies).

55. See Thompson and Thomas, supra at 5–7 (finding that such cases "dominate all other forms of state court shareholder litigation" and that in Delaware alone during the two-year period 1999–2000 such cases "equaled about half the total number of federal securities fraud class actions filed in *all* federal district courts during that same two-year period."

56. Ibid., 7–8.

57. But see ibid., supra at 5. (Arguing that "good policy must balance the positive management agency cost reducing effects of these acquisition-oriented shareholder suits against their litigation agency costs" and that these suits may have "positive management agency cost reducing effects that may offset the litigation agency costs that accompany them.")

58. See E. Merrick Dodd Jr. (1932), For whom are corporate managers trustees? *Harv. L. Rev., 45*, 1145; A. A. Berle Jr. (1932), For whom corporate managers are trustees: A note, *Harv. L. Rev., 45*, 1365.

59. Stephen M. Bainbridge (2003), Director primacy: The means and ends of corporate governance, *N.W. U.L. Rev., 97*, 547.

60. American Law Institute (1994), *Principles of corporate governance: Analysis and recommendations*.

61. Karmel, 29–30.

62. For a detailed and thorough discussion of these duties and the cases discussing them, see Block et al., supra note 22.

63. See, for example, *Graham v. Allis-Chalmers Mfg. Co.*, 188 A.2d 125, 130 (Del. 1963) (holding that in managing the affairs of the corporation directors are "bound to use that amount of care which ordinarily careful and prudent men would use in similar circumstances"); *Norlin Corp. v Rooney*, Pace, Inc. 744 F.2d 255, 264 (same).

64. See, for example, *Smith v. Van Gorkum*, 488 A.2d 858, 872–873 (Del. 1985) (citing *Aronson v. Lewis*, 473 A.2d 805, 812 (Del.1984)).

65. *Smith v. Van Gorkum*.

66. See Del. G. Corp. Law sec. 102(b)(7). Under section 102(b)(7) there are four enumerated exclusions to the ability of a corporation to eliminate (or limit) director liability: (i) a breach of the duty of loyalty; (ii) acts or omissions not taken in good faith or involving intentional misconduct or knowing violations of law; (iii) unlawful payments of dividends; or (iv) self-interested transactions. Interestingly, a number of recent Delaware cases have raised questions concerning the scope of a so-called "duty of good faith," which may give rise to another type of cause of action. See generally, Sean J. Griffith (2004, December 17), *The good faith thaumatrope: A model of rhetoric in corporate law jurisprudence* (draft).

67. However, it should be noted that the standard of liability and judicial review is, of course, different from a standard of care. Thus the change in liability standards does not change the expected care with which directors are to act. See generally, William T. Allen, Jack B. Jacobs, and Leo E. Strine Jr. (2001), Function over form: A reassessment of standards of review in Delaware corporation law, *Bus. Law., 56*, 1287.

68. Block et al., supra note 22.

69. 5 A.2d 503, 510 (Del. 1939).

70. See *Aronson v. Lewis*, 473 A.2d at 812.

71. Ibid.; see also *Beam v. Stewart*, 845 A.2d 1040, 1048–49 (Del. 2004); *Rales v. Blasband*, 634 A.2d 927, 933 (Del. 1993).

72. See, for example, *Orman v. Cullman*, 794 A.2d 5, 15 (Del. Ch. 2002); Block et al., supra at 19–28.

73. Aronson, 473 A.2d at 812; Van Gorkum, 488 A.2d at 872–73; Block et al., supra at 19–28.

74. *Emerald Partners v. Berlin*, 787 A.2d 85, 91 (Del. 2001).

75. See *Weinberger v. UOP*, Inc., 457 A.2d 701, 710 (Del. 1983).

76. See *Unocal Corp. v. Mesa Petroleum Co.*, 493 A.2d 946, 954 (Del. 1985). The court applies this stricter scrutiny to director conduct because, in part, of "the omnipresent specter that a board may be acting primarily in its own interests" rather than for shareholder interests. Idem. The cases discussing these standards, and the factual situations that determine what a "threat" is and whether a response is "reasonable" have been the subject of lengthy (and ongoing) debate. The most thorough summary is probably in Block et al., supra at 631–659.

77. See, for example, Marleen A. O'Conner (1993), The human capital era: Reconceptualizing corporate law to facilitate labor-management cooperation, *Cornell L. Rev.*, 78, 899; John C. Coffee Jr. (1990), Unstable coalitions: Corporate governance as a multi-player game, *Geo. L.J.*, 78, 1495.

78. See, for example, Blair and Stout, A team production theory of corporate law, supra; Stephen Bainbridge (2003, July 28), *The business judgment rule as absention doctrine*, UCLA Law and Economics research paper.

79. Bainbridge, supra at 4.

80. See generally, Dirk Zetzsche (2004, September 23), *Explicit and implicit system of corporate control: A convergence theory of shareholder rights.*

III
IMPROVING CORPORATE GOVERNANCE

8

Empowering the Board, Revisited

JAY W. LORSCH

I f the 1980s was the decade when the movement to empower U.S. factory and office workers took root, the 1990s was the decade when empower ment spread to corporate boardrooms. Empowerment means that outside directors have the capability and independence to monitor the performance of top management and the company; to influence management to change the strategic direction of the company if its performance does not meet the board's expectations; and, in the most extreme cases, to change corporate leadership. This trend seemed positive, and most observers felt that corporate boards were at last acting like the potentates the law intended them to be. Then came the dawning of the twenty-first century and the scandals of Enron, Tyco, WorldCom, and others. Were the failures of the boards involved in these scandals exceptions to the trend toward empowerment? The answer to this question, it seems to me, is that the scandals did occur at companies where the CEO still dominated the board not only in relative power, but also in terms of withholding information from the directors. Obviously not all boards had achieved the desired degree of empowerment in relation to their CEO, and those at companies involved in these notorious scandals were among the laggards. These events do not mean that empowerment of boards was an illusion, only that it was not occurring at all companies. In fact, there were, and still are in 2004, many American CEOs who are resisting the idea of board empowerment.

Because the chief executive is also the board chair in more than 80 percent of America's publicly held corporations, it is not surprising that a reluctant CEO can stifle board empowerment. Historically, corporate leaders considered a powerful, active board to be a nuisance at best and a force that could improperly interfere in the management of the company at worst. They preferred directors who were content to offer counsel when asked and to support management in times of crisis.

Chief executives who are ambivalent about empowered boards must change their attitude. If they do not, they and their companies will be the losers because the empowered board is here to stay. The Sarbanes-Oxley law and the revised listing requirements of the stock exchanges, to say nothing about pressure from investors, make it clear that empowered boards are going to be a fixture of the corporate landscape. Thus, even recalcitrant CEOs must recognize that empowered directors are a reality they must accept.

Empowerment does mean that directors and the chief executive must redefine their relationship. The CEO must understand clearly the power and responsibility of the board. Directors must recognize and respect the boundary between monitoring management and actually managing the company. What is required is a new form of teamwork in which directors and top-level managers understand one another's roles and responsibilities and collaborate effectively to achieve corporate success. Their newly defined relationship will strengthen the board's ability to advise management and to monitor corporate performance and make the necessary decisions. The CEO will retain the power to lead the company while obtaining the guidance and support of informed and active directors, as long as corporate performance is satisfactory.

PRESSURES FOR EMPOWERMENT

There are several driving forces to empower outside directors. The most obvious one is the major spate of scandals just mentioned and the resulting changes in laws and regulations. This has been accompanied by continuing pressure from institutional investors for more effective corporate governance. Most institutional investors do not want to sit on boards and play a direct role in governing companies, but they have become more active in pressing boards to challenge management and have been effective in getting the media to apply similar pressure. Further, performance difficulties of many major companies and the removal of their CEOs have generated more public interest in active boards. Finally, the move to empower directors has been fueled by the ongoing controversy about CEO compensation—or, more precisely, by the perception that many CEOs are substantially overpaid relative to their companies' performance. As long as shareholders, the media, and the public are uncomfortable with what and how CEOs and other top managers are rewarded, there will be pressure on boards to be more active in overseeing not only executive pay, but also corporate performance.

INVALID ASSUMPTIONS ABOUT EMPOWERING DIRECTORS

Many CEOs and others who have reservations about empowering directors proceed from incorrect premises about power in the boardroom.

Power Is Zero-Sum

This is a serious misconception. As U.S. factories and offices illustrate, one party (employees) can gain power without the other party (management) losing it. The same is true in the boardroom. In companies such as Target Corporation and Medtronic, where directors have long been empowered to monitor corporate and management performance, there is no evidence that the CEO and other top-level managers have found their power to lead the company diminished. What they have found is that directors are better informed, communicate their ideas more effectively, and in general provide better advice. For example, at the steel company Lukens, the chairman and CEO asked several outside directors to serve on a board committee to consider a major acquisition in great detail. Each director reviewed all the data used by management to recommend the acquisition, and then the committee met for a daylong session with the management team. In the end, the committee recommended the acquisition to the full board, which approved it with understanding and enthusiasm. The CEO commented that as a result of the process, the full board had become more active, involved, and communicative, and that the change in procedure had been valuable.

Advising and Monitoring Are in Conflict

Advice is what CEOs want most from outside directors, and many chief executives worry that if directors become more forceful monitors, their usefulness as advisers will diminish. That concern is misguided because directors require the same two ingredients to perform both roles: access to useful information and the time to discuss it with one another and with management. In fact, directors on empowered boards are likely to be more knowledgeable and involved and therefore to be better advisers. It is true, of course, that if top management consistently disregards the directors' advice, an empowered board is more likely to be forceful in expressing its opinions. While such forthrightness may be uncomfortable to managers at first, it should lead to better decisions if directors and managers are working together effectively.

There Is No Need to Act Unless a Crisis Strikes

The assumption that boards can safely remain passive until there is a crisis implies that directors are like firefighters who sit around the station playing checkers until there is a fire and then spring into action. However, firefighters must practice in order to cope with an emergency, and so must directors. Directors who passively await a crisis will have neither the necessary information nor the decision-making and communication mechanisms they need to resolve issues quickly if a crisis does strike.

Moreover, as the events at so many companies have illustrated, the most difficult crises confronting boards occur gradually. Boards that do not actively monitor performance, even in apparently good times, are likely to have great difficulty spotting and understanding problems in a timely fashion. An important virtue of board empowerment is that it enables directors to prevent crises. By being active monitors, they can encourage and support their CEO in making the changes necessary to keep small difficulties from turning into large ones. In fact, in organizations whose boards removed CEOs because of poor corporate performance, the boards themselves usually had failed to monitor management and company performance in the years before the crisis.

One Size Fits All Companies

Many managers incorrectly assume that empowerment should entail identical procedures and processes in all boards. While there are certain essential activities for any board, as I will explain below, the specifics of how the board should carry out those activities and, more broadly, act as advisers and monitors must depend on the company's particular circumstances.

At least three factors influence the processes and procedures that outside directors should use. First is the confidence the directors have in the CEO and the nature of the relationship between them. If the CEO is new and the directors do not have a good understanding of his or her ideas, they may want to monitor those ideas and the CEO's actions more frequently and carefully. If the CEO has been leading the company successfully for several years, directors can be effective monitors with less detailed annual assessments. In the latter situation, however, outside directors must satisfy themselves that neither they nor the CEO is overlooking significant changes in the circumstances facing the company.

A second factor that affects the way a board should think about empowerment is the company's performance. If a company has been having problems, the directors will clearly want to be more involved in understanding management's thinking and decisions than if the company has not. Again, at the least, the directors should feel sure that they and management are anticipating the future and not overlooking potential problems.

The board's role as monitor will also depend on the complexity of the decisions facing managers and directors. Beyond problems with company performance, the factor that most influences such complexity is the diversity of the company's businesses—in other words, the number of different products and markets and also the number of countries in which the company operates. For example, the board of a company such as General Electric, which operates different businesses all over the world, has more complexity to deal with than the board of Coca-Cola, which basically is in only one business, even though it operates globally.

Some would argue that a company's size is also a determinant of the complexity of the decisions it faces. While that argument has some merit, size alone has less of an effect on complexity than diversity does. In essence, a bigger company has to make bigger decisions about the same issues, but if a company engages in a greater number of businesses, that means more and *different* issues for the board.

Another factor that affects the complexity of decisions is the rate of market and technological change in the company's businesses. Clearly, a company such as IBM, which not only has multiple businesses operating globally but also deals with constant and rapid technological and market changes, faces immense complexity. The task of keeping abreast of those changes is enormous.

Complexity as determined by such factors presents a serious challenge. The more complexity a company faces, the more difficult it is for directors to be effective monitors, because they constantly must be alert to changes, especially ones that are hard to anticipate.

What monitoring involves in a given company will change over time, as conditions change. Directors must have the information they need to focus on the right issues and use their time together productively. The effectiveness of the group is the true source of their empowerment. To understand why, let's consider the sources and limits of directors' power.

THE SOURCES AND LIMITS OF DIRECTORS' POWER

In theory, the directors' mandate to govern a company comes from the laws of the state in which it is incorporated. To the layman, those definitions of the board's role are surprisingly vague and broad. For example, according to Delaware law, "The business and affairs of every corporation organized under this charter shall be managed by or under the direction of a board of directors." Directors usually delegate the responsibility of operating the company to management. In carrying out their residual responsibility of overseeing management, they are expected to demonstrate care and loyalty (have no conflicts of interest) and to exercise sound business judgment. Laws defining directors' powers in other states generally follow those of Delaware.

Of course, these broad duties have been interpreted and refined by court decisions in the individual states and especially in Delaware and by new laws like Sarbanes-Oxley. In addition, the stock exchanges and the Securities and Exchange Commission have developed rules and regulations that further define directors' duties. For example, the exchanges require audit, compensation, and governance committees to be composed entirely of independent directors, and the SEC has prescribed how compensation committees should report top management's pay to shareholders.

While such actions enhance a board's ability to govern, the broader legal framework really does little more than provide a board with the legitimacy to govern. Its real power and ability depend on two other sources: the knowledge that directors have, and their cohesion as a group. Each source must be considered in relation to the CEO, because a board's real power depends on its relationship with its CEO and with other top executives.

One important factor is that directors are part-timers and the CEO is a full-time employee whose entire career may have been with the company. Not surprisingly, CEOs have knowledge about their companies that directors do not. From the directors' perspective, it is not an exaggeration to say that a primary purpose of board meetings is to learn about the organization from the CEO. Directors may obtain any data they want, but such information must be converted into useful knowledge through the prism of a broader understanding of the company and its markets and operations—information that inevitably must come from management at board meetings. The financial and written data tell only part of the story, and directors usually come to meetings armed with many questions: Why are revenues up or down? What are customers and dealers doing? Why are manufacturing costs declining? What is the status of a new product in a test market? Why are negotiations on a proposed acquisition taking so long?

Superior knowledge about such matters provides even the most well-intentioned CEO with a real power advantage over the outside directors. If we add to this advantage the fact that the CEO usually determines the board's agenda and leads its meetings, it is clear why CEOs must be convinced of the value of empowered directors. If they resist the idea, they can easily inhibit progress.

Directors, however, have a critical source of power that they can use to their advantage: their solidarity as a group. Given the experience and ability of the directors on most boards, only a stubborn and arrogant CEO would resist a unified board. As we have seen in the past few years, when a united board decides that it's time for a change in corporate direction or leadership, it prevails. Previously, the process of building such consensus may have taken too long because boardroom norms inhibited directors from communicating freely with one another. An empowered board, however, can facilitate the necessary dialogue and build solidarity among its members.

WHAT MAKES AN EMPOWERED BOARD?

Much has been said and written lately about the characteristics of an empowered board. These characteristics, which are being adopted to varying degrees in different boardrooms, can be summarized as follows:

- Most of the directors are independent.
- The board is small enough to be a cohesive group. Its members understand their common objectives and are willing to dedicate the time to accomplish

them. They recognize that their primary obligation is to monitor the company's management and performance, not to manage the company. Members represent a range of business and leadership experiences, which are pertinent to understanding the issues the company faces.

- Members communicate freely with one another in both committee meetings and board meetings and outside such settings—with and without management.
- If the CEO is also chair of the board, the outside directors select a leader from among themselves. This person leads their deliberations when they meet without management and works closely with the CEO to plan board activities.
- Committees are made up entirely of outside directors. While management is consulted on matters discussed within the committees, they also meet regularly without management.
- Members receive information about the company's financial and product-market performance in a format that is intelligible and enables them to understand their company's performance relative to the competition's.

Such characteristics are the foundation on which board empowerment is being built, but the critical and less explored issues are what empowered boards should do differently as they monitor and advise, and how they should carry out their activities without interfering with management's duty and capacity to run the company.

Three activities are crucial if the board is to be an effective monitor: ensuring legal and ethical conduct by the corporation's officers and employees; approving the company's strategic direction and evaluating its progress; selecting, evaluating, rewarding, and, if necessary, removing the CEO, and ensuring that appropriate top management succession plans are in place.

For years, directors have identified those three activities as being their most important responsibilities. The first is the one with the longest history and the one that is accomplished most uniformly across the broad spectrum of U.S. companies, especially with the passing of the Sarbanes-Oxley Act. Audit committees made up of outside directors in all public companies ensure that financial reports are accurate and transparent, that accounting rules are followed, and that assets are not misappropriated. Many audit committees also review officers' and employees' compliance with other rules and standards of conduct. While some boards have failed in handling this responsibility, in recent years it now appears that audit committees have been reinvigorated by the new legislation. This does not mean accounting fraud or misconduct has been abolished, but it is less likely to occur.

To monitor effectively, boards must also use their greater power to review and approve corporate strategy and to evaluate CEO performance and succession planning at least annually. A brief review of how most boards have been carrying out those two responsibilities will illustrate why they are the areas requiring change.

Traditionally, boards became involved in thinking about strategic direction when they approved specific capital or acquisition proposals. During the past decade, in a growing number of companies, boards have held one- or two-day strategic retreats. While that development is commendable, what happens at the retreats varies considerably. In some companies managers inform directors of their intended strategy either through briefing books provided in advance or through oral presentations made at the retreat. Directors share their reactions and concerns at the retreat or later in private discussions with the CEO. Alternatively, strategic retreats have been used for directors and senior officers to have an open, no-holds-barred discussion of changes in their industry.

While such approaches to involving board members represent an advance over the traditional practice of simply asking them to approve major projects individually, they do not go far enough. What is needed is for more boards to approve explicitly the strategic directions proposed by management and to review progress annually. Today too few boards take that approach.

The practice of evaluating the CEO realistically has also, until recently, been restricted to a few companies. The acknowledged pioneer was Dayton Hudson Corporation (now Target Corporation), and its directors and managers have gradually spread the gospel around the Twin Cities and beyond, so that more and more boards have developed explicit CEO reviews. But in too many companies, the practice is still a casual conversation between the chair of the compensation committee and the CEO about the latter's compensation and how it relates to his or her and the company's performance. More companies need a thorough evaluation process if the board's monitoring is to succeed. Part of such an evaluation process must be a look at the state of management development and succession planning under the CEO's leadership. While the board can oversee such a process and in the end will decide who the next CEO is to be, it's the incumbent CEO's responsibility to make sure there is an internal candidate as a successor.

A final aspect of the board's monitoring work is implementing an annual schedule of planning and review for the board and management. This calendar should designate specific board meetings for strategic planning and review, for discussing CEO performance, and for reviewing management succession plans. Not only does such a schedule organize and focus the board's work, it also emphasizes for directors and management alike the interconnectedness of the key facets of the directors' work.

EFFECTIVE EMPOWERMENT

While empowered directors have many concerns, including insuring compliance with accounting rules and laws, they are now focusing more and more of their attention on CEO performance evaluation and corporate strategy. They hope that by doing a better job on these matters, they will avoid the problems that plagued many major companies in the past decade, when both directors and managers failed to recognize changes in technology and markets that adversely affected their companies.

Evaluating the CEO annually is central to effective monitoring for several reasons. Fundamentally, it is a major step toward empowering the board because it delivers a clear message to both the CEO and the directors that the former is accountable to the latter. It also provides outside directors with an impetus to engage in an open and frank discussion about the CEO's and the company's performances at least once a year. As a result, they will understand their company and its leader better and will be more effective monitors. A director who has served on two boards that have conducted CEO evaluations says that on most boards without careful CEO reviews, the outside directors don't have much opportunity to talk to one another. On the two boards with such evaluations, directors don't necessarily want to criticize the CEO, but they find it useful to converse openly about issues they may not want to bring up in front of the CEO. That director adds that such discussions allow directors to learn more about the organization and provide a forum for addressing concerns.

Finally, an evaluation benefits the CEO personally by directly communicating the directors' concerns and suggestions for improvement, as well as their praise. If it is done properly, it also allows the CEO to discuss his or her reactions with the directors. All corporate leaders realize that such feedback and dialogue are invaluable but all too rare.

As the list of companies whose boards evaluate the CEO has grown, unique approaches to such evaluations have been developed. However, certain criteria are essential to an effective evaluation:

- It should be conducted at least annually.
- It should assess the company's annual and long-term performance in comparison with that of similar organizations.
- The CEO's accomplishments should be judged against individual goals as well as against the goals for the company's performance. The CEO's individual goals should cover initiatives like starting a major quality-improvement program or making an acquisition. While such goals will vary from year to year, the CEO should continuously plan for top-management succession.
- The CEO should provide an assessment of his or her own performance.
- The outside directors should make their assessments individually. Their judgments should be combined by one director, a committee of directors, or an independent party so that they indicate the general tenor of the directors' assessments as well as the range of their views. This feedback should be transmitted to the CEO confidentially.
- The CEO should discuss the evaluation face-to-face with one or more outside directors and should have the opportunity to discuss his or her reactions to the review with all the directors.

Once a board and its CEO have implemented such a review, the roles of each party are quite clear. The CEO will set his or her objectives and do a self-appraisal, and the directors will assess and communicate how well they think the CEO is performing. Once the CEO and the board agree that such a process is desirable, there should be little dispute about the division of responsibility between CEOs and directors.

The related question of when and how deeply the board should become involved in strategic matters is less clear and likely to remain more controversial. A long-standing concern of both managers and directors is where to draw the line that separates management and board prerogatives. An outside director at Lukens who was actively involved in developing strategy said there is a fine line between having a director contribute ideas to the company's strategic direction and having that director try to manage the company. Once a director crosses that line, the board has real problems, because directors should not run the company. The director suggested that in such cases, maybe management should hold back information at board meetings.

Withholding information from the board is certainly not a good solution to the problem, but the question about where to draw the line is important. A senior executive at Lukens was clear about the distinction between directors and managers: "As each side moves closer to the dividing line, the responsibilities of each begin to look the same. But they are not the same, so the line needs to be drawn in such a way to ensure that managers manage and the board approves. You cannot have the whole group managing and approving together."

At a minimum, directors should approve corporate strategy and review and evaluate its results. How involved they should become in specific strategic decisions depends on specific circumstances. For example, at Lukens, the chairman and CEO asked the committee of outside directors to become involved in an acquisition proposal because the decision was of great importance to the future of the company. Furthermore, the CEO was new and wanted to be certain that the directors supported the initiative. In such circumstances, it is prudent for directors to be more deeply involved in strategic decisions.

Even in companies that have established CEOs and are performing well, some decisions may be of such magnitude that management seeks or the board desires involvement. For example, at AT&T, the chairman and CEO held a strategic retreat with the board to discuss the impact of wireless communication on the company. The purpose of such informal meetings is for the CEO to get the directors' advice as well as to prepare the directors for a possible major decision. At AT&T, these discussions prepared the board for a major acquisition more than a year later.

While in both examples, management invited the board's involvement in strategy, the legal responsibility to determine where to draw the line between the board's monitoring and management's development and implementation of strategy belongs to the board. Monitoring will not work if directors and top management have not agreed about their respective roles. One of the tenets of American democracy has always been that the government rules with the consent of the governed. In a different sense, the same must be true as boards become empowered. Corporate leaders, who are the governed, must believe that the means the board has chosen to monitor strategy are reasonable and viable, and do not interfere with management's prerogatives. For that reason, both CEOs and directors must have a means of reviewing and adjusting the line between the board's and management's prerogatives. I shall return to this point, but first let's consider the major factor in how effective directors can be as monitors: the knowledge they need in order to carry out their activities.

DIRECTORS' KNOWLEDGE

To contribute effectively to discussions of corporate strategy and evaluate CEO performance competently, directors obviously need adequate knowledge. I use knowledge here instead of the more frequently used *information* because the directors' biggest problem is not just lack of information, but its context. One director says that most boards spend too much time watching presentations when what they really need is to understand the material presented so they can participate more effectively. In the 1989 survey of boards for *Pawns or Potentates,* the book I coauthored with Elizabeth MacIver, and in subsequent interviews with many directors, very few directors expressed a concern about getting enough information. Their real concern is having too much information to digest in the time they had available. Under the U.S. system of governance, outside directors are part-timers. No matter how diligent they want to be, there is a limit to how much time they can devote to a particular board.

Directors receive information in two ways. The first is written reports. Typically, they contain information about the company's financial results as well as about specific proposals to be discussed at a particular meeting. The second is oral presentations by managers; especially important is the CEO's report, which is a central feature of most board meetings. While the specific content may vary from one boardroom to another, the CEO's remarks about the state of the company and events affecting it since the previous meeting are an important source of knowledge for directors.

In the past, directors absorbed all of that data over many years of service and gradually converted it into knowledge about the company. In many boardrooms of the past, such a gradual approach to building knowledge was adequate. However, in companies faced with rapidly changing market and technological conditions, this approach is inadequate. Directors would be no more aware of the significance of external events than top-level managers. One reason for such myopia is that managers were the providers of information to the board. But another may have been that directors are long on financial knowledge and short on knowledge about changing markets and technology. It is not that management willfully withholds information about products and markets, but that, traditionally, such data was not judged to be within the board's purview.

If boards are to be effective in evaluating the CEO and approving corporate strategy, they need to develop knowledge not only about the company's financial results, which are an indication of past performance, but also about the company's progress in accomplishing its strategy. That means understanding progress in developing new technology and new products and services, and in entering new markets. It means understanding changing customer requirements and what competitors are doing. Similarly, directors need the data to build knowledge about the organizational health of the company. In essence, they need their own version of the "balanced scorecard," which Robert S. Kaplan and David P. Norton recommend for managers in "Putting the Balanced Scorecard to Work" (*HBR*, September–October 1993).

As in other aspects of a board's work, directors and managers must decide what mix of knowledge is appropriate to the company's circumstances. Again, there are certain minimal requirements. The data must be balanced between financial and strategic issues and focused on future prospects as well as past performance. Information must be grounded in strategic objectives and competitive demands, and it must paint a broad picture of the conditions the company is facing. The data should also shed light on the CEO's progress toward achieving his or her individual goals.

The challenge for directors is to take what may be a greater quantity and a broader array of information and turn it into useful knowledge quickly. Some boards deal with this challenge by increasing the capital limits of projects requiring board approval, thus freeing up time to devote to broader strategic issues.

Another practice followed by some boards is to ask directors periodically for their assessment of the information they receive. This practice encourages directors to provide one another and management with an explicit review of information and discourages the company from supplying the same types of data because "we have always done it that way." Another solution to the problem of more information is to ensure that data is organized efficiently and provides a concise but comprehensive overview of the company's strategic progress. Data should be sent to the directors in advance so they can study it, formulate questions, and identify issues they would like to discuss at board meetings. Directors should have the option of meeting alone to develop their collective understanding of the company's situation and decide which questions and issues they want to discuss with management. A growing number of boards are now doing that.

Such steps should enable directors to keep up with events in a rapidly changing world so they can make informed approvals of specific strategic issues and in-depth judgments about the CEO's accomplishments and goals. Those steps are essential to the board's role as an effective monitor.

SELF-MONITORING

In this dynamic world, no set of board activities is likely to constitute effective monitoring for very long. Conditions facing the company will change, as will the membership of the board. The inevitability of change and the fact that even the most talented and well-motivated directors and managers will find that their best-laid plans do not always work mean that an empowered board must periodically monitor its own performance. Many boards already monitor themselves, and the new listing requirements make this necessary for all U.S. companies. At some companies the outside directors use an annual questionnaire to solicit opinions from themselves and from managers, and then review the results of the survey to find opportunities for improvement. At other companies, directors simply devote part of a meeting, usually annually, to a discussion of how well the board has been conducting its affairs and how its performance can be improved.

The idea of the entire board's reviewing its own activities annually is sound because it enables all directors to contribute their ideas for improvement and thus be committed to any changes in process. Regardless of the specific process used, how well a board is conducting its duties must be assessed in light of the conditions the directors are confronting: What is their relationship with the CEO, and how much confidence do they have in him or her? How well has the company been performing? How complex are the issues facing the directors?

In the context of such circumstances, directors need to assess how well they are understanding and monitoring the company's strategy. How well is the process of CEO evaluation working? How effectively do the directors use their time together? How well are board committees functioning? Are directors getting the appropriate information, and is it well organized? Those are some of the major concerns that should be addressed to make boards more effective monitors.

The review of procedures will be conducted most efficiently if the directors have designed in advance an explicit set of principles about how they intend to function as a board. Creating such guidelines causes directors to reason together about what changes they may want to make. Once such principles have been established, they also provide directors with a clear framework against which to judge their performance. In addition to reviewing their processes and procedures, a few boards are conducting explicit reviews of individual directors.

While the full board can be involved in both aspects of evaluation, the board's committees can also play a role in monitoring the board's work. The compensation committee can focus on the CEO review process. The audit committee, already familiar with the company's information system, is an ideal group to monitor and improve the information directors are receiving. The corporate governance committee, in addition to evaluating individual directors, can orchestrate the annual review of the board's activities. Each committee thus makes a unique contribution to the board's oversight of its own functioning.

Empowering directors will enable them and their organizations to deal more successfully with the turbulence and demands of the future. U.S. companies today face great challenges and uncertainty. The continuing growth of the world's marketplace, with customers and competition in Asia, Eastern Europe, and South America, as well as the accompanying shift in the domestic economy, present U.S. companies with unprecedented challenges and opportunities. Empowered boards are most likely to contribute to meeting them if their growing power is developed in collaboration with that of the managers they oversee. That means both groups must work together to establish and understand the role of empowered directors.

Throughout this discussion, I have refrained from mentioning what may be the greatest challenge any board can face—deceit and even fraud on the part of its company's executives. When this article was originally written, the idea that events like Enron, Tyco, and WorldCom could occur was too far-fetched to contemplate. Yet as we all know, management malfeasance occurred at these companies and many others, not just in the U.S., but in other countries as well. If managers aim to deceive and intentionally withhold information from their boards, directors have an almost insurmountable problem. Even boards with the most diligent audit committees, and the other practices I have described, will find it difficult, if not impossible, to detect deliberate deception.

Clearly boards are not investigative bodies. However, their best hope to prevent such occurrences is through developing the power to oversee management and to also assure that the company's auditors—internal and external—are doing their jobs.

NOTE

This chapter was adapted from the *Harvard Business Review* article, Empowering the board, by Jay W. Lorsch (January–February 1995), 108–117.

9

Measuring the Effectiveness of Corporate Boards and Directors

MARC J. EPSTEIN and MARIE-JOSÉE ROY

Recent corporate accounting and governance scandals have focused increased attention on how corporate boards can be more effective. Regulators have reacted to past corporate scandals and collapses by establishing new governance requirements that have significant implications for boards of directors, senior managers, and financial and accounting professionals. Among the most prominent, the Sarbanes-Oxley Act of 2002 has already caused profound changes in corporate governance practices. However, as recent controversies demonstrate, strict compliance with regulations and requirements does not guarantee effective boards. Investors have also reacted to these scandals by increasingly including governance criteria in their investment decisions. This increased investor focus has generated a growing number of published scoring systems that evaluate and rank the corporate governance practices of public companies.

There are numerous new codes and guidelines of best governance practices. However, these guidelines often provide only minimum performance standards and lack the specificity to move boards to a higher level of performance. They can aid in the formulation of general policies and rules for board functioning, but do not provide much insight into internal processes that should be implemented to promote high-performance boards. Without appropriate systems, particularly for measuring and reporting performance, changes will only be superficial and will not yield the much-needed improvements.[1]

In recent years, companies have placed increasing importance on the development of performance metrics to better measure and manage corporate performance. Information systems have been developed to provide a broader set of metrics to incorporate into new strategic management systems.[2] Although attention has been placed on the development of improved performance measures, these have generally not been applied to senior corporate leadership, including corporate boards. So, boards have been operating without measures that permit an effective evaluation of board performance by senior corporate managers, the board, and board members, or by external stakeholders.[3] This lack of performance metrics has led in part to the lack of both actual and perceived accountability of corporate boards to their various stakeholders.

Drawing on prior research on performance measurement and board governance, and on our examination of corporate board governance practices, we found that board performance can be improved only by paying careful attention to both inputs and processes. Further, we found that the lack of measurement of board performance is a significant barrier to improving internal governance and external accountability. In a recently released report, we have carefully examined the key success factors for improving corporate governance and developed measures for the evaluation of performance of corporate boards, individual board members, and CEOs. In the report, we introduced a strategic management system to guide the measurement and improvement of the performance of corporate boards.[4]

We present a strategic management system that can help companies establish the drivers of superior board performance and evaluate how that performance affects shareholder value. However, these management systems rely on a thorough identification of strategic objectives, key performance drivers, and a broader set of both financial and nonfinancial performance measures.

We first present the main elements of a board evaluation system (BES) that can provide a process for better defining and articulating board strategy, implementing the strategy, and measuring and improving both board and corporate performance. Second, a carefully developed set of key performance indicators is developed as a basis for a comprehensive performance measurement and management system that is essential to drive improvements in corporate governance and in the performance of boards and board members. Third, we examine the growing phenomenon of governance scoring systems and their implications on reporting decisions. Investors are increasingly considering corporate governance issues in their decision-making process and may be willing to pay a premium for well-governed companies.[5] To capture this premium, companies must actively consider their governance practices and adopt an effective disclosure strategy to signal their commitment to high standards of corporate governance. Given the growing popularity of corporate governance rating systems, corporate communication strategies must consider the impact of governance decisions. Although the actual value of these rating systems has not yet been demonstrated, the factors and metrics considered by these systems must be well understood by companies to either take advantage of positive scores or to alternatively avoid negative publicity, and many of the metrics are critical for effective corporate governance.

IMPROVING THE BOARD'S PERFORMANCE: IDENTIFYING KEY INPUTS AND PROCESSES

Over time, there have been changes in the definition of the roles and responsibilities of corporate boards.[6] Though there are differing current perspectives as to what a board's key responsibilities are, most agree that the board has a fiduciary duty to represent the corporation's interests in protecting and creating shareholder value and must determine whether the company is managed well to achieve long-term success. As such, high-performance boards must achieve three core objectives:

1. Provide superior strategic guidance to ensure the company's growth and prosperity;
2. Ensure accountability of the company to its stakeholders, including shareholders, employees, customers, suppliers, regulators, and the community;
3. Ensure that a highly qualified executive team is managing the company.

Numerous decisions concerning board operations will have significant impact on the board's ability to achieve these objectives. These include decisions related to board composition, structure, and the supporting systems. Based on various guidelines, codes of best practices, requirements from stock exchanges, and regulations, and our extensive research, the key inputs and processes leading to superior board performance are identified. Further, as they are essential to superior board performance, these key success factors become the foundation for the development of rigorous performance evaluation systems for boards.

Figure 9.1 describes the inputs, processes, outputs, and outcomes of board activities. Corporations make important choices in board composition (inputs) that have a significant impact on board performance. The board systems and structure (processes) also significantly affect the board decisions and performance. The manner in which the board prepares, deliberates, and decides on important decisions is affected by the board's composition and does affect the board's success at fulfilling its roles and responsibilities and improving board performance (outputs) and ultimately improving corporate performance (outcomes). Further, continuous feedback provides the basis for improvement for the directors, the board, and the corporation. Thus, as seen in Figure 9.1, there are four key inputs and six key processes that lead to success in the three core objectives and ultimate outcome of corporate profitability.

The link between board performance and corporate performance has been examined extensively by academics and others, and there is still not a clear understanding of this complex relationship that involves many variables.[7] Some

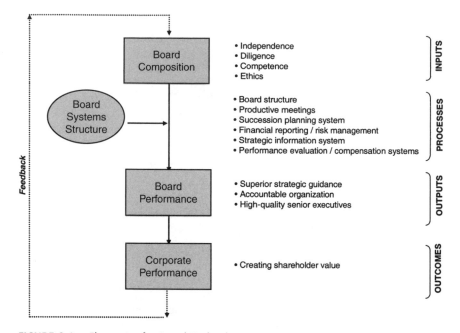

FIGURE 9.1.   Elements of a Board Evaluation System

studies have focused on a limited set of governance variables, examining one or a few governance issues such as board independence, board size, or the leadership the board.[8] Other studies have focused on a larger set of governance issues by either developing a governance ranking measure as a proxy for governance quality that includes several governance elements or by using existing rating systems.[9] Among these studies, Gompers et al. found that if a fund had taken long positions in companies scoring in the top decile of their governance ranking measure and short positions in companies in the bottom decile, it would have outperformed the market.

Although prior empirical research findings are not completely consistent regarding the impact of corporate governance on corporate performance, there is evidence that good corporate governance pays.[10] From either an internal long-term profitability or an external shareholder perspective, it is clear that modern governance practices inject a huge measure of shareholder and investor confidence into the management decision-making process and thus also contribute to corporate performance. Good governance improves both the reality of better corporate performance as well as the market's perception of better performance, thus having an impact on stock prices. As recent events have shown, companies failing to implement sound governance practices can find themselves in substantial difficulty that places the future of the organization in jeopardy.

Measures to support a comprehensive board performance evaluation system are critical. These measures are essential to monitor the key performance drivers (inputs and processes) and assess whether the board is achieving its stated objectives (outputs) and thus contributing to the long-term success of the corporation (outcomes). Given their specific challenges and areas of concern, boards should adopt metrics that are most appropriate to fit the strategy and objectives of the company and the board. Although Continental European governance systems are already converging toward the Anglo-Saxon, the model can also reflect elements such as country-specific legal frameworks.[11] For each metric, a specific target reflecting best industry practices and the company's commitment to superior corporate governance should be identified, and results should be compared against these targets. The metrics should all be a part of a causal chain that includes both leading and lagging indicators of performance.

Measuring Key Inputs

As shown in Figure 9.1 and Table 9.1, four specific aspects of board composition must be evaluated and monitored closely through appropriate metrics: independence, diligence, competence, and ethics. Historically, many board members were selected by CEOs based on personal relationships, affiliations, or friendship, and were expected to vote with the CEO. In the current environment, with increased public expectations and personal liability of corporate board members, the board should comprise a panel of objective overseers who counsel corporate managers and monitor performance.[12] However, many directors have not been the active counselors, vigilant monitors, or skeptical judges that are necessary for high-performance boards and high-performance organizations.

TABLE 9.1.   Metrics for Board Evaluation System: Key Inputs

Input	
Independence	• Level of compliance of corporate definition of independence with NYSE's definition
	• % of independent directors
	• Interlocking directorships
Diligence	• # of hours spent on preparation
	• Overall attendance of meetings
	• # of boards directors serve on
	• # of visits to company sites by individual directors
Competence	• % of directors "financially literate"
	• Diversity of board—race and gender (% represented)
	• # of hours of training for directors
Ethics	• Existence of a code of conduct for directors
	• Results of ethics audit

INDEPENDENCE

In response to increased pressure, corporations globally have been improving the independence of boards. In order to limit the input of the CEO in the director selection process, many firms have chosen to nominate new directors solely through their nominating committee comprised only of independent directors. Many of the decisions about board composition will affect the overall independence of the board. Among the issues that must be determined are: the definition of "independent director" and the number of independent directors on the board.

Many companies have also forbidden interlocking directorships (multiple directors being on common boards). In the past, this practice has generated indebted and obliged directors and reduced at least the perception of objectivity in their judgments.

DILIGENCE

Directors usually face many competing demands for their time, and some do not devote enough time and effort to successfully accomplish their responsibilities. In addition to near-perfect attendance at board and committee meetings, significant preparation before meetings is essential. Members should be proactive by seeking additional relevant information from other sources, and not relying only on the information provided by the CEO. In addition, though challenging the CEO in board meetings is sometimes difficult, a culture is desirable where these challenges are welcomed as an opportunity to fully vent topics of concern and avail the CEO of the best possible counsel.

Board members are being asked to take a far more active and time-consuming role than previously. The number of boards that any individual can participate in should be smaller and the compensation must be commensurate with the increased effort. Existing executives must consider whether they have any available time to sit on additional company boards given the time constraints of their own executive positions and outside board responsibilities. In many of the recent financial scandals, the boards appeared to have exercised too little oversight and too readily blamed others for an obvious lack of board investigation and oversight.

COMPETENCE

To provide strong oversight and relevant input into strategic decisions, companies must ensure that board members have the right mix of skills and knowledge. Board members should possess both functional knowledge in the traditional areas of business such as accounting, finance, legal, or marketing as well as industry-specific knowledge that will enable members to truly understand specific company issues and challenges. Indeed, board members must have enough general knowledge to provide good inputs in all topics of discussion and be encouraged to ask questions of all specialists until they are comfortable enough to cast votes.

Though there is some discussion about the level of "financial literacy" that should be required of board members, it is increasingly evident that all board members must possess enough knowledge of financial issues to be able to understand, evaluate, and contribute to discussions of corporate financial and accounting issues. Educational and training programs for board members should be a continuing part of corporate learning activities, and broader sets of competency should be considered in the screening and selection process of potential board members.

Boards should also build a diverse board that includes minorities and primary stakeholders as they surely possess knowledge and points of view that are valuable for the organization. To help build a board that has the right pool of talent and qualities, boards can develop tools to evaluate current expertise against needed competencies and use this information in the director selection process. Further, as companies grow and evolve over time, the mix of skills required to provide strategic guidance may change. A continuous reevaluation of board needs often leads to changes in board composition and to the renewal of ideas and skills. That is why some companies have decided to put a limit on the number of years a director can serve on a board.

ETHICS

Examination of recent lapses in corporate governance indicates that having independent, diligent, and competent directors alone does not produce good governance. The board members individually and the board collectively must have established a code of conduct and high ethical principles for the conduct of the board and the corporation. The formulation and enforcement of these ethical principles along with the establishment of systems and a culture for implementation are critical to ensure that ethical business practices are maintained and that any abuses are promptly reported and punished. The board must establish ethical principles for itself and oversee that they are developed and enforced throughout the corporation.

Measuring Key Processes

Once board composition (inputs) is determined, boards can focus on the processes necessary to drive superior board performance. Recent studies have certainly showed that board composition elements alone do not ensure good board performance nor superior corporate performance. As illustrated in Figure 9.1, six fundamental processes for good board performance must be monitored closely: (1) board structure (committees, size, and leadership of the board; (2) productive meetings; (3) succession planning system; (4) financial reporting and risk management system; (5) strategic information system; and (6) performance evaluation and compensation systems.

Several metrics associated with each of the six processes are presented in Table 9.2. Regulators have focused more attention on some of these processes than on others. In particular, the integrity of the financial reporting process

TABLE 9.2.   Metrics for Board Evaluation System: Processes

Processes	
Board structure	• Leadership of the board (CEO, or lead director, independent chairman)
	• % of meetings without CEO (executive sessions)
	• # of committees
Productive meetings	• # of meetings with management other than CEO
	• # of days in advance that agenda and material are sent
	• Average duration and number of meetings
	• % of meeting time allocated to opposing points of view
	• of meeting time for discussions
Succession planning system	• Existence of a position description for CEO
	• Annual report on succession planning
	• Interim CEO identified
Financial reporting and risk assessment systems	• Adherence to code of ethics / code of conduct
	• # of ethical / legal violations
	• # of voluntary disclosures
	• # of risk audit performed and results
Strategic Information system	• of meetings with stakeholders
	• Evaluation of list of information provided to board to assess projects (financial and nonfinancial)
	• # of hours spent on long-term strategic issues
	• Existence of communication channels with board
Performance evaluation and compensation systems	• Regular performance evaluations conducted (for CEO, board, directors)
	• Evaluation systems include nonfinancial data
	• Evaluation systems include external and objective data
	• % of compensation linked to performance
	• % of performance linked to nonfinancial performance (social, environmental)
	• % of compensation linked to stock ownership
	• # of board members owning stock
	• Goals and objectives clearly defined (for CEO, board, directors)

and the role of the audit committee have been examined closely. However, all of these processes must be evaluated and monitored since they all are essential to maintaining superior board performance.

BOARD STRUCTURE

Choices about the type and number of committees required to support the board's activities, the leadership of the board (including how the meetings are conducted), and board size are key structure issues that must be addressed.

Board committee structure. Most large companies have adopted a board committee structure to address some of their fundamental functions and responsibilities more effectively.[13] Indeed, committees allow directors to share responsibility and focus the necessary resources on a specific issue. Committee chairs report on their meetings and require approval from the board of directors. Typically, companies have developed three board committees, each with its own processes and systems, to support its efforts in meeting the responsibilities of the board (audit, compensation, and governance/nominating).

Leadership of the board. Many corporations have tried to improve the independence of their boards through ensuring that the board leadership is also independent. This can be done through either a separation of the role of CEO and chairman of the board or by the appointment of a lead director. In both cases the goal is to provide a board leader who is independent of all day-to-day corporate activities and is devoted solely to providing oversight and fulfilling a fiduciary duty to the shareholders. Of course, it is essential that a good working relationship exist between the two.[14] Lead directors also represent the board's contingent of outside directors. These directors may often meet regularly in executive session without the CEO. Meetings of outside directors, without management present, are of paramount importance to improve board independence.

Board size. The board size is also an important factor, as it affects board performance. While larger boards will likely offer a broader set of knowledge and skills to choose from and may provide some beneficial redundancy, coordinating these larger boards can be complex. Discussions and decision-making can also be more difficult, reducing board member involvement. Larger boards often become more symbolic and are less part of the management process. As a matter of fact, empirical evidence suggests that board size and firm value are negatively correlated.[15]

Recent surveys have suggested that the optimal board size is about ten directors.[16] Some have suggested that a board of nine to thirteen members is typically right for most companies, but too small for larger ones.[17]

PRODUCTIVE MEETINGS

Some companies have had high-quality inputs to their boards but still very-low-quality board performance. If competent and independent board members do not question CEO decisions and provide a rubber stamp instead of oversight, governance fails. To fulfill their fiduciary responsibilities, board members have an obligation to independently discuss and challenge proposed decisions and contribute to the success of board meetings.

The level of input the directors have into the agenda is critical and a good measure of board independence. If the CEO controls the agenda, the board hears, discusses, and votes on the issues of the CEO or management. This may reduce the opportunity to learn about controversial issues, hear both supporting and dissenting positions on major strategic decisions, and fully explore difficult topics. If an independent chairman or lead director controls the agenda, then the topics, invited guests, and speakers at board meetings may be significantly different and allow for the board to discuss and investigate issues of their concern. Employees, customers, suppliers, and investors should have direct access to the board, independent of management, to provide important inputs to the decision-making and oversight processes.

Finally, the agenda and supporting material should be distributed well in advance of meetings to encourage and facilitate preparation. The board should be provided with all of the necessary materials and resources to enable it to carry out its own independent analyses. Board members must be adequately prepared and must all contribute to open discussions of the issues.

SUCCESSION PLANNING SYSTEM

To ensure that there is always a highly qualified team managing the company, an effective succession plan must be in place. Succession events have significantly increased in number in recent years and have the potential to both greatly disrupt companies and create significant uncertainty about a company's future from many critical stakeholders such as employees, major customers, and investors.

The board should have a clear agreement of the desired qualifications of potential CEOs and should explicitly articulate this in a succession plan. This is part of understanding the drivers of improved performance and starts with the necessary inputs. Thus, qualified, competent, and motivated senior managers are required, and the process of training is identified for continuous development of the necessary skills to enable them to make a greater contribution to company performance. This is among the most important responsibilities of boards and should be reviewed on a regular basis.[18]

FINANCIAL REPORTING AND RISK MANAGEMENT SYSTEM

In the wake of recent accounting scandals, ensuring the integrity of the company's financial reporting process has become essential. Audit committees, responsible for these duties, have received a lot of attention and are asked to be more aggressive and vigilant. The committee's responsibilities will typically include reviewing and overseeing the following elements of the financial reporting process:

- Internal controls and risks assessment
- Internal and external auditing processes
- Financial reporting
- Compliance with law, regulations, and codes of ethics

These systems are essential to stakeholders' satisfaction, as they are necessary to create accountability and reduce shareholder risk. Thus, the committee should review and evaluate the effectiveness of the company's process for assessing risks and the steps that management is taking to monitor and control those risks. It should also evaluate and assess the integrity of internal controls surrounding the process including information systems and security. The financial reporting process requires a good understanding of corporate risks and internal controls. Hence, it requires a sound risk management system, a reliable compliance system, and effective internal controls. This includes a wide spectrum of risks that can be categorized as external environment risks, business process and asset loss risks, and information risks.[19]

New regulations have brought substantial modifications to the running of the committee in charge of this process in order to both promote the financial transparency of the company and improve the reporting process. For example, committee members must meet "financial literacy" and independence criteria so they can play a more active role in the financial reporting process and assure credibility. The Sarbanes-Oxley Act also requires that the audit committee include at least one "financial expert."[20]

The committee is responsible for asserting compliance to law, regulations, and codes of ethics. Shareholders expect the boards of directors and the audit committees to exercise more control and direction over the external audits being performed. They want both groups to ensure that an effective internal control system exists and that any weaknesses are being corrected. Further, shareholders want assurance that the auditors, management, and board of directors are responsible for the prevention and detection of errors and fraud.

The audit committee and the board also have an opportunity to be proactive in the financial reporting process to increase corporate transparency and accountability. Through more voluntary disclosures of both financial and non-financial information, corporations can "tell the corporate story" to external users. Financial analysts commonly believe that companies tend to provide only the information that is legally required unless they have additional good news they want to broadcast. If corporate disclosures are to be credible, full disclosure must occur in both good times and bad. A corporate communications strategy that recognizes the importance of open and honest communications to both financial analysts and shareholders is important to the fair valuation of a company's stock. One of the most important elements of a good corporate communications strategy is that those communications must be consistent, honest, and forthright.[21]

STRATEGIC INFORMATION SYSTEM

As boards are asked to play a more significant and active role in corporate oversight, the need for information is mounting.[22] This need to improve the quality of the information provided to boards is a dramatic departure from most existing company practices. For example, the discussion of the information about alternate strategies considered by management (including comparative analysis) and best, worst, and most likely case scenarios that will allow boards to independently assess the level of risk involved are beyond what many boards include. It provides for a fuller and more consultative role for board members in addition to their oversight responsibilities. These new informational needs force senior managers to share more information with the board and open more decisions to discussion and evaluation. It requires a secure and confident CEO to provide for full disclosure and discussion of information and critical management decisions.

PERFORMANCE EVALUATION AND
COMPENSATION SYSTEMS

A compensation system's objective is to develop, monitor, evaluate, and reward senior corporate executives. Traditionally, this required only a cursory review of performance and relatively standard pay increases. In recent years, with the downturn in the economy, employee layoffs, and the decline in stock prices, shareholders have become increasingly uneasy with executives receiving high salaries when corporate performance and share prices decline.

A decade ago, many suggested that to better align shareholders' and managers' interests, companies should adopt pay plans that "pay for performance"— that is, pay that is linked to increases in stock price.[23] However, because many of the measures of performance were short-term, executives received large bonuses as stock prices went up but were not required to return it when stock prices ultimately fell. Further, since performance was often not benchmarked against industry averages, a steadily rising stock market pushed many corporate stock prices higher for companies with only average performance.[24] Thus, many CEOs with below-industry-average performance received bonuses in the tens of millions of dollars.

Compensation programs should align executives' interests with those of the shareholders and establish an explicit link between corporate performance and executive compensation. That is why an increasing number of companies are compensating their senior managers with equity. However, equity compensation must be carefully designed to avoid dysfunctional consequences.[25] For executives receiving large stock option grants every year, small changes in prices can translate into enormous gains but draw criticism because they permit executives to benefit from stock gains without risks. Thus, many compensation committees are looking at mechanisms to correct unwanted effects. Further, practices such as option repricing have created significant controversy. Adjusting downward the exercise price of options as a means to retain executives has angered shareholders and often does not properly align incentives.

It is critical that performance and success should not be measured only by short-term changes in stock value. Companies should consider a broad set of performance indicators that are in line with the company's mission, vision, and values, and that are consistent with the company's long-term interests. This is likely to include both leading and lagging indicators of performance and both financial and nonfinancial indicators of success.[26]

Compensation for board members is also an important issue. Many boards insist that directors own significant stock in the company they oversee.[27] The board must put processes and compensation policies in place to encourage each board member to maximize the contribution of both individual board members and the board as a whole. Compensation should reflect time, effort, and risk exposure for directors.

Performance evaluation systems play an essential role in providing boards with relevant and reliable information so they can give superior strategic guidance to management, ensure accountability to a broad range of stakeholders, and make more informed decisions regarding succession planning and compensation. The systems can also be the basis for continuous improvement for the organization. As board responsibilities are increased, new information, measurement, evaluation, and reporting systems are needed to fulfill their responsibilities. Specifically, performance evaluation systems must provide information to evaluate:

- Overall corporate performance
- The CEO's performance
- The board's performance (including individual board members)

MONITORING AND EVALUATING
CORPORATE PERFORMANCE

Boards must assess the success of both the formulation and implementation of strategy. They must then evaluate corporate performance and adapt future strategies accordingly. Typically, boards are provided with traditional accounting-based performance measures such as earnings and return on investment to assess corporate performance. However, financial accounting has limited value as a management tool. Often, it actually hampers decision-making because it turns attention toward historical figures. Boards need to know if the strategy is working, and financial numbers alone rarely tell them.[28]

Traditional financial measures tend to be lagging indicators, measuring current and past performance but not adequately predicting future performance or motivating behavior that will attain future performance goals. To link corporate activities with corporate strategic objectives, performance measures must include leading indicators that give insight into the organization's ability to improve its competitive position in the future and are predictors of future performance. Companies must provide boards with access to pertinent information that will allow board members to participate actively and meaningfully in the development and evaluation of the strategic plans.

MONITORING AND EVALUATING THE CEO'S PERFORMANCE

In too many companies, CEO evaluations are performed in a perfunctory manner. CEOs have appointed many or most of the board members and the boards are neither independent nor assertive enough to critically evaluate the CEO's performance. Yet, ensuring that the corporation has the right person at its helm is a major board responsibility. This should include a process to evaluate and monitor whether the CEO is fulfilling current company responsibilities and is the best person to lead the company into the future. When boards develop open and honest evaluations of CEOs, they can provide important feedback on both strengths and weaknesses and make suggestions on performance improvement.

Given recent concerns over excessive executive compensation, conducting a rigorous performance evaluation and explicitly linking it to compensation can provide improved governance and accountability on the part of both CEOs and boards. The identification of the performance objectives should be a joint effort between the board and the CEO and should identify objectives and goals that reflect the CEO's roles and responsibilities.

The measures should be linked to strategy and include both leading and lagging indicators of performance and a wide variety of both financial and nonfinancial metrics. Evaluations should include full 360-degree performance reviews, including self-assessments, along with assessments from subordinates, board members, and various outside stakeholders. These stakeholders including employees, customers, shareholders, partners, and the community, can provide valuable inputs to the evaluation process. Other external information, including benchmarks from other companies, can also be helpful. The process should be seen as being interactive, encouraging an open discussion of issues rather than just listing simple diagnostics, and should be conducted often enough to identify and correct any potential problems.

A particular challenge when constructing a performance evaluation system for the CEO is to develop one that will adequately capture the inherent distinctions between corporate performance and the CEO's performance. The performance evaluations and rewards should not result in rewarding poor performance or in overlooking superior performance. For example, CEO performance can be only marginal even though the stock price is higher. Or, the reverse may be true. It is the board's responsibility through the development of effective measurement and evaluation systems to distinguish between the performance of the CEO and the performance of the corporation.

It is important that the strategic plans and decisions included in the CEO's performance evaluation system be those of this CEO and should not be confused with previous strategic decisions made by predecessors. Often CEO performance evaluations are tainted by the inclusion of financial metrics that are the results of decisions made by previous executives. To adequately evaluate current CEOs, it is necessary to include a significant amount of leading indicators of performance along with the tracking of prior decisions.

MONITORING AND EVALUATING THE BOARD'S AND INDIVIDUAL BOARD MEMBERS' PERFORMANCE

Just as corporate performance evaluations provide feedback to improve performance, board and board members' evaluations represent a valuable opportunity to carefully assess both strengths and weaknesses and evaluate the board's role and contribution in improving corporate performance. It is an opportunity for boards to examine how they are contributing to protecting and creating shareholder value and should unveil specific opportunities, directions for improvements, and standards of performance. The board evaluation should be focused on how it can improve the board's inputs and processes so that the board's contribution to overall corporate performance can be increased. Furthermore, the NYSE requires that its listed companies develop and perform annual performance evaluations for the board and its committees.

The evaluation process should include individual board member evaluations to further encourage all directors to focus on individual responsibilities and accomplishments, related to improving board and corporate performance. This is particularly important as board needs are identified and the evaluation of board requirements point to specific board member skills that must be obtained through either new members or additional board member training.[29] Though some are concerned that a comprehensive evaluation process could deter some good board candidates, responsible board members should be committed to rigorous evaluation and continuous improvement for the directors and the board.

Some of the metrics presented in Tables 9.1 and 9.2 are evaluations of overall board performance. Others are indicators of board performance but are derived through an aggregation of measures of individual board members' performance. It is important to separately evaluate the performance of both the board and the individual board members. Though overall board performance may be satisfactory, evaluating the performance of individual members provides an opportunity to determine whether there are board needs that are not being met and whether certain members should be replaced.

For example, an analysis of overall attendance at board meetings can be disaggregated into specific results for each director and provide additional information for board actions. When monitored individually, an overall attendance level of 90 percent may reveal a poor attendance record for only one particular director. These metrics are necessary to ensure that each board member is making a significant contribution to the functioning of the board and improving corporate performance. They also provide a gap analysis that allows the board to determine what other contributions are required to meet overall board requirements.

Other individual metrics might include the number of hours of preparation for meetings, the number of visits to company sites, the quality and quantity of individual contributions in board meetings, and the level of individual skills and capabilities. It is useful for individual board members to have a small set of measures to better assess and highlight the directors' individual contributions. Evaluations should include full 360-degree performance reviews including self-assessments, along with assessments from subordinates, board members, and various outside stakeholders. Self-assessments alone have significant weaknesses, and unless they are supplemented with other inputs and metrics, a complete evaluation of performance cannot be accomplished.

Although most directors acknowledge the importance of board evaluations, until recently, only 40 percent of major North American companies conducted formal evaluations of their board, and individual evaluations were even less frequent.[30] But today, even when evaluations are completed, they are often only self-evaluations or lack the rigor that is necessary to provide useful input to making significant improvements in board performance. They often do not focus on the inputs, the processes, the outputs, and the outcomes—all of which are necessary to make significant improvement in the performance of both the boards and the companies. Objectives for each of these must be clear, and measures for each are necessary for the evaluation of performance.

Measuring the Outputs and Outcomes: Board and Corporate Performance

The inputs and processes lead to improved performance of the board (output) and ultimately to a successful outcome of improved corporate performance. As seen in the model in Figure 9.1 and the metrics in Table 9.3, these should all be linked in a cause-effect relationship. Metrics associated with outputs and outcomes are an important part of a comprehensive BES. These performance indicators empower the board with information to evaluate whether it is achieving its stated objectives and contributing to the long-term success of the company. For example, metrics such as "The percentage of projects accepted by the board that met or exceeded projected ROI" is a good indicator of the quality of the strategic guidance the board provides the executive team.

TABLE 9.3.   Metrics for Board Evaluation System: Outputs and Outcomes

Outputs	
Strategic guidance	• % of projects accepted by board that met or exceeded projected ROI
	• Risk profile (industry audit)
Accountable organization	• # of complaints (employees, community, customers)
	• Stakeholders satisfaction survey
	• Evaluation of quality of external disclosures by stakeholders (survey) or by experts
	• Credit rating
High qualified executive team	• % of major projects that met operating goals
	• % of major projects that met or exceeded projected ROI
	• Turnover rate among senior executives
	• Revenue per employee
	• Earning growth trends
	• Market growth
Outcomes	
Creating shareholder value	• EVA
	• Cash flow
	• ROI
	• Stock price
	• Earnings (overall and per business units)

A weak performance on these output metrics should signal a need to examine the board's inputs and processes so that the board's contribution to overall corporate performance can be increased. It is indeed an opportunity for boards to examine how they are contributing to protecting and creating shareholder value and should unveil specific opportunities, directions for improvements, and standards of performance. The BES should highlight the specific contribution of the board's activities, decisions, and interventions in addition to providing valuable feedback that can lead to future board improvements.

IMPLEMENTATION ISSUE AND USE OF THE BALANCED SCORECARD

In the last section, we presented the elements of a board evaluation system and how it can provide a process for better defining, articulating, and implementing board strategy. We also provided a carefully developed set of performance metrics for board evaluation. Though the discussion was set in a specific framework, the metrics and analysis of linkages can be utilized in any strategic management or performance measurement system. Among these strategic management systems, the balanced scorecard has certainly established itself as a useful reference for the development of strategic management and performance systems.[31]

Consistent with the board evaluation systems we proposed, companies already familiar with the balanced scorecard framework can develop a "board" balanced scorecard and use it to help in evaluating corporate performance and can be applied to the evaluation and improvement of board performance. By developing a board balanced scorecard, boards should be able to both understand and identify the cause-and-effect relationships of their actions on shareholder value, thus focusing attention on the drivers of corporate success and the levers that boards can pull to improve both board and corporate performance. The balanced scorecard will clearly indicate how boards can specifically impact shareholder value through the same causes and effects of learning and growth, internal processes, stakeholders' satisfaction, and financial performance. Further, the balanced scorecard will allow the board to evaluate whether it is achieving its objectives.

The four dimensions connect in a chain of cause-and-effect relationships where one dimension of drivers impacts performance in the next. These should be mutually reinforcing and all contributing to improving the implementation of the board's strategy. For example, as shown in Figure 9.2, the impact of improving the quality of information provided to board members could be illustrated in the following form:

Strategic information availability leads to: Reviewing system of strategic plan, which leads to: Stakeholders' satisfaction, which leads to: Project profitability.

To develop the board's balanced scorecard, directors and top management must first discuss and explicitly define for each of the dimensions four basic elements: (1) objectives, (2) performance drivers, (3) measures, and (4) targets. For each dimension, *objectives* should provide additional specificity to the board's roles and responsibilities. The objectives should specify what the board must accomplish to be successful in each of the four dimensions of the balanced scorecard, each capturing a distinct and essential aspect leading to financial performance. Identifying strategic objectives requires that board members along with management articulate a shared understanding of their specific duties. The objectives should reflect both the board's responsibilities and the domain of its possible interventions since it is not the board's responsibility to micromanage the company.

Performance drivers should then be explicitly identified. They are actions that boards of directors could take to implement the strategy to improve both board and corporate performance. They are the key inputs and processes that must be monitored closely, as the failure to successfully complete the actions will likely hinder performance.

In the **learning and growth** dimension, the board must identify the key activities it needs to complete to learn, improve, and develop relevant skills

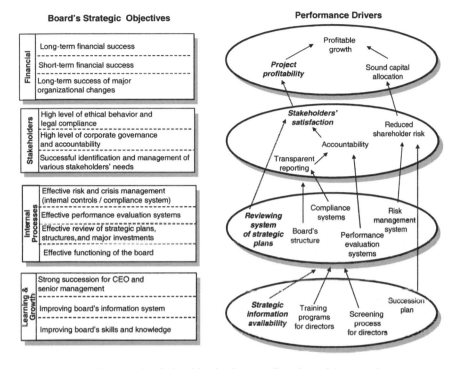

Board's Strategic Objectives

Financial
- Long-term financial success
- Short-term financial success
- Long-term success of major organizational changes

Stakeholders
- High level of ethical behavior and legal compliance
- High level of corporate governance and accountability
- Successful identification and management of various stakeholders' needs

Internal Processes
- Effective risk and crisis management (internal controls / compliance system)
- Effective performance evaluation systems
- Effective review of strategic plans, structures, and major investments
- Effective functioning of the board

Learning & Growth
- Strong succession for CEO and senior management
- Improving board's information system
- Improving board's skills and knowledge

Performance Drivers

Profitable growth

Project profitability

Sound capital allocation

Stakeholders' satisfaction

Reduced shareholder risk

Accountability

Transparent reporting

Compliance systems

Risk management system

Reviewing system of strategic plans

Board's structure

Performance evaluation systems

Strategic information availability

Training programs for directors

Screening process for directors

Succession plan

FIGURE 9.2. The Causal Relationships in the Board's Balanced Scorecard
Source: Adapted from Kaplan and Norton (1996), *The balanced scorecard,* Cambridge: Harvard Business School Press.

and knowledge for the future. The board should also identify the key **internal processes** to be implemented so it can satisfy company customers and other stakeholders. Effective internal processes will enable boards to achieve their core objectives, such as ensuring a reliable financial reporting system or ensuring a sound reviewing process of strategic plans. As it relates to the **customer and other stakeholders'** dimension, boards should try to achieve a high level of both ethical and legal compliance and accountability. They should also ensure the successful identification and management of the various stakeholders' needs. Finally, in their scorecard, boards should also demonstrate how they are contributing to success in the **financial** dimension. As they frequently approve major organizational changes, capital allocation decisions, financial plans, mergers and acquisitions, and other significant material transactions, boards share responsibility for these decisions with the CEO and other top management.

Each performance driver should be associated with specific *measures* and *targets*. Targets should reflect both industry best practices and the company's commitment to superior corporate governance. Results should be monitored regularly and used to identify areas of weakness, challenge the plans and systems in place, and establish new initiatives to improve deficiencies. Much like the metrics supporting the board evaluation systems we introduced, the selected metrics will include a combination of input, process, output, and outcome metrics to effectively measure performance. The metrics described earlier can be easily grouped into a balanced scorecard format.[32]

REPORTING ON CORPORATE GOVERNANCE DECISIONS

As reported previously, the link between corporate governance and corporate performance is still not clear. However, some studies have suggested that companies with better corporate governance records can, over time, create greater shareholder value and be more attractive investments than companies with relatively poorer governance. Furthermore, some investor surveys have shown that corporate governance has become an important factor in investment decisions and that a formal review of the corporate governance practices is often part of the investment decision-making process.

As investors require increasingly reliable information on governance practices, numerous rating systems that evaluate and rank the relative corporate governance practices of public companies have surfaced. Their levels of accuracy and relevancy have certainly been widely discussed. Regardless of whether these ratings are empirically sound or valuable, investor relations departments must consider these ratings as they develop their communication strategy. A strong investor relations communication strategy will enable companies to signal potential investors, creditors, and the public information about their commitment to high standards of corporate governance. Companies must obtain a good understanding of the content and methodology of these ratings systems and their evaluation criteria for governance practices. Companies must understand the factors being considered by the various corporate governance ratings services and may wish to implement or adapt their practices accordingly. Further, companies should actively monitor the information being used by rating companies to avoid potentially negative publicity. Because the ratings are typically based on publicly available information, there can be occasions of incorrect or incomplete information on a particular company.

Corporate Governance Rating Systems

In addition to large institutional investors—organizations such as TIAA-CREF or CalPERS that have developed their own guidelines and systems to assess corporate governance practices—many other organizations have developed corporate governance scoring systems that are available to shareholders, potential investors, creditors, and others. Rating agencies, shareholders' rights advocate organizations, debt rating agencies, and shareholder and investor advisory groups have all become involved in governance scoring.

Table 9.4 presents the factors being considered by some of the most well-known corporate governance ratings services. To provide better insight into these factors, Table 9.4 includes factors from different types of organizations: Standard and Poor's and Moody's are leading credit rating companies; ISS and the Corporate Library are important investment and research firms that provide numerous institutional shareholder services, while GMI focuses specifically on governance rating; Deminor Rating is a subsidiary of a European-based consulting firm that is dedicated to corporate governance services; Davis Global Advisors (DGA) is a consulting firm specializing in global corporate governance. However, unlike the other organizations presented in Table 9.4, DGA's annual Leading Corporate Governance Indicators report focuses on country-average governance practices results.

For all these organizations, the rating systems are composed of a limited set of factors. While there is some variation on the factors adopted by the scoring organizations, there are four main underlying factors:

1. Attitude toward shareholder rights and takeover defenses
2. Board structure and processes
3. Executive compensation
4. Level of disclosure

For many of these organizations, those factors are built on internationally accepted standards (for example, OECD, ICGN, World Bank, Conference Board), listing requirements, national codes of best practices (for example, Cadbury Report in the UK, Preda Code in Italy), and other standards issued by recognized organizations (for example, CalPERS, TIAA-CREF). Each of the factors includes a subset of criteria. The total number of criteria and corresponding weight vary substantially from one organization to another.[33] Except for S&P, which incorporates interviews with the management and other officials of the company, methods used for obtaining data are typically similar.

They are primarily based on publicly available data such as proxy statements, annual reports, and company websites, and the results are usually sent to the corporation before publication for accuracy verification.

Differences in methodology account for some of the inconsistencies and in widespread criticisms of the scoring systems. For example, opinions about Maytag's governance practices vary widely.[34] Maytag appeared on CalPERS's focus list and is also one of the low-rated companies at the Corporate Library. However, the ISS and GovernanceMetrics reports tell a different story. ISS awarded the company a 95.3 percent governance rating against other companies in its consumer-durables and apparel group, while GovernanceMetrics, in its January 2004 report, considered Maytag to be "above average" (i.e., 8/10).

Another methodological aspect of external ratings that is often discussed is the difficulty of assessing the quality of corporate governance by only examining public information. Qualitative ("soft factors") and process aspects of

TABLE 9.4. Factors of Major Governance Rating Systems

ISS "Corporate Governance Quotient"	GMI "Basic and comprehensive rating"	The Corporate Library TCL "Board Effectiveness Rating"	Standard & Poor's "Corporate Governance Score"	Moody's Investors Services "Corporate Governance Assessment"	Davis Global Advisors "Leading Corporate Governance Indicators"	Deminor Rating "Deminor rating standard"
1. Board structure and composition 2. Charter and bylaw provisions 3. Laws of the state of incorporation 4. Executive and director compensation 5. Quantitative factors such as financial performance 6. Director and officer stock ownership 7. Director education 8. Audit	1. Board accountability 2. Financial disclosure and internal controls 3. Executive compensation 4. Market for control and ownership base 5. Corporate behavior and CSR issues 6. Shareholder rights	1. Ownership director shareholdings 2. Board composition 3. CEO compensation 4. Shareholder responsiveness 5. Litigation & fines 6. Problem directors	1. Ownership structure 2. Financial stakeholder relations 3. Financial transparency and information 4. Board structure & process	1. The board of directors 2. Compensation arrangements and related practices 3. Public disclosure 4. Legal/regulatory structure and arrangements by which the public corporate entity exists 5. Shareholder voting and other ownership prerogatives	1. Best practice codes 2. Nonexecutive directors 3. Board independence 4. Split chairman/CEO 5. Board committees 6. Voting rights 7. Voting issues 8. Accounting standards 9. Executive pay 10. Takeover	1. Rights and duties of shareholders 2. Range of takeover defenses 3. Disclosure on corporate governance 4. Board structure and functioning

corporate governance, such as how board meetings are conducted, are more difficult to measure, especially for an external rating agency. Further, including these factors in assessing corporate governance practices also implies a certain degree of subjectivity, even though it may be more relevant and more reliable.[35]

Other criticisms relate to the fact that the scoring systems are based on elements that often have little theoretical foundation, and that the lack of conceptual framework has led to recommendations that cover some aspects of corporate governance and ignore others.[36] Although the scoring systems are increasingly being tested for their predictive ability,[37] the link between a good governance score and a firm's financial performance has yet to be truly established.[38]

Finally, there is substantial concern over the influence these scoring systems could have on companies as some companies may choose to adopt cosmetic changes only to "accommodate" a particular scoring system. Surely, companies making decisions regarding corporate governance should go beyond mere compliance to scoring systems. Instead, companies should focus on identifying the key inputs and processes that can be implemented and lead to improved board and corporate performance. Once companies have decided on those aspects of corporate governance they want to adopt or modify to appeal to investors and other stakeholders, they must find the appropriate communication strategy to signal their commitment.

The board evaluation system (and balanced scorecard) and associated metrics that were introduced here represent a new and rich pool of metrics that companies can choose from to improve communication with their stakeholders. They include metrics that are financial and nonfinancial, leading and lagging, and are from both internal and external sources that have typically not been externally reported.

There are some who would like all of the information to be open and publicly available. Many company executives would prefer that very little were disclosed. The decision of what information should be disclosed to various stakeholders is complex. The decisions reflect on both corporate governance and overall corporate accountability. Some stakeholders suggest that since it is the shareholders who own the company and elect the board of directors, they are entitled to receive the information that they desire from the companies that they own. Further, since they do vote for the board members, they need information that permits an evaluation of the performance of the board, board members, the CEO, and the corporation.

Most stakeholders agree that some proprietary information should not be disclosed as it could hinder competitive advantage. However, much of the information in the board evaluation system we presented is not proprietary or could be disclosed in a way that does not divulge sensitive information. Companies that are striving for higher levels of transparency and accountability should provide investors with disclosures of both historical and forward-looking information and more access to understanding organizational past performance and future direction so they can make their own more informed predictions of future organizational success.

The board should also ensure that the company provides timely disclosure of information about its products, services, and activities, permitting stakeholders to both assess the validity of claims made by the company and make informed decisions. This will include information that is already publicly reported to governmental agencies and voluntary disclosures that go far beyond minimum regulatory requirements.

Financial measures are important as they tell a significant part of the corporate story. However, forward-looking metrics, such as the ones related to learning and growth and the other dimensions of the balanced scorecard, will provide stakeholders with additional critical information to inform better decisions. Companies are often reluctant to report adverse information. However, if corporate disclosures are to be credible over the long term, they must include both favorable and unfavorable information.

Boards have a responsibility to improve corporate accountability. In part, this requires increasing credibility and trust in corporate disclosures. Trust can be attained only if stakeholders believe that they are receiving full and fair disclosures and that both good news and bad news are fully and promptly reported. Stakeholders are rightly angered when they have made investment decisions of various resources (including time) based on false representations. The information included in the board evaluation system provides an opportunity for companies and their boards to dramatically improve both corporate governance and corporate transparency. It is an opportunity to develop metrics that both improve internal operations and performance and external disclosure and accountability. Stakeholders have a right to understand the performance of the corporations that they own, the boards and board members they elect, and the top managers that they pay to operate the companies on a daily basis. Boards can effectively use this new set of metrics to both satisfy stakeholders and improve corporate governance and accountability.

As there are still some inconsistencies with governance rating systems, and there is still not a clear understanding of the effect of certain elements of corporate governance such as board independence and leadership of the board on corporate performance, suggesting that maybe "one size does not fit all," disclosure and transparency issues have become fundamental. Indeed, through an appropriate disclosure strategy, investors and other stakeholders can assess company governance practices based on more complete information and in the end choose to either reward good governance practices or punish bad ones according to the specific context of the company.

CONCLUSION

Improving board performance is not just about complying with new regulations. The value is in taking the voluntary actions necessary to improve long-term corporate profitability and recognizing the critical role of the corporate board in corporate oversight. Better information and measurements are necessary to improve the overall strategic management systems throughout organizations. But these have not been implemented at the board of directors' level. Boards haven't been evaluated and performance of individual board members hasn't been measured, nor have the directors been accountable for their performance. Implementing a board evaluation system is critical to improving a board's performance as well as the market's perception of better performance.

We have provided a framework for improving the measurement and performance of corporate boards. It provides guidance on the use of performance metrics to improve the evaluation and performance of boards of directors and individual board members. This is an important part of an overall program that should be in place to improve overall corporate governance and overall corporate accountability. If corporations want to move toward improved accountability, the framework and recommendations for measurements and improvements that are included here can be important steps in that process. Further, it is becoming evident that increased accountability is not only critical in our current environment but is also in the long-term best interests of the corporation and its stakeholders.

With these new performance measurement and management frameworks, companies can empower their boards by providing them with improved information for improved and more independent decisions on critical corporate issues. However, creating independent boards and providing them with comprehensive and strategic information is only a partial solution. Board members need to assume new responsibilities and sometimes make very complicated and difficult decisions.

NOTES

1. A. Cadbury (1999), What are the trends in corporate governance? How will they impact your company? *Long Range Planning, 32* (1), 12–19. D. P. Forbes and F. J. Milliken (1999), cognition and corporate governance: Understanding boards of directors as strategic decision-making groups, *Academy of Management Review, 24* (3), 489–505. J. A. Sonnenfeld (2002, September), What makes great boards great, *Harvard Business Review,* 106–113.

2. R. S. Kaplan and D. P. Norton (2000), *The strategy-focused organization: How balanced scorecard companies thrive in the new business environment,* Cambridge: Harvard Business School Press. M. J. Epstein and R. A. Westbrook (2001, spring), Linking actions to profits in strategic decision making, *MIT Sloan Management Review,* 39–49.

3. J. A. Conger, D. Finegold, and E. E. Lawler III (1998, January–February), Appraising boardroom performance, *Harvard Business Review,* 136–148. The Conference Board (1999), *Determining board effectiveness: A handbook for directors and officers.* Julie I. Siciliano (2002, November–December), Governance and strategy implementation: Expanding the board's involvement, *Business Horizons,* 33–37.

4. For the complete report, see the Society of Management Accountants of Canada (2002), Measuring and improving the performance of corporate boards, Hamilton, ON, http://www.cma-canada.org

5. McKinsey and Company (2002, July), Global investor opinion survey: Key findings.

6. R. Charan (1998), *Boards at work: How corporate boards create competitive advantage,* San Francisco: Jossey-Bass. Jay A. Conger, D. Finegold, and E. E. Lawler III (2001), *Corporate boards: new strategies for adding value at the top,* San Francisco: Wiley.

7. B. E. Hermalin and M. S. Weisbach (2003, April), Boards of directors as an endogenously determined institution: A survey of the economic literature, *Federal Reserve Bank of New York Policy Review,* 7–26. D. L. Rhoades, P. L. Rechner, and C. Sundaramurthy (2000, spring), Board composition and financial performance: A meta-analysis of the influence of outside directors, *Journal of Managerial Issues, XII* (1), 76–91. N. Korac-Kakabadse, A. K. Kakabadse, and A. Kouzmin (2001), Board governance and company performance: Any correlations? *Corporate Governance, 1* (1), 24–30.

8. S. Bhagat and B. Black (2002, winter), The non-correlation between board independence and long-term firm performance, *Journal of Corporation Law,* 27 (2), 231–273. D. R. Dalton, C. M. Daily, A. E. Ellstrand, and J. L. Johnson (1998), Meta-analytic reviews of board composition, leadership structure, and financial performance, *Strategic Management Journal, 19,* 269–290. These studies suggest that companies that have independent boards or have established a distinction between the functions of CEO and chairman of the board do not perform better than other companies.

9. L. D. Brown and M. L. Caylor (2004), Corporate governance study: The correlation between corporate governance and company performance, *Institutional Shareholder Services,* 1–13. W. Drobetz, A. Schillhofer, and H. Zimmermann (2003, February 11), Corporate governance and expected stock returns: Evidence from Germany, *Finance Working Paper, 11,* 1–36. Document available at http://papers.ssrn.com/sol3/papers.cfm?abstract_id=379102. See also P. A. Gompers, J. L. Ishii, and A. Metrick (2003, February), Corporate governance and equity prices, *Quarterly Journal of Economics, 118* (1), 107–155. P. W. MacAvoy and I. Millstein (1999, fall), The active board of directors and its effect on the performance of the large publicly traded corporation, *Journal of Applied Corporate Finance, 11* (4), 8–20.

10. P. A. Gompers et al. (2003); P. W. MacAvoy and I. Millstein (1999); McKinsey and Company (2002); W. Drobetz et al. (2003).

11. W. Drobetz et al. (2003).

12. J. W. Lorsch (1995, January–February), Empowering the board, *Harvard Business Review,* 107–117.

13. A. Klein (1998), Firm performance and board committee structure, *Journal of Law and Economics, 41,* 275–303.

14. J. D. Westphal (1999), Collaboration in the boardroom: Behavioral and performance consequences of CEO-board social ties, *Academy of Management Journal, 42* (1), 7–24. J. Roberts and P. Stiles (1999), The relationship between chairmen and chief executives: Competitive or complementary roles? *Long Range Planning, 32* (1), 36–48.

15. B. E. Hermalin and M. S. Weisbach (2003).

16. Korn/Ferry International (2002), Twenty-ninth annual board of directors study.

17. J. A. Conger et al. (2001).

18. J. W. Lorsch and R. Khurana (1999, May–June), The board's role in CEO sucession, *Harvard Business Review*, 96–105.

19. W. R. Kinney Jr. (2000), *Information quality assurance and internal control for management decision making*, New York: Irwin McGraw-Hill.

20. While the term "financial literacy" typically indicates that directors should be able to read and understand financial statements and the usual financial ratios, the term "financial expert" refers to (1) "an understanding of generally accepted accounting principles and financial statements"; (2) "experience in the preparation or auditing of financial statements of generally comparable issuers and the application of such principles"; (3) "experience with internal accounting controls"; and (4) "an understanding of audit committee functions." See Sarbanes-Oxley Act 2002, available at http://banking. senate.gov/pss/acctfin/conf_rpt.pdf

21. M. J. Epstein and K. Palepu (1999, April), What financial analysts want, *Strategic Finance*, 48–52.

22. T. McNulty and A. Pettigrew (1999), Strategists on the board, *Organization Studies*, 20 (1), 47–74. Gordon Donaldson (1995, July–August), A new tool for boards: The strategic audit, *Harvard Business Review*, 99–107.

23. B. J. Hall and J. B. Lieberman (1998), Are CEOs really paid like bureaucrats? *Quarterly Journal of Economics, 113* (3), 653–691.

24. K. J. Murphy (2000), Performance standards in incentive contracts, *Journal of Accounting and Economics, 30* (3), 245–278.

25. B. Stephen, L. Hwang, and S. Lilien (2000), CEO stock-based compensation: An empirical analysis of incentive-intensity, relative mix, and economic determinants, *Journal of Business, 73* (4), 661–693.

26. C. Ittner, D. F. Larcker, and M. V. Rajan (1997), The choice of performance measures in annual bonus contracts, *Accounting Review, 72* (2), 231–255.

27. D. C. Hambrick and E. M. Jackson (2000, summer), Outside directors with a stake: The linchpin in improving governance, *California Management Review, 42* (4), 108–127.

28. J. I. Siciliano (2002); J. W. Lorsch (2002, September–October), Smelling smoke: Why boards of directors need the balanced scorecard, *Balanced Scorecard Report*.

29. J. A. Conger and E. E. Lawler III (2002, May–June), Individual director evaluations, *Ivey Business Journal*, 28–31.

30. J. A. Conger and E. E Lawler III (2002).

31. The balanced scorecard is a strategic management system that links performance to strategy by using a multidimensional set of financial and nonfinancial performance metrics. It focuses on better understanding the causal relationships and linkages within organizations and the levers that can be pulled to improve corporate performance. The traditional model contains four dimensions that relate to the core values of the company: financial, customer, internal business processes, and organizational learning and growth. R. S. Kaplan and D. P. Norton (2000).

32. See the Society of Management Accountants of Canada (2002), Measuring and improving the performance of corporate boards, Hamilton, ON, at http://www .cma-canada.org. For an application of the balanced scorecard to corporate governance,

see Robert S. Kaplan and Michael Nagel (2003), *First Commonwealth Financial Corporation,* Harvard Business School Case #9-104-042.

33. L. A. A. Van den Berghe and A. Levrau (2003, spring), Measuring the quality of corporate governance: In search of a tailormade approach? *Journal of General Management, 28* (3), 71–86.

34. For investors, is glass half full or half empty? As Maytag's feud with calpers shows, there's little consistency in corporate-governance ratings (2004), *Wall Street Journal,* C1.

35. L. A. A. Van den Berghe and A. Levrau (2003).

36. P. Linden and Z. Matolscy (2004), Corporate governance scoring systems: What do they tell us? *Australian Accounting Review, 14* (1), 9–16.

37. L. D. Brown and M. L. Caylor (2004), Corporate governance study: The correlation between corporate governance and company performance, *Institutional Shareholder Services,* 1–13.

38. Standard and Poor's Governance Services (2003, July), Standard and Poor's corporate governance scores and evaluations: Criteria, methodology, and definitions; and L. A. A. Van den Berghe and A. Levrau (2003).

10

International Corporate Governance: A Gradual If Incomplete Convergence

HOLLY J. GREGORY

The past decade has graphically demonstrated that, when seismic events shake investor confidence, the global landscape of public company governance changes. In this interconnected world, corporate scandals or financial crisis in one nation or region reverberate in the reform efforts of distant economies. The Asian financial crisis of 1997–98 spurred governance reforms across a broad swath of developing and emerging market nations; the U.S. scandals of 2001–02 had a similarly broad impact in more developed markets.

The issues that corporate governance reforms seek to resolve are common throughout the world and relate to the very real human tendency to put one's own interests first, even when charged with managing the assets of another.[1] This agency problem may play out in concerns about controlling shareholders' potential to abuse minority shareholders—or in concerns about management entrenchment or fraud, but the fundamental problem is the same.

Nations face similar regulatory choices about how to control this common problem: What is the appropriate amount of governmental intervention necessary to protect against insider misdeeds while still allowing the flexibility necessary for entrepreneurial activity? Where is the appropriate locus of regulation: the supranational (for example, EU), national, or more local level? What elements should be covered in company law versus security regulation versus listing rules? What mix of regulatory methods should be used? How much (and what) should be strictly mandated in rules versus subject to evolving affirmative principles? What should be addressed in disclosure obligations versus left to voluntary "best practice"? Whatever the ultimate mix, achieving appropriate balance between regulation and governance flexibility—and between supranational, national, and local regulation—will remain a common challenge in reform efforts, whether in the United States, the EU, or elsewhere.

As law and regulation attempt to address our common human weaknesses, efforts to find workable solutions in fixing apparent gaps in legal frameworks are similar. Throughout the world, legislative and regulatory efforts to reform corporate governance are building on the fundamental tenets first set out in the Millstein Report to the OECD[2]—the fundamentals of accountability, transparency, fairness, and responsibility that are the basis for investor confidence. Thus, the universal desire for assurance that invested capital is being put to productive use, and not being misused by corporate insiders—whether they are managers, directors, or controlling shareholders—is eroding national differences. This force is apparent not only in government-driven reform efforts, but in shareholder activism efforts and more subtly through market forces. Across the United States and Europe, but also in Asia, South America, and to a limited extent in Africa as well, institutional investors, investment funds, and investor associations are paying close attention to the corporate governance practices of the companies in which they invest and in which they are contemplating an investment. Interest in shareholder activism is growing in many regions, along with a cottage industry of corporate governance advisers and rating services. In turn, many individual companies appear to be paying closer attention to investors.

Of course, forces for variation in corporate governance practices remain significant, as different cultures, values, legal traditions, business financing arrangements, and levels of ownership concentration result in different emphases and approaches. Path dependency will certainly influence the ultimate mix of regulatory solutions, but the common nature of the agency problem and ever-increasing needs for investor capital are driving common practices.

Throughout the world, enterprises organized as limited liability joint stock corporations typically have the following characteristics:

- The providers of equity capital—the shareholders—hold a property interest in the corporation (usually proportional to the amount of investment) and as a collective body they "own" the corporation; this property interest is (usually) associated with proportional rights of control and participation in both risk and profit;
- The property interests held by equity capital providers are transferable;
- The liability of the equity capital providers is limited to the amount of capital invested;
- In exchange for limited liability, the equity providers delegate large elements of control over the corporation to a distinct supervisory body and retain only limited decision rights; and
- The corporation has full legal personality, including the authority to own assets, to bind itself to contracts, and to be held legally responsible for its actions.

Such corporations are commonly subject to the control of three bodies—a shareholder body, typically organized through a general meeting (the "GM" or "AGM") with decision rights limited to major fundamental issues; a supervisory body (a supervisory board in a two-tier board system or a board of directors in a unitary board system) charged with selecting and providing oversight of the management team hired to run the business; and a management body (a management board in a two-tier board system or a less formally structured management team in a unitary board system) that has responsibility for running the day-to-day operations of the business. Auditing bodies are also common. In some jurisdictions (for example, the United States) the auditing body is formed as a committee of the supervisory body (to provide oversight of financial reporting and of the audit and to select—or recommend to shareholders for selection—the outside auditor). In other jurisdictions (for example, Japan) the auditing body is formed as a separate corporate organ. Most jurisdictions recognize that the role of a corporate director (on a board of directors in a unitary board system or on a supervisory board in a two-tier board system) is to provide oversight of the management of the corporation, acting through the board as a collective body. Directors are generally expected to act with a certain level of prudence (care) in the best interests of the company (loyalty) rather than in their own self-interests.

Notwithstanding these commonalities, legal systems around the world reflect different choices about how best to ensure that the interests of equity capital providers and other key constituents are protected. For example, they express different conclusions on issues such as the degree to which employees and creditors can be protected sufficiently by contract and other specific laws tailored to address such concerns, or whether such concerns are better addressed through board structures and other company law requirements. They also express different conclusions about the degree to which shareholders, as providers of risk capital, should participate in company decisions, and the degree to which company managers and supervisory bodies should consider shareholder interests in relation to other interests.

Interest in corporate governance reforms has increased throughout the world in the last several years. The focus of reform efforts often emphasizes:

- Improvement of the scope and quality of financial disclosure;
- Enhancement of auditor independence;
- Strengthening the independence and role of nonexecutive directors—with these directors often having exclusive responsibility for audit supervision and executive compensation decisions;
- Enhanced transparency of corporate governance practices and principles, executive and director compensation, corporate group and affiliate structure and relations, and insider transactions;
- The role that stakeholders (employees, creditors, suppliers, and the local community) play in the vitality of a company; and
- The critical importance of business ethics.

Another important trend in reform efforts around the world is the emphasis on "soft law" in the form of codes of best practice, which express model or ideal practices—often with a "comply-or-explain" requirement. Most of these codes are supplemental to company law and securities regulation. They are flexible and nonbinding. Even when a comply-or-explain disclosure mandate exists, a company is still free to choose not to follow the code's prescriptions, so long as it discloses and explains such noncompliance. This approach recognizes that there are often justifiable reasons for adopting practices that differ from the model. In addition to encouraging adoption of best practices, soft law in the form of such codes has proven influential in:

- Stimulating discussion of corporate governance practices;
- Educating investors and other interested parties about corporate governance practices and related laws and regulations;
- Benchmarking the practices of corporate boards; and
- Paving the way for necessary legal reform.[3]

Throughout the last decade the number of codes of best practice adopted throughout the world has steadily increased, and the content of such codes exhibits a remarkable degree of similarity, indicating strong international convergence about employing effective governance practices.[4]

The recent round of reform activity often reflects a move to embed soft law concepts about effective governance practices into regulation. Such activity has been most pronounced in the United States and Europe, reflecting reactions to recent governance scandals and failures. However, reform interest is also apparent in countries as diverse as the Russian Federation, Brazil, China, and South Africa.

In the United States, corporate governance reform efforts peaked in 2003–2004 as regulators adopted, and companies implemented, various rules relating to the Sarbanes-Oxley Act of 2002,[5] the broadest piece of federal legislation to address corporate governance since the adoption of the Securities Exchange Act in 1934. The Sarbanes-Oxley Act, and related regulations adopted by the Securities and Exchange Commission (SEC) to implement aspects of the act, set forth requirements with respect to, among other things, the disclosure of off–balance sheet transactions and contingent liabilities, the use of non-GAAP financial information, protections for corporate whistle-blowers, the adoption of a code of ethics for the chief executive and senior financial executives, audit committee independence and responsibilities, independence of outside auditors, and review and certification of internal controls.[6]

In addition to adopting Sarbanes-Oxley implementing rules, the SEC also adopted new rules and proposed another controversial set of rules aimed respectively at increasing the transparency of the process for the nomination of directors and providing enhanced shareholder participation in that process in certain circumstances.[7] The new disclosure rules require that public companies establish a means by which shareholders can communicate with directors. Companies must also disclose how director-nominees are chosen, whether independent directors control the nomination process, and whether nominees suggested by shareholders are considered. The more controversial proposed rules would, under certain circumstances, require companies to include in their proxy materials the names of shareholder nominees for election to the board of directors. Although the controversial provisions have not been adopted and compromise proposals are under consideration by the SEC, they reflect regulatory interest in increasing the voice of shareholders in the nomination of directors. Together with the new disclosure requirements, they could greatly affect the way shareholders interact with the U.S. companies in which they invest. (Neither the new disclosure rules nor the proposed shareholder access rules would apply to foreign private issuers.)

In 2003 and 2004 the SEC also approved various amendments to New York Stock Exchange and NASDAQ corporate governance listing standards.[8] These amendments address board composition; nominating, compensation, and corporate governance committee structures and responsibilities; the role and definition of independent directors; and requirements for a company-wide code of conduct and ethics. Taken together, the new governance-related listing standards are designed to better position boards to hold management accountable for the performance of the company and, in particular, for the accurate portrayal of the company's financial condition. Through related disclosure requirements, they are also designed to assist shareholders in monitoring corporate governance practices. For example, companies listed on the New York Stock Exchange must adopt and disclose corporate governance guidelines, various committee charters, and a code of business conduct and ethics. (Listed foreign private issuers are subject to some but not all of these new requirements.)

The discussion of modern corporate governance reform in the United Kingdom dates to 1992, when the seminal Cadbury Report was published.[9] Since then a number of other important recommendations—the Greenbury, Hampel, Turnbull, Higgs, and Smith Reports[10]—have been united with the Cadbury recommendations in the Combined Code applicable to companies traded on the London Stock Exchange.[11] As most recently revised, the Combined Code addresses board independence from management, external auditor independence, internal control systems, disclosure accuracy, and executive and director compensation, among other things. The revised Combined Code became effective on a comply-or-explain basis for listed UK companies as of November 1, 2003. Companies must disclose whether they comply with its provisions and if not, why not.

Similarly, in 2002, the German Transparency and Disclosure Act[12] amended section 161 of the German Stock Corporations Act to provide that German publicly listed companies either comply with the German Corporate Governance Code (the "Cromme Commission" code)[13] or explain noncompliance.

Significantly, the German code recommends that the supervisory board of each company establish an audit committee. Prior to the code's promulgation in February 2002, only about 40 percent of German listed companies had an audit committee. The code also makes important recommendations regarding financial reporting requirements, risk management, and external auditor independence.[14]

The Combined Code has clearly influenced the development of rules and regulations governing public companies in other jurisdictions; the comply-or-explain methodology of compliance is the most visible example. In addition to Germany, codes with comply-or-explain disclosure requirements have been adopted by a number of other nations.[15] As discussed below, disclosure against national voluntary governance codes is also a component of the EU's Action Plan for governance reform.

The EU has recently considered, proposed, ratified, or implemented at the national level a number of directives[16] and recommendations that relate to corporate governance issues, including the *Prospectus Directive,*[17] which harmonizes standards for the issuance of securities offered to the public and requires implementation by member states by July 1, 2005, and the *Directive on Market Abuse,*[18] which is intended to protect investors and the market generally against insider trading and market manipulation, and had an October 12, 2004, deadline for member state implementation. In addition, the *Takeover Bid Directive,*[19] setting an EU-wide minimum standard of protection for shareholders of companies subject to takeover bids, completed the European legislative process on April 21, 2004, and should be implemented into member state law by May 20, 2006, and the *Transparency Directive,*[20] which seeks to improve the quality of information for investors included in periodic reports and increase the frequency with which periodic reports must be issued by listed companies, received final approval in 2004 and will become law in 2006. (Under this directive, company directors who accidentally omit important information from their annual reports could face lawsuits from investors throughout Europe if an investor loses money as a result.)

In May 2003 the EU issued two communications setting forth plans for specific corporate governance reforms impacting boards of directors and performance of the statutory audit: *Modernizing Company Law and Enhancing Corporate Governance in the European Union: A Plan to Move Forward* (the Action Plan),[21] and *Reinforcing the Statutory Audit in the EU* (the Statutory Audit Communication).[22] Both the Action Plan and the Statutory Audit Communication are designed to further European market integration by creating a regulatory framework that fosters a transparent, sound, and competitive capital market while aligning EU governance norms with international expectations. They underscore the EU's claim to regulate the corporate governance and auditing standards of corporations organized under the laws of its member states.

The Action Plan incorporates a set of legislative and nonlegislative proposals that extend over three phases to be implemented through 2009. Unlike the fast track of U.S. reforms, the European plan envisions a more lengthy implementation period, stretching, for some of the reforms, to the end of the decade. Each of the Action Plan's proposals require further development and eventual implementation through either nonbinding recommendations or directives to each member state to achieve the result, thereby providing national authorities discretion in choosing both the form and the method of implementation. The Action Plan would require each member state to designate a corporate governance code against which listed companies based within its jurisdiction would be required to disclose their governance practices on a comply-or-explain basis.[23] Initiatives in the Action Plan's first phase include:

- Expanding disclosure requirements for director compensation, governance policies, and corporate group and affiliate structures and relations;
- Confirming the collective responsibility and liability of board members for key nonfinancial statements;
- Strengthening the independence and role of nonexecutive (and supervisory) directors by establishing minimum standards of independence and by making executive compensation and audit supervision the exclusive responsibility of nonexecutive, preferably independent, directors;
- Facilitating shareholder communication, decision-making, and participation in shareholder meetings and proxy voting by harmonizing and integrating the legal framework of the various member states and by promoting the use of modern technology;
- Creating a European Governance Forum to coordinate the corporate governance efforts of member states;
- Simplifying the current EU Directive on minimum capital maintenance requirements for listed companies; and
- Facilitating cross-border mergers between companies from member states.

These proposals cover issues remarkably similar to those addressed by the U.S. reforms. The Action Plan also outlines a number of medium- and long-term corporate governance reforms, including:

- Requiring the disclosure of institutional investor investment and voting policies;
- Examining whether to allow EU-wide choice between one-tier and two-tier board structures;
- Enhancing the responsibilities and accountability of board members by establishing special investigation rights, additional insider trading rules, and director disqualification provisions;
- Examining the consequences of an EU-wide one-share/one-vote rule; and
- Considering regulation of company groups, subsidiaries, and private limited liability entities.

Not as broad in scope as the Action Plan, the Statutory Audit Communication is another key component of EU reform efforts to promote a transparent

EU-wide capital market. Important elements of the Statutory Audit Communication include:

- Requiring International Auditing Standards for all EU statutory audits from 2005 onwards;
- Implementing a mechanism to coordinate national systems of public oversight into a cohesive, pan-EU network;
- Defining principles for the appointment, dismissal, and compensation of auditors, and auditor independence (including restrictions on the provision of nonaudit services);
- Examining the auditor's role in reviewing and assessing company internal control systems;
- Considering the advisability of a harmonized EU code of ethics for auditors;
- Implementing quality assurance mechanisms by the end of 2003;
- Reexamining current EU auditor education curriculum requirements, and considering continuing education principles;
- Developing disclosure requirements concerning relationships between audit firms and their networks; and
- Studying the economic impact of auditor liability regimes, with an eye toward regulation.

Again, these proposals cover issues similar to those that U.S. legislators, regulators, and listing bodies addressed in their recent reform efforts.

In October 2004 the European Commission issued more detailed recommendations for implementation of the Action Plan.[24] These recommendations, which are not legally binding, call on member states to adopt at a national level, whether by legislation or by a comply-or-explain approach, provisions concerning the role of nonexecutive directors as well as the transparency of director remuneration. The recommendation regarding nonexecutive directors provides both basic principles intended to strengthen the role of nonexecutive directors as well as additional guidance to assist the member states in interpreting these principles. In particular, it provides that a unitary or supervisory board should include a sufficient number of independent nonexecutive directors to ensure that any material conflicts of interest involving management directors are properly addressed. Even prior to the release of this recommendation, a number of codes in the member states already expressed the principles set forth in the recommendation regarding nonexecutive directors—for example, in addition to the UK's Combined Code, the Dutch and Swedish codes mandate a majority of independent directors, while Spain's Olivencia Report recommends that outside directors should outnumber executive directors. Note that this recommendation would also hold directors collectively responsible for the accuracy of the companies' financial statements. (The U.S. law, by contrast, requires only the chief executive and chief financial officers to certify financial statements.) The recommendation relating to the remuneration of directors invites member states to adopt measures that promote mandatory disclosure of compensation and to provide that certain director remuneration policies be submitted to shareholder vote. In addition, a European Corporate Governance Forum consisting of fifteen experts was set up in October 2004 to advise the European Commission and member states on corporate governance reform.[25] Matters it will address include coordination and convergence of national codes.

Oversight of internal control systems relating to financial reporting has been the focus of significant reform interest in the United States, as evidenced in Section 404 of the Sarbanes-Oxley Act, and in the UK as evidenced in the Turnbull Report and the Combined Code. The European Commission may turn attention to internal controls in the near future. The French stock market regulator, the AMF, is calling for a common European standard in internal corporate controls. The AMF said in January 2005 that it planned to approach the European Commission in a few months with EU-wide guideline proposals.[26]

Throughout the European Union, corporate governance reforms are taking root in practice. According to Jaap Winter, chairman of the high-level group of company law experts who advised the European Commission on governance-related reforms across Europe, governance practices are changing "relatively fast." "In all Member States things are happening, codes are produced, legislation is changed, boards are starting to operate differently." There is a "sense of urgency that things must be transparent, that conflicts of interest must be dealt with, and that nonexecutives have a real role to play."[27]

The sense of reform urgency that has been apparent in the United States and Europe over the past several years is somewhat attenuated in other areas of the world. Governance reform efforts continue throughout Asia, Africa, and Latin America, albeit at a lesser pace than following the 1997–98 economic crisis. The immediate aftereffects of recent U.S. scandals have been less potent in these regions, in part because in the 1997–98 period the economic crisis heightened recognition of governance-related failures and a number of nations had already engaged in a recent round of reforms. However, in some nations, the U.S. governance scandals have provided an excuse to stall corporate governance reform, as reform skeptics have pointed to the inability of U.S.-style corporate governance to prevent fraud. Nonetheless, governance reforms progress along familiar lines:

- In Russia, the Federal Securities Commission issued a *Corporate Governance Code* in 2002.[28] It has since been implemented on a comply-or-explain basis. Progress has been made over the past few years in several important areas, including the use of cumulative voting, improvement in board composition and management expertise, a reduction in asset stripping by requiring shareholder approval of major asset sales, and standardized calculation and payment of dividends.[29] All listed companies are, as of this year, required to adopt International Financial Reporting Standards.[30] Between 2005 and 2007, A-level stock market listings will be required to phase in at least three independent board members; to have audit, nomination, and compensation committees consisting of independent directors; and to offer extensive disclosure of directors' remuneration. B-level listings will be required to have at least one independent director and will not face requirements regarding the independence of board committees.[31]

- The China Securities Regulatory Commission (CSRC) issued in December 2004 a *Decree to Further Safeguard the Rights of the Investing Public,* which is designed to protect the rights of minority investors in matters where a decision by the majority shareholder would otherwise impact their rights.[32] Together with the State Economic and Trade Commission, the CSRC has also promulgated a *Code of Corporate Governance for Listed Companies*[33] as a mechanism for improving the confidence of investors in listed companies. The code calls for boards to include independent directors and to evaluate management performance and determine management compensation. It also requires adoption of internal control systems and imposes requirements for the independence of outside auditors.[34]
- In South Africa, the JSE Securities Exchange launched the Socially Responsible Investment (SRI) Index in May 2004 to encourage companies to adopt socially and environmentally responsible policies—and good governance.[35]
- In Latin America, within the past decade Argentina, Brazil, Chile and Mexico, among other countries, have enacted laws designed to strengthen minority shareholder rights and the powers of market regulators.[36]

The 2004 revised edition of the *OECD Principles of Corporate Governance,* by comparison with the original 1999 edition, further demonstrates in its greater level of detail the growing global convergence of ideas concerning what constitutes effective corporate governance practices.[37] The OECD *Principles* were first adopted in 1999 to articulate what is required for an effective framework for corporate governance both within OECD countries and beyond. They have become widely accepted global benchmarks to measure the effectiveness of a nation's legal and regulatory framework, addressing areas such as transparency in financial reporting, ownership and governance, shareholder relations, and board accountability. Although nonbinding, they provide important reference points in the ongoing dialogue on experiences and improvements adaptable to the social, legal, and economic frameworks of individual companies.

On April 22, 2004, the governments of the thirty OECD countries approved revisions to the original *Principles,* adding new recommendations to reflect evolving ideas about the role of governance in building and maintaining public trust in companies and stock markets. The revisions provide more detail on board elections, including nominating procedures and director election processes. They emphasize the need for transparent lines of management and board responsibility as well as the importance of a regulatory framework that facilitates effective enforcement and defines the responsibilities between different supervisory, regulatory, and enforcement authorities.

The OECD *Principles* are stated in six primary points, as follows:

1. *Ensuring the basis for an effective corporate governance framework.* The corporate governance framework should promote transparent and efficient

markets, be consistent with the rule of law, and clearly articulate the division of responsibilities among different supervisory, regulatory, and enforcement authorities;

2. *The rights of shareholders and key ownership functions.* The corporate governance framework should protect and facilitate the exercise of shareholders' rights;

3. *The equitable treatment of shareholders.* The corporate governance framework should ensure the equitable treatment of all shareholders, including minority and foreign shareholders. All shareholders should have the opportunity to obtain effective redress for violation of their rights;

4. *The role of stakeholders in corporate governance.* The corporate governance framework should recognize the rights of stakeholders established by law or through mutual agreements and encourage active cooperation between corporations and stakeholders in creating wealth, jobs, and the sustainability of financially sound enterprises;

5. *Disclosure and transparency.* The corporate governance framework should ensure that timely and accurate disclosure is made on all material matters regarding the corporation, including the financial situation, performance, ownership, and governance of the company; and

6. *The responsibilities of the board.* The corporate governance framework should ensure the strategic guidance of the company, the effective monitoring of management by the board, and the board's accountability to the company and the shareholders.

The *Principles* provide additional detail through subparts and annotations. Specific areas of focus include:

Institutional Investors

- Institutional investors should be required to disclose their voting policies and how they intend to manage conflicts of interest that may compromise their voting;
- Institutional investors should be free from restrictions on consultations with other stockholders and obstacles to the exercise of cross-border voting rights.

Stockholder Rights

- Stockholders should have the right to remove board members and to participate in the nomination and election processes;
- Stockholders should be able to make their views known on the policy for executive and board remuneration, and any equity component of remuneration should be subject to their approval.

Conflicts of Interest and Auditor Responsibility

- Boards should be required to approve and disclose conflicts of interest and transactions between related parties;
- Rating agencies, analysts, and investment banks should be required to avoid or disclose conflicts of interest that could compromise the nature of their advice;

- Auditors should be held accountable to stockholders and exercise due professional care when conducting an audit;
- Auditors should be required to be wholly independent and not be compromised by other relationships with the company.

Stakeholder Rights and Whistle-Blower Protection

- The *Principles* acknowledge that stakeholders have rights established both by law and through mutual agreement;
- Boards should develop a code of ethics and a procedure to ensure compliance with the law;
- Mechanisms should be designed to provide protection for whistle-blowers, including by providing a communication means through which complaints can be made in a confidential manner.

Board Responsibilities

- Boards should be required to act objectively and independently, and be accountable to stockholders;
- The duties and responsibilities of the board should include responsibility for corporate ethics, compliance with laws and standards, and oversight of internal control systems covering financial reporting;
- Boards should be required to monitor, disclose, and otherwise manage potential conflicts of interest.

The OECD is likely to continue to encourage member countries to adopt a legal framework in line with the *Principles* and to participate in a continuing exchange of information about implementation practices—both at the government and corporate levels. It is also expected that the World Bank and OECD will continue to use the *Principles* to encourage non-OECD nations to improve their own legal frameworks.

These are just a few of the reform initiatives over the last several years that indicate both an increased awareness of the importance of corporate governance and a convergence around common solutions. Activist investors have long recognized the value-enhancing potential of good governance practices. Increasingly, regulators are recognizing the link between economic growth and development, investor confidence, and a sound framework of governance regulation. At the same time, boards of directors, corporate managers, and shareholders are more conscious of the role that governance plays within individual corporations. Achieving an appropriate balance between regulation and governance flexibility remains the central challenge in reform efforts and the focus of some debate. If balance is to be achieved, however, private sector players—primarily corporate directors and managers, but also shareholders and various professionals upon whom the corporation relies (auditors, bankers, lawyers)—need to adopt the mind-set and act in the capacity that the governance framework contemplates. Throughout the world, the contemplative mind-set eschews self-interest in favor of prudence in the best interests of the company. Throughout the world, self-interest and lack of due care are likely to be met with more regulation.

NOTES

Frederick W. Philippi, a paralegal specialist, assisted in the drafting of this chapter.

1. Adam Smith (1776), *The wealth of nations* (1776); Adolf Berle and Gardiner Means (1932), *The modern corporation and private property*, 337; W. O. Douglas (1934), Directors who do not direct, *Harv. L. Rev., 47,* 1305.

2. Ira M. Millstein (1998, April), et al., *Corporate governance: Improving competitiveness and access to capital in global markets.* A report to the OECD by the Business Sector Advisory Group on Corporate Governance.

3. Holly J. Gregory and Robert T. Simmelkjaer (2002, January), *Comparative study of corporate governance codes relevant to the European Union and its member states, on behalf of the European Commission, Internal Market Directorate General* (Weil, Gotshal and Manges LLP), available at http://www.odce.ie/_fileupload/services/EU%20Comparison.pdf

4. Holly J. Gregory (2005, January), *International comparison of selected corporate governance guidelines and codes of best practice* (Weil, Gotshal and Manges LLP), available at http://www.weil.com/wgm/cwgmhomep.nsf/Files/CorpGovGuide_Am_Eu_As_Af/$file/CorpGovGuide_Am_Eu_As_Af.pdf

5. The Public Company Accounting Reform and Investor Protection Act of 2002 ("the Sarbanes-Oxley Act of 2002"), H.R. 3763, Pub. L. No. 107-204, available at http://news.findlaw.com/hdocs/docs/gwbush/sarbanesoxley072302.pdf

6. SEC (2003, January 22), *Final rule: Conditions for use of non-GAAP financial measures,* Release Nos. 33-8176; 34-47226; FR-65; File No. S7-43-02 (adopting rules implementing Sarbanes-Oxley provisions that require the disclosure of non-GAAP financial information); SEC (2003, January 23), *Disclosure required by sections 406 and 407 of the Sarbanes-Oxley Act of 2002,* Release Nos. 33-8177; 34-47235; File No. S7-40-02 (adopting rules implementing Sarbanes-Oxley provisions that require disclosure of financial experts on company audit committees and the adoption of a code of ethics); SEC (2003, January 27), *Final rule: Disclosure in management's discussion and analysis about off–balance sheet arrangements and aggregate contractual obligations,* Release Nos. 33-8182; 34-47264; FR-67; File No. S7-42-02 (adopting rules implementing Sarbanes-Oxley provisions that require the disclosure of off balance sheet and contingent liabilities); and SEC (2003, January 28), *Strengthening the commission's requirements regarding auditor independence,* Release Nos. 33-8183; 34-47265; 35-27642; IC-25915; IA-2103, FR-68, File No. S7-49-02 (adopting rules implementing Sarbanes-Oxley provisions that strengthen requirements with respect to auditor independence). See SEC (2003, January 22), *Insider trades during pension fund blackout periods,* Release No. 34-47225; IC-25909; File No. S7-44-02 (adopting rules implementing Sarbanes-Oxley requirements with respect to insider trades during pension blackout periods); SEC (2003, January 24), *Final rule: Retention of records relevant to audits and reviews,* Release Nos. 33-8180; 34-47241; IC-25911; FR-66; File No. S7-46-02 (adopting rules implementing Sarbanes-Oxley requirements with respect to the retention of audit records); and SEC (2003, January 29), *Final rule: Implementation of standards of professional conduct for attorneys,* Release Nos. 33-8185; 34-47276; IC-25919; File No. S7-45-02 (adopting rules

implementing Sarbanes-Oxley requirements with respect to professional conduct standards for attorneys).

7. SEC (2003, November 24), *Disclosure regarding nominating committee functions and communications between security holders and boards of directors*, Release Nos. 33-8340; 34-48825; IC-26262; File No. S7-14-03 (adopting rules requiring disclosure of the director nomination process and facilitating communications between shareholders and boards of directors); SEC (2003, October 14), *Proposed rule: Security holder director nominations*, Release Nos. 34-48626; IC-26206; File No. S7-19-03 (proposing rules regarding shareholder nominations of candidates for election to boards of directors).

8. NYSE (2003, November 4), *Final NYSE corporate governance rules* (for companies listed on the NYSE), available at http://www.nyse.com/pdfs/finalcorpgovrules.pdf, amended, SEC Release No. 34-50625, File No. SR-NYSE-2004-41 (November 3, 2004), available at http://www.nyse.com/pdfs/2004-41app.pdf; NASDAQ, *Corporate governance—Rules 4200, 4200A, 4350, 4350A, 4351 and 4360 and associated interpretive material* (as of April 15, 2004) (for companies listed on NASDAQ), available at http://www.nasdaq.com/about/CorporateGovernance.pdf, amended, SEC Release No. 34-49753, File No. SR-NASD-2004-081 (May 20, 2004), available at http://www.sec.gov/rules/sro/nasd/34-49746.pdf; SEC, Release No. 34-49901, File No. SR-NASD-2004-080 (June 22, 2004); available at http://www.sec.gov/rules/sro/nasd/34-49901.pdf; SEC Release No. 49903, File No. SR-NASD-2004-086 (June 22, 2004), available at http://www.sec.gov/rules/sro/nasd/34-49903.pdf

9. *Report of the committee on the financial aspects of corporate governance* ("Cadbury Report") (December 1, 1992, reissued April 1996).

10. Study Group on Directors' Remuneration (1995, July), *Directors' remuneration* ("Greenbury Report"); Committee on Corporate Governance (sponsored by the London Stock Exchange, et al.) (1998, January), *Final report* ("Hampel Report"); Institute of Chartered Accountants in England and Wales (1999, September), *Internal control: Guidance for directors on the combined code* ("Turnbull Report"); Financial Reporting Council Group (2003, January 20), *Audit committees: Combined code guidance* ("Smith Report"); Derek Higgs (2003, January 20), *Review of the role and effectiveness of non-executive directors* ("Higgs Report").

11. The Financial Reporting Council (July 1998, revised July 2003), *The combined code on corporate governance*, available at http://www.asb.org.uk/documents/pdf/combinedcodefinal.pdf

12. Gesetz zur weiteren Reform des Aktien- und Bilanzrechts, zu Transparenz und Publizität (Transparenz- und Publizitätsgesetz) (2002, July 25), BGBl. I, 2681 ("TransPuG").

13. Government Commission German Corporate Governance Code (the "Cromme Commission"), *German corporate governance code* (February 26, 2002, revised May 21, 2003), available at http://www.gurn.info/topic/corpgov/kdd03.pdf

14. Peter Etzbach and H. Elizabeth Kroeger (2003, March), Audit committees in German companies, *International Financial Law Review*.

15. See, for example, Australian Stock Exchange Corporate Governance Council (2003, March), *Principles of good corporate governance and best practice recommendations* the Korea Stock Exchange, et al. (1999, September), Committee on Corporate Governance, *Code of best practice for corporate governance*, V.2.3; Russian Federal Securities

Commission (2002, April 4), *Corporate governance code,* Ch. 7, sec. 3.3.6 and current regulations; and Consejo Coordinador Empresarial y la Comisión Nacional Bacaria y de Valores (1999, June 9), *Corporate governance code for Mexico,* Motive and Intent. In addition, codes issuing in many countries propose disclosure on a comply-or-explain basis. See, for example, Corporate Governance Committee (the "Lippens Committee") (2004, December 9), *The Belgian code on corporate governance,* Provision 9.2; Indonesian National Committee for Corporate Governance (2001, April), *Code of good corporate governance,* sec. VII, Principle 7.3; Corporate Governance Committee ("the Tabaksblat Committee") (2003, December 9), *The Dutch corporate governance code: Principles of good corporate governance and best practice provisions,* Best Practice Provision I.1; and La Comisión Especial para el Estudio de un Código Etico de los Consejos de Adminis-tración de las Sociedades (1998, February), *The governance of Spanish companies* ("Olivencia Report"), Recommendation 23.

16. In addition to the directives discussed in the text, the following directives progressed in 2004: (i) The *Product Directive,* which harmonizes rules for collective investment vehicles such as mutual funds and unit trusts to ensure freedom of in-vestment choices, entered into force on April 30, 2004, and requires member state implementation by April 30, 2006 (2004 O.J. (L 145) 1); (ii) The *Markets in Financial Instruments Directive* (MiFID) (also called the *Management Company Directive*), up dates the *Investment Services Directive* of 1993 and governs how investment firms should be set up, how they are authorized to trade, and what products they may deal in. Among other things, it provides investment firms with a "single passport" to oper-ate across the EU, using approval from their home member state. It is scheduled to come into force April 30, 2006 (2004 O.J. (L 145) 1); (iii) The *European Company Statute,* which enables companies to operate across Europe under a single legal structure (as a Societas Europea or SE) without having to set up a network of subsidiaries governed by different national laws, comprises two legal instruments: a regulation directly ap plicable in all EU member states, and a directive, intended to have been transposed into national laws by October 8, 2004 (2001 O.J. (L 294) 1).

17. Directive 2003/71/EC of the European Parliament and of the Council of 4 No-vember 2003 on the prospectus to be published when securities are offered to the public or admitted to trading and amending Directive 2001/34/EC, 2003 O.J. (L 345) 64.

18. Directive 2003/6/EC of the European Parliament and of the Council of 28 January 2003 on insider dealing and market manipulation (market abuse), 2003 O.J. (L 96) 64.

19. Directive 2004/25/EC of the European Parliament and of the Council of 21 April 2004 on takeover bids, 2004 O.J. (L 142) 12.

20. Directive 2004/109/EC of the European Parliament and of the Council of 15 December 2004 on the harmonization of transparency requirements in relation to information about issuers whose securities are admitted to trading on a regulated market and amending Directive 2001/34/EC, 2004 O.J. (L390) 38.

21. Communication from the Commission to the Council and the Parliament—Modernizing Company Law and Enhancing Corporate Governance in the European Union: A Plan to Move Forward, COM(03)284 final (May 21, 2003), available at http://europa.eu.int/eur-lex/en/com/cnc/2003/com2003_0284en01.pdf. This communication recommends corporate governance-related reforms that are informed by the November 2002 *Report of the high level group of company law experts* (the "Winter Report") as well

as by a study by Holly J. Gregory and Robert T. Simmelkjaer (2002, January), *Comparative study of corporate governance codes relevant to the european Union and its member states, on behalf of the European Commission, internal Market Directorate General* (the "Weil Study") (Weil, Gotshal and Manges LLP), available at http://www.odce.ie/_fileupload/services/EU%20Comparison.pdf. The Weil Study recommended that the commission focus not on an EU-wide corporate governance code—the forty codes and sets of guidelines analyzed in this study showed a remarkable degree of convergence—but rather on: (i) reducing the information and participation barriers faced by investors throughout the various EU member states; (ii) encouraging listed companies to provide information about internal governance, including information about corporate ownership structure, board composition, and governance processes, and (iii) creating a forum in which policymakers for member states could share ideas and approaches. The commission's Action Plan reflects these recommendations.

22. Communication from the Commission to the Council and the Parliament—Reinforcing the statutory audit in the EU, COM(03)286 final (May 21, 2003), available at http://europa.eu.int/smartapi/cgi/sga_doc?smartapi!celexapi!prod!CELEXnumdoc&lg=EN&numdoc=52003DC0286&model=guichett

23. See, supra, note 16.

24. Commission recommendation on fostering an appropriate regime for the remuneration of directors of listed companies, COM(03)284 final (2004, October 6), available at http://europa.eu.int/comm/internal_market/company/docs/directors-remun/2004-recommendation_en.pdf; Commission recommendation on the role of nonexecutive or supervisory directors and on the committees of the (supervisory) board, COM(03)284 final (2004, October 6), available at http://europa.eu.int/comm/internal_market/company/docs/independence/2004-recommendation_en.pdf. In addition, in September 2004 the European Commission initiated public consultation on the cross-border exercise of shareholder rights (Fostering an appropriate regime for shareholders' rights: Consultation document of the services of the internal market of the directorate general (2004, September 16)). In the fall of 2004 the European Commission also introduced proposals amending the fourth and seventh company law directives, dealing, respectively, with annual and consolidated accounts, by tightening the rules in several respects, with the aim of restoring public confidence in corporate financial statements (Proposal for a directive of the European Parliament and of the council amending council directives 78/660/EEC and 83/349/EEC concerning the annual accounts of certain types of companies and consolidated accounts (2004, October 28)), and modernizing the second company law directive on the formation of public limited liability companies and the formation and alteration of their capital, with safeguards to protect the interests of minority shareholders, including reciprocal squeeze-out and sell-out rights, and the interests of creditors through harmonization of national legal provisions in the event of a capital reduction (Proposal for a directive of the European Parliament and of the council amending council directive 77/91/EEC, as regards the formation of public limited liability companies and the maintenance and alteration of their capital, COM(04) final (2004, September 21)).

25. The European Commission, Internal Market (2004, October 18), *Commission creates European Forum to promote convergence in Europe* (press release), available at http://europa.eu.int/rapid/pressReleasesAction.do?reference=IP/04/1241&format=HTML&aged=0&language=en&guiLanguage=en

26. Peggy Hollinger (2005, January 14), French call for common standards, *The Financial Times*, 16.

27. Ian Bickerton and Brian Groom (2004, December 27), Softly, softly on EU convergence, says lawyer, *The Financial Times*, 19.

28. Russian Federal Securities Commission (2002, April 4), *Corporate Governance Code*.

29. Russian Federal Laws Nos. 5-FZ (2004, February 24), and 17-FZ (2004, April 6); Institute of International Finance (IIF) Equity Advisory Group (2004, October), *Corporate governance in Russia: An investor perspective*, 2.

30. IIF, *Corporate governance in Russia*, 4.

31. Decision of the Federal Commission for Securities Market No. 03-54/ps of December 26, 2003, on the Endorsement of the Regulation on the Activities in Organization of Trade at Securities Market, sec. 4, Annex I and II of (December 26, 2003). Notwithstanding corporate governance reforms, weaknesses in the country's equity culture and judicial system continue to compromise shareholders' rights. IIF, *Corporate governance in Russia*, 5–6, 8.

32. CSRC (2004, December 23), *Decree to further safeguard the rights of the investing public*. Shenzhen Stock Exchange, press release.

33. CSRC and the State Economic and Trade Commission (2001, January), *Code of corporate governance for listed companies in China*, available at http://www.ecgi.org/codes/documents/code_en.pdf

34. Notwithstanding these advances, and three years after China's entry into the WTO, some analysts view widespread corruption and political interference with the judiciary in China as a continuing obstruction to the rule of law. Both the United States and the EU continue to deny China market economy status due to state interference, and other reasons. *See statement from commerce secretary Donald L. Evans on America's economic relationship with China* (2004, April 28), available at http://usinfo.state.gov/eap/Archive/2004/Jun/30-239352.html; see also *EU-China summit: New steps in a growing relationship* (2004, December 6), available at http://europa.eu.int/comm/external_relations/china/summit_1204/ip04_1440.htm

35. JSE Securities Exchange (2004, May), *Socially responsible investment index*. The specific criteria for inclusion on the SRI index were developed in reliance on a number of sources, including the Institute of Directors in Southern Africa's *King Report on Corporate Governance* (November 1994; revised March 2002). In recognition of South African realities, the SRI index takes an incremental approach to compliance. To be included, a company's corporate governance practices must comply with—or within two years plan to comply with—at least 60 percent of the elements of the *King Report* that relate to the board, board committees, and the separation of management, oversight, and audit functions.

36. OECD (2001, March), *Rights and equitable treatment of shareholders: Recent advances in Latin America* (second meeting of the Latin American Corporate Governance Roundtable) (regarding Argentina, Chile, and Brazil); and Institute of International Finance (IIF) Equity Advisory Group (2003, May), *Corporate governance in Mexico: An investor perspective* (regarding Mexico). In November 2003 the Latin American Corporate Governance Roundtable unveiled a blueprint for reform in the region. It includes calls to safeguard minority investors, curb cronyism, adopt international accounting standards, and establish a more muscular regulatory function. See

OECD (2003), *White paper on corporate governance in Latin America.* In a parallel development, the Financial Stability Forum (FSF) held its third Latin American regional meeting in Santiago, Chile, in November 2003. While noting the improved implementation of auditor oversight mechanisms throughout the region and the continuing effort to reach consensus on accounting standards, the FSF underscored that strengthening corporate efficiency and transparency, as well as improving judicial and legal systems, are necessary to bolster investor confidence in Latin America. See Financial Stability Forum, Press Release: (2003, November 17–18), *Third FSF Regional Meeting, Latin America.* In 2002 a group of sixteen asset management firms with U.S. $70 billion in equity in emerging and developing markets released a set of corporate governance guidelines that addresses, among other things, the treatment of minority shareholders, the structure and responsibilities of boards of directors, and the transparency of ownership and control of companies. *See* IIF Equity Advisory Group (2002, February), *Policies for corporate governance and transparency in emerging markets.* The group is encouraging regulators and companies in Latin American markets to implement the code.

37. Organisation for Economic Co-Operation and Development (OECD) Steering Group on Corporate Governance, *OECD principles of corporate governance* (April 1999, revised April 2004), available at http://www.oecd.org/dataoecd/32/18/31557724.pdf

IV
APPLICATION AND EXTENSIONS OF CORPORATE GOVERNANCE

11

Internal Investigations in the Spotlight

JONATHAN C. DICKEY and WENDY HOULE

In today's toxic environment of corporate scandal and aggressive prosecutions, the discovery of potential misconduct within your organization requires swift and sure investigation, and prompt remedial action. This has become an essential feature of good corporate governance.

Recent SEC enforcement actions make clear that in addition to strong "self-policing," companies will be expected to promptly "self-report" to the government. It is now a given that prompt disclosure of the company's discovery of potential misconduct, and the results of the company's internal investigation, are essential to minimize the company's exposure to government sanctions.

As important as it is to get the facts quickly and accurately, it is also important to demonstrate the company's cooperation with any government inquiries into suspected wrongdoing, and to avoid the kinds of mistakes that recently led to huge penalties against Banc of America Securities and other respondents for allegedly having failed to timely and completely cooperate with the Securities and Exchange Commission. Today the SEC's "cooperation" mandate has become an unfortunate game of "gotcha," as the staff makes increasingly onerous demands on the company. Any lapses in the company's compliance with such requests can quickly become evidence of the company's alleged "noncooperation." You can do an excellent job of investigating, but if it is not packaged and presented to the commission with optimum care, you may still pay a price. This chapter will discuss some of the ways to deal effectively with the SEC and to fulfill the letter and spirit of the commission's new co-operation mandate.

Perhaps not as well documented as the SEC's "self-policing" and "self-reporting" standards for the conduct of internal investigations are the evolving standards of corporate compliance that are the metaphorical "canary in the coal mine," the means by which corporate misconduct can be detected early on and promptly remedied. These corporate compliance policies and procedures need to be in place and operational months, even years, before a corporation is faced with material allegations of misconduct. The need for strong compliance mechanisms is underscored by recent changes to the U.S. Sentencing Guidelines. Below, we will discuss some of the new amendments to the Sentencing Guidelines that may require changes to public companies' compliance programs going forward.

In light of all these new pronouncements and guidelines, this chapter sets forth a brief discussion of "best practices" for the conduct of internal investigations in the new era. While there is no "one size fits all" checklist for how to conduct an effective internal investigation, the guidance we offer is designed to serve you well in the typical investigative situation.

ESTABLISHING A CULTURE OF COMPLIANCE AND IMPLEMENTING EFFECTIVE COMPLIANCE POLICIES AND PROCEDURES

An effective response to the discovery of suspected misconduct begins well before suspicions are raised or allegations made. The organization's responsibilities start with the implementation of a program to prevent and detect violations of the law. The existence of an effective compliance program will be a key factor in the government's decision on whether to bring an enforcement action against the company, or to bring criminal charges. Following is a summary of recent government pronouncements on how public companies should establish and implement "effective" corporate compliance programs.

U.S. Sentencing Guidelines

Since the first issuance of the U.S. Sentencing Guidelines in 1991, the U.S. Sentencing Commission has set the standards for corporate governance in the United States. The SEC and other government agencies look to the Sentencing Guidelines as the leading "benchmark" for evaluating the adequacy of corporate compliance. In April 2004 the United States Sentencing Commission (USSC) amended the existing guidelines for sentencing organizations, specifically, the requirements for an "effective compliance program." U.S. Sentencing Guidelines Manual, Section 8B2.1 (2004) (hereafter "Guidelines"). These new standards may have a profound impact on the way public companies manage their compliance function, and how they react to allegations of misconduct. The full text of the Guidelines may be found on the Sentencing Commission's website, www.ussc.gov.

An "effective compliance program" is a potential mitigating factor in the sentencing of an organization for accounting fraud or other criminal misconduct, and the lack of such a program can lead to enhanced criminal fines and penalties. The revised Guidelines not only make the requirements for an effective compliance program more stringent, but they broaden the purpose of the compliance program to encompass the prevention and detection of *any* violations of law (including rules and regulations).[1]

An effective compliance program must (1) exercise due diligence to prevent and detect violations of law, and (2) "promote an organizational culture that encourages a commitment to compliance with the laws." Section 8B2.1(b). The amended Guidelines retain the seven minimum steps necessary to satisfy these two prongs that are found in existing guidelines, but provide additional specifics to meet each step. Guidelines, Section 8B2.1(a)–(b).

Step 1 for an "effective compliance program," and the reduction of penalties, is to establish "compliance standards and procedures to prevent and detect violations of law." "Compliance standards and procedures" are conduct standards and control systems "that are reasonably capable of reducing the likelihood of violations of law." Guidelines, Section 8B2.1(b)(1).

Step 2—often overlooked in large corporations—requires the organizational leadership[2] of the company *and* the company's governing authority (that is, the board of directors) to be knowledgeable about the program. Specific high-level personnel must be assigned *direct responsibility* for the implementation and effectiveness of the program, while the *board* must "exercise reasonable oversight." In addition, the responsible individuals must be given adequate resources and authority to carry out their responsibility, and should report *directly* to the board. Guidelines, Section 8B2.1(b)(2).

Step 3 is related to Step 2's focus on a top-down culture of compliance. This step requires the organization to "use reasonable efforts" not to allow "any individual whom the organization knew, or should have known through the exercise of due diligence, has a history of engaging in violations of law or other conduct inconsistent with an effective program" to be in a position of substantial authority within the organization.[3] Therefore, in hiring and promoting, the organization should consider: the recency of an individual's violations or misconduct, if any; the relatedness of the individual's misconduct to the specific responsibilities in the organization; and whether the individual has engaged in a pattern of such misconduct. Guidelines, Section 8B2.1(b)(3) and app. 4(c).

Steps 4 through 6 relate to the content of the programs and the dissemination of the program's standards to personnel. Step 4 requires communication of the compliance program to personnel and adequate training of personnel, including the board, upper-level management, employees, and, where appropriate, agents of the organization. Pursuant to Step 5, the organization must establish auditing and monitoring systems designed to detect violations of law, and must periodically evaluate the systems to assess their effectiveness. The internal systems should provide guidance for behavior and a mechanism for anyone to *anonymously* report potential or actual violations. In conjunction with this, Step 6 requires the internal systems to include both disciplinary measures and appropriate incentives for compliance with programs. Guidelines, Section 8B2.1(b)(4)-(6).

Finally, under Step 7, the organization must take reasonable steps to respond appropriately to violations of law and to prevent further similar violations of law, including any necessary modifications to the compliance programs. Guidelines, Section 8B2.1(b)(7). Similarly, the amendment separately requires ongoing risk assessment and modifications to ensure an effective compliance program. Guidelines, Section 8B2.1(c). Risk assessment includes consideration of the type of business (and the potential violations attendant to that business) and the prior history of the organization. Guidelines, Section 8B2.1(c), app. 6(A).

Each of these steps in the amended Sentencing Guidelines attempt to put "teeth" into corporate compliance—and also hold senior management and the board accountable for supervision and oversight of the compliance system. To borrow an old adage, "An ounce of prevention is worth a pound of cure." All companies should carefully review their existing compliance programs in light of these new guidelines.

The SEC's "Seaboard Report"

The Guidelines are not the only example of the government placing high importance on the existence of an effective compliance program designed to prevent and detect violations.

In October 2001 the SEC issued a "Report of Investigation Pursuant to Section 21(a) of the Securities Exchange Act of 1934."[4] This report, known as the "Seaboard Report" after the Seaboard Corporation (Seaboard), the public company involved in the proceeding, derived from a cease-and-desist proceeding against the former controller of Seaboard's subsidiary. The former controller caused Seaboard's books and records to be inaccurate and its periodic reports to be misstated, and then covered up these facts. Notably, the SEC decided not to take action against Seaboard, and detailed its reasoning in a "Statement on the Relationship of Cooperation to Agency Enforcement Decisions." This statement sets forth a blueprint for companies dealing with suspicions of misconduct. It stresses four key concepts—self-policing, self-reporting, cooperation, and remediation—and lists a detailed set of factors the SEC may consider when bringing an enforcement action. The SEC warned that enforcement decisions are highly fact-specific and that its criteria are nothing more than points for consideration, but this report remains a good indicator of SEC concerns and expectations.

While the Seaboard Report is discussed in greater detail below, the first of its four concepts, self-policing, is relevant here as it echoes the "effective compliance program" standards in the Sentencing Guidelines. The Seaboard Report notes that public companies should institute effective compliance procedures *prior* to the discovery of alleged wrongdoing, asking: "What compliance procedures were in place to prevent the misconduct now uncovered?" and "Why did those procedures fail to stop or inhibit the wrongful conduct?" In a variation on the "culture of compliance" standards in the Guidelines, the report queries: "How did the misconduct arise? Is it the result of pressure placed on employees to achieve specific results, or a tone of lawlessness set by those in control of the company?" Other points of consideration touch upon the seniority of the individuals involved in the misconduct and whether the misconduct was a symptom of the way the entity conducts business. Today's companies must be aware of these concerns, and should probe their own compliance structure and conduct.

The Department of Justice's "Thompson Memo"

On January 20, 2003, Deputy Attorney General Larry D. Thompson issued a memorandum setting forth factors that should be considered by federal prosecutors in deciding whether to charge a business organization with a criminal offense (Thompson Memo).[5] Developed from the combined efforts of the DOJ's Corporate Fraud Task Force and the Attorney General's Advisory Committee, the Thompson Memo places increased emphasis on a corporation's cooperation with government authorities, but discusses a number of factors a prosecutor should consider when deciding whether to bring criminal charges against a corporate defendant. Among these factors is the "existence and adequacy of the corporation's compliance program" and the corporation's history of similar conduct.

Like the Sentencing Guidelines, the Thompson Memo emphasizes the importance of keeping employees fully educated on the company's compliance policies and management's commitment to those policies. As well, the Thompson Memo stresses the importance of establishing effective informational and reporting systems. The DOJ will not accept cookie-cutter programs; rather, each organization's program must be designed with an eye toward the particular business and its specific susceptibilities to criminal misconduct. The Thompson Memo urges corporations to meet with state and federal agencies that have the expertise to evaluate the adequacy of a program. Finally, the company should question not only whether the program is adequately designed, but whether it has been adequately enforced (that is, "Does the corporation's compliance program work?"). "Paper" compliance simply is not enough.

While the existence of an effective compliance program does not absolve a corporation of responsibility, it may help curtail prosecution against a corporation under a *respondeat superior* theory for the act of a rogue employee. At the least, it is a factor going to the severity of the charges brought against the corporation.

INVESTIGATION AND COOPERATION

We have discussed the steps a corporation should take to prevent and detect violations. We now turn to the responsibilities attendant to the investigation of suspected wrongdoing. An organization has dual roles in the investigation of misconduct: (1) the role of a fact-finder, conducting a thorough and objective internal investigation to reach the bottom of the allegations and potential problems; and (2) the role of a "self-reporting" agent of the government, providing prompt, voluntary, and comprehensive cooperation to investigating agencies.

Internal Investigations Generally

The Seaboard Report provides guidance for a corporation's conduct in an internal investigation and underscores that the manner in which an investigation is carried out can be a factor in the decision to bring an enforcement action against a corporation.[6] The Seaboard Report warns that the SEC will carefully consider *how* the internal investigation proceeds and *who* is involved. Among the relevant factors relating to *how* the investigation proceeds are the timeliness of the corporation's response to the discovery of misconduct, the steps taken to inform the audit committee and the board of directors, the steps taken to ferret out the necessary information, the limitations placed on the scope of the company's review, and whether the company did a thorough review of the extent of damage and consequences of the conduct. Pursuant to the Seaboard Report, the SEC also will consider *who* was involved in the investigation—whether the management, the board, or a committee of outside directors oversaw the investigation, and whether outside persons were retained. If outside consultants or counsel were used, an inquiry will be made into their independence.

Prompt "Self-Reporting"
Seaboard's response provides a model for the type of action a company should take when confronted with suspected wrongdoing: "Within a week of learning about the apparent misconduct, the company's internal auditors had conducted a preliminary review and had advised company management who, in turn advised the Board's audit committee." The full board was advised, and the board promptly hired an outside law firm. Additionally, within a couple of weeks of the first report of wrongdoing, and upon confirming the need for restatement in its internal investigation, the company disclosed publicly and to the SEC that its statements would be restated.

This final step of self-reporting to the government and to the public is clearly a key factor for both the SEC and the DOJ. The Seaboard Report asks:

"Did the company promptly, completely and effectively disclose the existence of the misconduct to the public, to regulators and to self-regulators?" The SEC has even taken pains to reward companies for their prompt investigations and disclosures. In an April 2004 speech, SEC director for the Division of Enforcement, Stephen Cutler, praised Reliant Resources for having voluntarily undertaken an internal investigation into "roundtrip trades," and when the internal investigation revealed that the roundtrip transactions had occurred, for promptly reporting this to the SEC and to the public in a press release. Likewise, the Thompson Memo impresses upon prosecutors the importance of a company's "timely and voluntary disclosure of wrongdoing."

On the flip side, any significant delay in "self-reporting" can penalize the company. Under the Sentencing Guidelines, for example, there is no downward adjustment in sentencing for an effective compliance program if, after becoming aware of the offense, the organization unreasonably delays in reporting to the government. Guidelines, Section 8C2.5(f)(1)–(3).

Independence

The importance of having independent directors, auditors, and counsel involved in an internal investigation cannot be understated. Not only is this subject important to the SEC, it is also the subject of recent attention from courts in derivative actions.

For example, in In re Oracle Corp. Derivative Litigation, 824 A.2d 917 (Del. Ch. 2003), the court held that the Special Litigation Committee (SLC) of three outside directors created by Oracle was not independent, and, on that basis, rejected the SLC's report and recommendation. The SLC included two outside directors employed as tenured professors at Stanford University, an institution that had ties with a number of the targeted individuals: one was a fellow Stanford University professor, one an alum and frequent donor, and the third a generous benefactor. Although there was no explicit evidence of a direct financial or business relationship between the SLC members and the individuals under investigation, the court concluded that the entangled relationships between Oracle, its directors, and Stanford University raised sufficient questions as to the disinterestedness of the SLC.

Similar to the judicial skepticism reflected in the Oracle decision, in Biondi v. Scrushy, 820 A.2d 1148 (Del. Ch. 2003), the Chancery Court questioned a number of actions taken in regard to HealthSouth's investigation of potential claims against Richard Scrushy, its former CEO. One member of the SLC was a close personal friend of Scrushy and the other a chairman of a foundation to which HealthSouth, under Scrushy, had contributed significant amounts of money. And the same day HealthSouth formed its SLC, it hired outside counsel to investigate the alleged wrongdoing. Only six days after forming the SLC and hiring outside counsel, and before the SLC completed its investigation, HealthSouth issued a press release disclaiming any wrongdoing on the part of Scrushy and the company as a whole. A couple of weeks later, still before the SLC completed its investigation, HealthSouth issued yet another press release proclaiming that outside counsel had cleared Scrushy of any wrongdoing. The court concluded that under these circumstances, in particular the public statements of exoneration, there was no way it could find that the SLC acted independently, and it rejected a motion to stay the litigation until the SLC completed its investigation.

Finally, in a recent decision by the Southern District of Florida, *Klein v. FPL Group, Inc.,* 2004 WL 302292 (S.D. Fla. Feb. 5, 2004), the court questioned the independence of both the Evaluation Committee (EC) assigned to investigate derivative claims related to payments under a Long-Term Incentive Plan (LTIP) and the outside counsel hired to assist in the investigation. First, the EC and the board consisted of those individuals who had initially approved the LTIP and the payments under the plan. Second, the members of the EC were nominated by the individual that received the most significant payments, and it was unclear whether the board or the EC had decision-making authority in regard to the derivative claims. Third, original counsel for the EC was the law firm that advised on the LTIP, and substitute counsel was hired approximately eight months into the investigation. Although new counsel reinterviewed witnesses and reviewed thousands of documents, it did not revisit the formation of the EC or the issue of the EC's independence. Additionally, new counsel was hired to represent both the board and the EC, and it drafted the report and recommendation presented to the board. According to the court, new counsel's dual representation made it nearly impossible to give neutral advice to the board. The court found that under the totality of the circumstances, the company failed to establish the independence of the EC and the decision-making process.

Cooperation with Government Agencies

Although an effective compliance program, self-policing, and voluntary disclosure are important factors in minimizing the potential exposure of a company to a governmental action, recent SEC enforcement actions make clear that an equally key factor is ongoing cooperation with the government in connection with the government's inquiry into the alleged wrongdoing.

SEC investigations frequently begin with a request for informal cooperation by a corporation in providing information to the SEC staff. While a corporation and its employees are under no obligation to comply with such a request, as the discussion below makes clear, it is usually in the company's interest to do so. The securities laws also permit the SEC to issue subpoenas to compel the production of documents and to compel witnesses to appear and to testify under oath in connection with investigations of possible violations of securities laws. If the staff believes that securities law violations have occurred, they will recommend to the SEC that an enforcement action be brought. If approved, the staff will be authorized to commence an action, usually in a federal district court. The SEC may seek injunctive relief, disgorgement of the money obtained as a result of the alleged violations, corrective disclosure, a structural change in corporate governance, a bar on an individual's service as an officer or director, and/or civil money penalties.[7]

The Seaboard Report devotes a considerable amount of its discussion to cooperation, detailing the questions the SEC will ask regarding the company's voluntary cooperation with its investigation: Did the company make the results of its investigation available for review? Voluntarily disclose information not specifically requested? Encourage employees to cooperate? Seaboard itself "pledged and gave complete cooperation":

> It provided the staff with all information relevant to the underlying violations. Among other things, the company produced the details of its internal investigation, including notes and transcripts of interviews of [the former controller] and others; and it did not invoke the attorney-client privilege, work product protection, or other privileges or protections with respect to any facts uncovered in the investigation.

Implicit in this view of cooperation is that "full" cooperation may require the company to waive its attorney-client privileges in connection with the investigation—and put those same privileges at risk in any parallel civil class action litigation. Recent court decisions have made clear that the voluntary production of otherwise privileged information to the government may constitute a waiver of privilege in other proceedings.[8] Accordingly, companies must carefully weigh the risks in deciding how much privileged information it will share with regulators.[9]

The SEC has not simply paid lip service to these principles of cooperation. On the contrary, it has imposed harsh penalties on uncooperative companies. A few recent examples:

American International Group. Beginning in July 2000 the SEC issued voluntary requests for documents to American International Group, Inc. (AIG). Document subpoenas to AIG followed in November 2001. In November 2002, AIG provided a sworn certification that its production of documents pursuant to the requests and initial subpoenas was complete. Yet, AIG subsequently produced a "large quantity of documents, many of which should have been produced before the certification was made." The SEC discovered that AIG had not searched the files of key individuals, had not searched locations in which responsive documents were likely to be found, and had not conducted an adequate search of the relevant computer drives prior to providing the sworn certification. These failures resulted in AIG producing documents two to three years after the first requests and subpoenas from the SEC. The SEC also found that AIG had failed to produce a white paper that was "directly relevant" to a position taken by AIG in the SEC proceedings, and that AIG was aware of the white paper's existence from near the beginning of the investigation.

Ultimately, in September 2003, the SEC issued a cease-and-desist order and instituted civil proceedings against AIG. AIG, anticipating the actions, offered to settle. The SEC accepted AIG's offer, finding that the need for relief was heightened by the "manner in which [AIG] conducted itself" during the investigation. The SEC ordered AIG to pay disgorgement of $100,000 and prejudgment interest. More important, due to its noncooperation in the investigation, AIG was required to pay a $10 *million* civil penalty. In re Am. Int'l Group, Inc., Exch. Act. Release No. 48477 (September 11, 2003).

Banc of America Securities. The SEC's investigation of Banc of America Securities LLC (BAS) began with SEC requests for documents, including e-mails, for seven managers over a three-year period. BAS undertook a "prolonged process for recovering e-mail and having it reviewed" for privilege and responsiveness. BAS missed more than one deadline for responding to the SEC's requests, but often failed to request extensions of time or otherwise explain the delay to the SEC staff. Six months after the initial request, only a small amount of the requested e-mail had been produced, and it was ultimately discovered that some responsive documents had been withheld. Although BAS blamed this on an unintentional technical glitch, the SEC determined that this was inaccurate. Production was not substantially complete until almost two years after the SEC's initial request. The SEC found that "BAS has repeatedly failed promptly to furnish documents that have been requested by the staff," and, therefore, BAS had engaged in a willful violation of Sections 17(a) and (b) of the Securities Exchange Act of 1934, under which the SEC is authorized to examine a broker-dealer's records, subject only to a reasonableness requirement. As a result of the violation, BAS was ordered to cease and desist from its action, censured pursuant to Section 15(b)(4), and ordered to pay a civil penalty of $10 million. In re Banc of Am. Sec. LLC, Exch. Act Release No. 49386 (March 10, 2004).

Lucent. In May 2004 the SEC imposed a $25 million penalty for Lucent's failure to cooperate. According to the SEC press release, Lucent: (1) provided incomplete document production, producing key documents after the relevant witness's testimony and failing to preserve relevant data; (2) after reaching an agreement in principle with the SEC to settle, Lucent's former chairman and CEO effectively denied the accounting fraud had occurred, thereby "undermin[ing] both the spirit and letter of its agreement" with the SEC; (3) after reaching an agreement in principle with the SEC to settle, Lucent voluntarily expanded the scope of employees that could be indemnified against the consequences of the SEC action; and (4) failed to provide timely and full disclosure regarding indemnification. Lucent Settles SEC Enforcement Action Charging the Company with $1.1 Billion Accounting Fraud (May 17, 2004); SEC Litig. Release No. 18715 (May 17, 2004).[10]

In light of these severe penalties for noncooperation, the SEC's cooperation mandate must be taken with the utmost seriousness. As well, cooperation will affect the company's potential criminal exposure. According to the Thompson Memo, "willingness to cooperate with the government's investigation" may be a factor in determining whether to charge a corporation. Cooperation may include identifying culprits, making witnesses available, disclosing the results of an internal investigation, and waiving attorney-client privileges and work product protections. On this last point, the Thompson Memo explains that while the DOJ does not consider waiver of privilege and work product protection an absolute requirement, "prosecutors should consider the willingness of a corporation to waive such protection when necessary to provide timely and complete information as one factor in evaluating the corporation's cooperation."[11]

Finally, full cooperation also helps an organization's culpability score under the Sentencing Guidelines. To count, however, the cooperation must begin when the company is officially notified of criminal investigation and include disclosure of all pertinent information. The recent amendments to the Guidelines add a provision to address privilege and work product issues. Consistent with the DOJ's position in the Thompson Memo, the Guidelines state that waiver of the attorney-client privilege and of work product protections "is not a prerequisite to a reduction in culpability score under subsection (g)[,]" but in some circumstances "may be required in order to satisfy the requirements of cooperation." Guidelines, Section 8C2.5(f), app. 12.

REMEDIATION AND RESTITUTION

The SEC, the DOJ, and common sense dictate that a corporation not only must identify and report the problem, but take prompt remedial action. A complete remediation plan includes taking steps to ensure that the misconduct is not repeated.

The Seaboard Report reveals that the SEC does not believe a corporation's obligations cease with the unveiling of misconduct, even if those responsible are charged by government authorities. The SEC not only looks to the action that the company has taken to remove those responsible for the misconduct, but also considers the steps the company has taken to develop more effective internal controls and procedures in response to the misconduct. The SEC approved of Seaboard's strengthening of its financial reporting processes with a detailed closing process, consolidation of its subsidiary accounting under the parent CPA, the hiring of additional finance personnel, the redesign of minimum audit requirements, and the requirement that the parent company is controller interview and approve all senior accounting personnel.

The SEC also implicitly recognized the importance of remedial measures in its enforcement action against Gateway, Inc. (Gateway). On November 13, 2003, the SEC instituted proceedings against Gateway, alleging that the company made misleading disclosures and reported false financial information in order to meet Wall Street's expectations in the year 2000. Gateway offered to settle with the SEC, and the SEC accepted the offer, stating:

> During the early stages of the staff's investigation, the Company's cooperation was not exemplary. In determining to accept Gateway's offer, however, the Commission has considered these undertakings, the limited duration of the violations, and the remedial measures undertaken by Gateway's current management and

board of directors, including the recent restatement of Gateway's financial statements, and substantial actions that Gateway has taken to enhance Gateway's internal controls and corporate governance.

The Gateway release suggests that subsequent remedial measures following noncooperation can undo at least some of the damage caused by earlier non-cooperation. In re Gateway, Inc., Sec. Act Release No. 8338 (November 13, 2003).

In the criminal context, the company's efforts to provide "restitution and remediation" also are factors in the decision whether to charge a company with a criminal violation. The Thompson Memo cites that "in determining whether or not a corporation should be prosecuted, a prosecutor may consider whether meaningful remedial measures have been taken, including employee discipline and full restitution." The Thompson Memo theorizes that companies that truly recognize the seriousness of their misconduct and accept responsibility "should be taking steps to implement the personnel, operational, and organizational changes necessary to establish an awareness among employees that criminal conduct will not be tolerated." Key factors for the DOJ are whether the wrong-doers were disciplined, whether necessary reforms to the company's program have been implemented, and whether the corporation has made restitution.

Federal statutes also provide companies with an additional motivation to take "timely and appropriate remedial action." Section 10A of the Securities Exchange Act of 1934, part of the Private Securities Litigation Reform Act of 1995, requires auditors to report certain suspected "illegal acts" to the audited company, and, under specific circumstances, notice to the SEC. Pursuant to Section 10A, if an auditor determines that it is likely an illegal act has occurred, it must inform the management of the company and assure that the audit committee or the board also is adequately informed. 15 U.S.C., Section 78j-1(b)(1).[12] Although the statute does not specify the type of remedial action required, supportive authority suggests that "possible remedial actions include disciplinary action against involved personnel, seeking restitution, adoption of preventative or corrective company policies and modifications of specific control procedures." Statement of Auditing Standards No. 54, Section 54.17.

"BEST PRACTICES" FOR THE CONDUCT OF INTERNAL INVESTIGATIONS

Respond Deliberatively, Not Hastily

First, companies must decide on a strategy for approaching the problem and assemble a team to respond to the inevitable inquiries. In doing so, companies should avoid making hasty statements about the nature of the problem or the propriety of the action. As the *Klein* decision involving HealthSouth discussed above indicates, statements of exoneration or denial of wrongdoing could be viewed as having compromised the organization's independence and that of any independent committee investigating the conduct. Further, statements to the government always must be accurate and complete, as mistakes are devastating to credibility.

The company also must think carefully about the composition of the investigating committee. For example, do any of the members have other business or social connections to the individuals under investigation? Was any member of the committee on the board or committee that approved of the action that is the subject of the investigation? The board must ensure that sufficient resources and authority are transferred to the investigating committee so as to avoid any implication that the result is a foregone conclusion. This is particularly important if a derivative suit is a possibility or reality.

Despite the powerful emphasis the SEC has placed on speedy reporting of alleged wrongdoing, it is incumbent on the company to pause, reflect, consult with counsel, and then decide on a course of conduct. A carefully focused investigation requires forethought—and avoids an unnecessarily overbroad and "over the top" inquisition into marginally relevant matters.

Hire a Lawyer

Companies are well advised to hire outside counsel to assist, but this also must be done deliberately and thoughtfully. Counsel should be given a clear mandate, and there must be no ambiguity surrounding who counsel is hired to represent. Counsel should be independent and not have any appearance of conflicting interests due to representing both the investigative committee as well as other constituencies (for example, the board, the company, or any member of management), nor should counsel have any history with those involved or the transaction at issue. For example, outside counsel should not be the firm that advised on the transaction that is now disputed. Additionally, the board or the investigating committee that hires outside counsel should be provided with more than one recommendation. You want to avoid the appearance that counsel was handpicked by the CEO or some other potentially interested party.

Secure Written Records

In conducting an internal investigation, or when faced with the prospect of a government investigation or civil suit, an early and important step is to identify employees whose paper and electronic files should be secured and reviewed for relevant information. Include the assistants and secretaries for key employees, and do not forget electronic files, including e-mails, individual hard drives, and shared drives. If any employees have recently left the organization, request that their hard drives be imaged and saved or otherwise preserved. The worst document is the one that has been lost or destroyed—and as the recent sanctions against Lucent demonstrate, companies will pay a steep price for having failed to adequately "lock down" relevant records.

Hire a Forensic Auditor If Accounting Issues Are Involved

In a financial misstatement situation, it is important to have extremely competent forensic accounting experts familiar with the financial and accounting matters involved. Forensic accountants can quickly assess potential fraudulent accounting and provide invaluable early guidance on the nature of the accounting issues and potential magnitude of the problem. They also may serve as important contributors in interviews with key witnesses, and in discussions with the audit committee and outside auditors.[13]

Be Actively Involved

Audit committee members, or members of other investigating committees, should have hands-on involvement in the investigatory process. Members should participate in key witness interviews, consult regularly with outside advisers, and attend any informational meetings. Members also should review all key documentary evidence and have a solid deliberative process before making final judgments.

Fix the Problem

If, in fact, there is an underlying business or financial statement problem, then it is important to correct it at the earliest possible time. Corrective action may include restating financials, disciplining or firing individuals involved in the transgression, redesigning control and reporting systems, and/or restitution. Such corrections not only make good business sense, but they may insulate the corporation from several forms of liability as a "controlling" person. Moreover, early corrective action will demonstrate good faith and negate any inference that enforcement action against the company is warranted to prevent future violations.

Be Forthcoming and Cooperative

If a problem is identified, prompt and voluntary disclosure to the public and to the relevant government authorities may be a necessary step. Early disclosure of problems often can greatly reduce the company's civil and criminal exposures, including reductions of fines, civil money penalties, and civil damages caused by the wrongdoing or by delayed disclosure.

In addition to prompt disclosure, the SEC's message is clear: cooperate, cooperate, cooperate. Failure to cooperate with investigating officials can lead to enhanced enforcement remedies and multimillion-dollar penalties. The company should make an early decision on whether to share the results of its own investigation with investigating authorities and encourage employees to cooperate with government investigators. The company also should keep open clear channels of communication with the government, assuring the government that the company is endeavoring to comply and providing prompt notification if problems arise.

Worry about Privilege

Of course, full cooperation with the government is easier said than done. Inevitably, a company under investigation will be faced with the decision of whether to waive attorney-client privilege and/or work product protection. Although the government has taken pains to assure corporations that waiver is not required, it also has stressed, in multiple formats, that waiver is a sign of cooperation and may be necessary in some circumstances. The advice of counsel will be essential in making the determination of whether such protections should be waived.

Enhancements to Compliance Programs

Finally, do not assume that once a particular problem is solved, the company's obligations are complete. Remember that effective compliance programs require frequent monitoring and updating, with new management and employees informed and trained. Also, once implicated in misconduct, the judge, jury, or the federal government will be less inclined to give a corporation a pass should it happen again. This means that a company that has a history of misconduct or compliance failures must place increased emphasis on internal controls and corporate compliance, and on maintaining an effective, anonymous internal reporting system.

CONCLUSION

Public companies are under intense scrutiny when faced with suspected wrongdoing. Directors and officers must be aware of the obligations that are attendant to, and potential pitfalls that arise from, the investigation and reporting of possible misconduct. The government's new "rules of engagement" make this process fraught with peril for company directors and officers, committee members, and investigating counsel. Acting quickly to detect and remediate problems, disclosing suspected law violations promptly to government authorities, and cooperating with any regulatory investigations, are key to minimizing the company's risks.

NOTES

1. The existing Guidelines limit the purpose of an effective compliance program to the prevention and detection of *criminal* violations.

2. Organizational leadership includes high-level personnel of the organization and a unit of the organization and those with substantial authority within a specific area, for examples sales manager, plant manager.

3. Note also that if a high-level person was involved in a violation, the amendment imposes a rebuttable presumption that effective programs did not exist. This is a change from existing guidelines precluding an organization from receiving any compliance credit if a high-level person was involved.

4. Report of investigation pursuant to Section 21(a) of the Securities Exchange Act of 1934 and commission statement on the relationship of cooperation to agency enforcement decisions (2001, October 23), Exch. Act. Release No. 44969.

5. Principles of federal prosecution of business organizations (2003, January 20), memorandum from Larry D. Thompson, deputy attorney general, to heads of department components, United States Attorneys.

6. In contrast, the DOJ in the Thompson Memo encourages corporations to conduct internal investigations, but does not discuss this as being a significant factor in deciding whether to bring criminal charges.

7. While the SEC does not have independent authority to prosecute criminal cases, willful violation of federal securities laws can be prosecuted as a crime by the DOJ. The SEC has a close working relationship with federal prosecutors and frequently refers more egregious violations of the federal securities laws to them. The most commonly prosecuted areas of securities laws violations are insider trading, financial fraud, and unregistered securities offerings.

8. See, for examples *McKesson HBOC, Inc. v. Superior Court*, 9 Cal. Rptr. 3d 812, 819–21 (Cal. Ct. App. 2004) (company waived attorney-client privilege and work product protection for interview memoranda and audit committee report produced to U.S. Attorney and SEC even though the disclosures were made pursuant to confidentiality agreements); In re Columbia/HCA Healthcare Corp. Billing Practices Litig., 293 F.3d 289, 304–07 (6th Cir. 2002) (defendant waived attorney-client privilege and work product protection for documents produced to the DOJ pursuant to a confidentiality agreement).

9. This weighing of the risks has often resulted in the decision to waive privilege entirely, in the interest of demonstrating full cooperation. For a recent discussion of this subject, see M. McDonough (2004, May), A tell-all approach: Opening corporate investigations fosters credibility with the feds, *ABA Journal*.

10. Other SEC enforcement actions resulting in penalties for a lack of cooperation include a) Xerox ($10 million penalty for its actions, including a "lack of full cooperation in the investigation." SEC Litig. Release No. 17465 (April 11, 2002)); and b) Dynergy ($3 million penalty, reflecting, in part, "dissatisfaction with Dynergy's lack of full cooperation in the early stages of the Commission's investigation." SEC Litig. Release No. 17744 (September 25, 2003)).

11. The DOJ expects companies to avoid conduct that appears to assist or protect culpable employees, including the advancement of attorneys' fees, or providing information from the government to the employees through a joint defense agreement. Companies must be mindful that these factors will weigh in favor of bringing serious charges against an organization.

12. After informing the appropriate parties, if the auditor concludes that the illegal act has a material effect on the company's financial statements, and the company has not taken "timely and appropriate remedial actions with respect to the illegal act," then the auditor shall directly report its conclusions to the board of directors. 15 U.S.C., Section 78j-1(b)(2). In that circumstance, the board of directors that receives such a report must notify the SEC within one business day after receipt of the report. If this action is not taken, the auditor shall notify the SEC directly. 15 U.S.C., Section 78j-1(b)(3).

13. For additional commentary on the use of forensic accountants in internal investigations, see Suzanne McGee (2004, May–June), Ding-dong: It's your forensic accountant, *Corporate Board Member*, 22.

12

Guiding Directors in Corporate Solvency and Insolvency

MYRON M. SHEINFELD

Private enterprise, usually conducted through the corporate vehicle, involves responsibility and ownership. Winston Churchill said, "Some see private enterprise as a predatory target to be shot, others as a cow to be milked, but few see it as a sturdy horse pulling the wagon." The director and the board can be likened to those responsible for maintaining and nurturing the "sturdy horse." The investors, or shareholders, own the "sturdy horse" and have the right and responsibility to expect that directors and the board, who are responsible for maintaining and nurturing their investment, act within the parameters of acceptable corporate governance and within the standards and rules that have been set forth as tests for their conduct. The directors and the board have the responsibility to supervise the enterprise management, which has overall responsibility, on a day-to-day basis, for the "sturdy horse pulling the wagon."

Recent developments, including the enactment of the Sarbanes-Oxley legislation, have created a day-to-day general public awareness of the concept of corporate governance. Corporate governance deals with corporate legitimacy, credibility, and duties and responsibilities of the corporate participants. The corporation exists for profitability to the investors, stable operations, creation of jobs, access to capital markets for growth, and repayment of borrowings. Corporate governance affects corporate management, from the chief executive officer to the directors and the board. No participant in the corporate structure is immune.

THE DIRECTOR'S ROLE

A director, as a member of a board of directors, is the overseer of the business and management of a corporation. Although corporations employ management staff and have chief executive officers, chief financial officers, and chief operation officers, the corporation's board as a whole and each director individually has the responsibility for management of the corporation's affairs.

Fiduciary Duties

Directors have duties and responsibilities that are legally imposed on them. These duties and responsibilities are those of a fiduciary. A fiduciary is a person or group of persons who have a special relationship of trust to another group of persons or entities. Fiduciaries must act in carrying out their responsibilities with the utmost good faith, honesty, and strict adherence to their duties. Because directors have fiduciary responsibilities, they have a special relation of trust and are required to act in good faith and responsibly to the beneficiaries of the trust to whom they owe these fiduciary duties. The responsibilities of fiduciaries are also set forth by various statutes in those states where the corporation is domiciled and by court decisions on that subject. These rules, statutes, and court decisions help directors determine how, when, why, and what duties and responsibilities they have and to whom these duties are owed.

In the instance of a solvent corporation, directors in performing their duties and responsibilities owe fiduciary duties and responsibilities to the investors, or shareholders, who own the corporation. This is understandable because shareholders made a monetary investment to acquire equity and ownership in the corporation, and by their vote select and determine who are to be directors to whom they entrust the control over management and supervision of the corporation's business.

THE RESPONSIBILITIES OF DIRECTORS
OF SOLVENT CORPORATIONS

A director must act in the best interest of the corporation to promote, sustain, and enhance the corporation's business. One aspect of this concept of fiduciary duty is described as the duty of care and loyalty.

The duty of care is self-explanatory. Briefly described, each director must be well informed and have knowledge of all material information that is reasonably available in order to act and make decisions. When acting and making decisions, each director must exercise the degree of care an ordinary, careful, and prudent person would use in similar circumstances.

The duty of loyalty requires that the director act in good faith, in the best interests of the corporation, in the best interests of the shareholders, and must not engage in self-dealing nor exploit corporate opportunities for his or her personal advantage. When a director does act for personal benefit, this becomes a clear breach of fiduciary duty and is an action against the best interests of the corporation and its shareholders. Such activity, usually determined after the fact and usually the subject of significant litigation, not only is harmful, financially and perhaps criminally, to the individual director, but is also damaging to the shareholder as a class. Examples of such activity are currently in the news, reporting recent corporate scandals with allegations of significant financial gain to the individual directors or the entire board.

Advice of Fiduciary Responsibility

Each decision made must be in the best interests of the corporation; it must be impartial; adequate inquiry to determine the facts should be undertaken before making a decision; each director should have the courage to inquire and act; each director should not act irresponsibly and should exercise the highest degree of skill, integrity, and honesty in his or her actions; each director should not be deterred from challenging and probing management, but basically should start with the premise that management is to be trusted, is honest, and acts in the best interests of the corporation. If management has neglected to be honest, forthright, and lacks integrity or conceals information and acts in its best interest and not in the best interest of the corporation, it is the director's responsibility to replace management. If the director needs help in performing his or her duties and responsibilities, the director may seek expert help within the corporation, or if the Director feels that outside independent advice is required to perform duties and responsibilities, independent counsel and consultants may be made available to represent the interests of a director and the board as a whole.

Independence from management is critical, but this does not mean you should be critical of, demeaning to, or mistrusting of management. Inquire, challenge, be informed, be intelligent, be courageous, and be persistent. Such activity does not mean using hostility or engaging in combative activity. Performing your duty as a director will create the correct relationship between you as a director, the management you supervise, and the ownership whose interests you have a duty to represent.

We have discussed in generalities the director's fiduciary responsibilities. What are the tests for determining whether you as a director have acted in a proper and reasonable manner in the performance of your fiduciary duties and responsibilities? We are dealing with the standards of review that have been established by the courts.

STANDARD OF REVIEW FOR A DIRECTOR'S CONDUCT

A review of a director's conduct is usually a "hindsight" investigation into a director's action, nonaction, or decision.

The Duty of Care

One of the doctrines discussed by the courts deals with the requirement that there be a finding that the action of the director is tainted with fraud or is ultra vires in order to find liability against a director.[1] In sum, negligence does not necessarily impose liability on the director and does not establish a breach of fiduciary duty if the director acts with discretion and in judgment and furtherance of the corporate enterprise.[2] One of the puzzling doctrines involves the concept of gross negligence. Some courts will impose liability on directors for their actions when these actions demonstrate an entire want of care or a conscious indifference to the rights of the shareholders.[3] This activity can be characterized by a director's abdication of the duties and responsibilities imposed by corporate law. Certainly this is more than gross negligence and is indifference and complete lack of care. It comes close to fraud.

Delaware courts have been active, informative, and authoritative on the duty of care. The leading authority on the director's duty of care is Caremark.[4] The concise doctrine, which is the generally accepted standard, imposes an obligation on the director to attempt in good faith to assure that the corporation's information and reports are adequate and accurate for the director to act within the scope of his or her fiduciary duty to make informed and meaningful judgments on the actions taken by the corporation. If a director fails to act and assure that the decision acted on is based on adequate and accurate information, there is reasonable ground to assert that the director's actions were not in good faith and are the basis for a claim that the director breached the fiduciary duty of care requirement.

The Business Judgment Rule

This is a standard for determining liability when a breach of the duty of care is asserted by shareholders or other aggrieved parties in litigation brought against the board or individual directors. It is a court-imposed test. This rule is applied when a board decision is challenged.[5] The business judgment rule presumes that a director's decisions and actions occur when he or she is fully informed and is acting in good faith and in the honest belief that the decision or action being taken is in the best interests of the corporation.

This presumption will carry forward in any litigation brought against the director or the board, but can be rebutted by proof that the elements of the presumption did not take place. The burden of proving the facts that rebut or overturn the presumption is on the party attacking the actions of the director or the board. The party attacking the director's action brings litigation derivatively on behalf of the corporation or its shareholders and seeks money damages against the director, the board, or the corporation, and usually alleges a breach of fiduciary duty and asserts that the action of the director or the board damaged the value of the shareholder's ownership interest.

The leading and most frequently cited case applying the business judgment rule in a judicial context is *Smith v. Van Gorkum.*[6]

Directors are afforded protection of the business judgment rule if they decide a corporate issue in good faith, after being fully and reasonably informed of all material information, act without any personal financial benefit, and vote in the honest and sincere belief that they are acting in the best interests of the corporation. Certainly any director who has a personal interest in the outcome of the matter, or is acting with a personal benefit, and with self-dealing, is not entitled to the benefit and defense of the business judgment rule.

An excellent recent example of how the business judgment rule works in connection with shareholder's attack on a board decision relating to compensation and severance of a corporate officer is the Disney case.[7] This case is an attack on the employment and severance package granted Michael Ovitz, the former Disney president. The court had to determine whether the board's conduct was a violation of its fiduciary duties and whether these decisions were protected by the business judgment rule. The court's detailed review of the facts led to the conclusion that the directors failed to inform themselves or adequately inquire and deliberate on the issue of compensation. The court concluded that there was a knowing or deliberate indifference by the directors to their duty to act faithfully and with appropriate care, and they did not act in good faith and honestly in the best interest of the corporation. The complaint asserted against the directors was determined to sufficiently allege that their actions fell outside the protection of the business judgment rule.

The Intrinsic Rule

This is another test utilized to determine whether the actions of the director or the board are substantively and procedurally fair. Each transaction that is under attack is reviewed to determine whether the terms of the transaction are fair to the corporation and in its best interests. The process of a director or board's decision will be reviewed in detail. Was the information on which the decision was made adequately and fully disclosed? Was the transaction for the benefit of certain directors and not negotiated on an arm's-length basis? Did the directors act free from coercion? Did the directors make proper inquiry? Did the directors seek outside and independent advice when they had the opportunity to do so? Was there anything in the transaction that "flagged" a duty for further independent inquiry? Was the entire transaction or series of transactions fair?

The Requirement of Independence

Recently the relationship of the director to the management of the corporation has come under scrutiny in connection with the director's fiduciary responsibility.[8] Directors must act independently and be independent of management and not controlled, beholden, or dominated by management or other outside interests. The concept of a controlled director is a developing concept and will be asserted by complaining parties aggrieved by the action of the board.

Reliance as a Defense

Many state statutes[9] grant protection to directors who rely in good faith on information furnished to them by the corporation. Such information comes from corporate records and corporate employees. This reliance is conditioned on the director's belief that the information has been furnished by reliable employees, corporate counsel, investment bankers, and accountants.

The Model Business Corporation Act

The Model Business Corporation Act, adopted by many states, covers the standards of conduct for directors and the standards of liability for directors. Additionally, the model act covers general standards for directors.[10]

In addition, the American Law Institute (ALI) has published and adopted the *Principles of Corporate Governance: Analysis and Recommendations*. The ALI *Principles* cover the duty of care of directors; the business judgment rule; reliance on a committee of a board; and reliance on directors, officers, employees, experts, and other persons.[11]

Good Faith

The duty of good faith is being discussed more frequently in recent cases. It is clearly required of directors. It requires that the director's actions be honest, not unlawful or contrary to public policy, and in the best interest of the corporation.[12] The Enron matter has heightened comment on this important aspect of a director's fiduciary responsibility.[13]

THE RESPONSIBILITIES OF DIRECTORS OF CORPORATIONS IN FINANCIAL DIFFICULTY

We have been dealing with the fiduciary duty of directors when the corporation is solvent. Now, what of the situation in which the corporation is in financial difficulty and is in the vicinity or zone of insolvency? Does the director's fiduciary duty move to others, and, if so, to what entities? Generally speaking, when the corporation nears insolvency, is in the vicinity or zone of insolvency, or is on the verge of or approaching insolvency, the director's fiduciary duty expands to encompass handling creditors. While many of the cases describe the situation in different terms (in the vicinity of, on the verge of, the zone of insolvency), the courts have determined that when the corporation operates in the vicinity of insolvency, a new director's fiduciary duty comes in existence, and that duty is to the creditors of the corporation.[14] The possibility of insolvency can expose "creditors to risks of opportunistic behavior and create complexities for directors".[15] The concept of when a corporation is in the vicinity of insolvency is described by different "subjective" tests and usually, in court decisions, after the fact. One of the issues is the definition of insolvency while another issue is whether the expansion of fiduciary duties includes shareholders as well as creditors. Is there further expansion of fiduciary duty to the community of interest of the corporate enterprise, such as shareholders, creditors, employees, or other groups interested in the corporation?

When the corporation is in the zone of or in the vicinity of insolvency, any decision made by the corporation's management and directors is subject to close and careful review from many constituencies. Directors act "under a microscope," and their actions become closely scrutinized by the corporation's creditors. Creditors are intent on getting paid in full and receiving the full benefit of their commercial bargained-for rights before any distribution is available for or made to the owners of the corporations. Creditors look to the management of the corporation to maximize the value of its assets. Creditors expect the board and the directors to assume responsibility and exercise fiduciary duty for the benefit of all creditors of the corporation. The corporation in the vicinity of insolvency is an enterprise existing primarily for the benefit of the creditors.

Another view of the corporation in the vicinity of insolvency reasons that all corporate assets are placed in trust for the benefit of its creditors, and the duty of directors and the board, as fiduciaries, is to administer this trust first for the benefit of corporate creditors, and then, after satisfying the creditors in full, for the benefit of the shareholders. This "trust fund" doctrine requires that all actions taken for and in behalf of the corporation when it is in the vicinity of insolvency must be to further and protect the value of the corporation's assets and interests of its creditors. The trust fund theory has been accepted by many courts.[16]

The concept of fiduciary duty of directors shifting to creditors when a corporation is in the vicinity of insolvency is dependent on which definition of insolvency is used to test the corporation's financial condition. This is a quagmire because there are many different definitions and tests of insolvency or financial inability to pay debts. Unfortunately, director's actions taken when financial difficulty seems "on the horizon" or is immediate are all subject to "hindsight" determination. This is an important reason for directors to be cautious and careful.

While there are factual issues as to when the corporation is on the verge of or in the vicinity of insolvency, this is subjective. The best approach is to regard insolvency as a situation when the corporation is unable to pay its debts as they fall due in the ordinary course.[17]

Another rationale for the expansion of a director's fiduciary duty to creditors when the corporation is in the vicinity of insolvency is premised on the theory that the creditor's claim against the corporation becomes an equitable interest in the corporate enterprise as creditors may no longer expect to be paid in accordance with their legal or contractual rights.[18]

The Director's Actions in the Vicinity of Insolvency

The director's fiduciary duty is to protect the value of the corporation's assets and the interests of its creditors. Creditors are intent on getting paid in full and receiving the full benefit of their commercial bargained-for rights before any distribution is available to be made to the owners of the corporation. Creditors look to the management of the corporation to maximize the value of its assets, and directors must be careful to insure that management's actions are directed to the maximization of asset value. Certainly creditors have the ultimate weapon to utilize if they are not being paid as their debts mature, that is, filing an involuntary bankruptcy, so that all the corporation's assets are then administered under the jurisdiction of the bankruptcy court and in accordance with the priorities of the bankruptcy code. In any event, directors must not forget the community of interests in the corporation when acting while the corporation is in the vicinity of insolvency. The community of interest includes the creditors, employees, and shareholders.

Fiduciary Duty of Directors When the Corporation Is Insolvent

When the corporation is in fact insolvent, the direct fiduciary duty of a director and the board is to the corporation's creditors. The directors and the board no longer represent the shareholders. The interests of the shareholders are subordinate to the interests of the corporation's creditors. The fiduciary duty in the insolvency situation is commonly known as the "trust fund doctrine." The trust fund doctrine is created by statute in many jurisdictions[19] and enforced by the courts.[20] The courts have generally interpreted the trust fund doctrine to place directors or the board in a position of trust, thereby imposing the duty on the director as a fiduciary or trustee. In many cases where creditors have recovered judgments against directors, the courts have used language indicating that the director's actions in the transactions involved a breach of the director's trust. For example, where directors diverted assets of the corporation when it was insolvent, whether by sale, dissolution, or transfer, the courts have characterized the director's action as being fraudulent[21] because the corporation's creditors were not paid out of the proceeds of the transaction. In fact, if a corporation dissolves and distributes its assets in a manner that is not fair and equitable, for example to shareholders, and the dissolution is approved by directors, such actions are not consistent with the director's fiduciary duties, and the assets distributed are burdened with a lien in favor of the creditors.[22] In such a situation where a lien is imposed, if the creditors cannot in fact recover the distributed assets, the directors are liable, jointly and severally, for the total amount of the assets distributed.[23]

Is there a methodology or test to determine what fiduciary duty is owed by directors to creditors in the insolvency situation? The simple answer is—no. Many of the cases seem to rely on duties likened to those of a trustee.[24] Some cases imply that the fiduciary duty prohibits self-dealing and giving preferred treatment to insiders.[25] Other cases speak in terms of the duty to minimize loss.[26] Another case imposes personal liability and characterizes the director's actions as wrongful conduct, prolonging insolvency by fraudulently misrepresenting corporate asset value and thereby breaching the director's duty of care.[27] Another case attacks the director's conduct in the insolvency situation as a violation of the duty of loyalty when the director acquired significant creditor claims without disclosing his ownership of the claim.[28] The business judgment rule applicable to directors in the insolvency situation requires that directors in the decision-making process closely examine the effect of the proposed action on the rights of creditors. This simply requires directors to carefully consider and analyze the consequences of any sale or transfer of some or all of the corporation's property. To do otherwise invites litigation and creates the likelihood of recovery against directors.[29]

CONCLUSION

Consideration of the director's fiduciary duty and ultimate responsibility for actions taken requires the exercise of great care. The entire concept of potential director liability is characterized by uncertainty. Courage, inquiry, access to, and reliance on the best information and advice available are the best guidelines.

The art of governing (it is emphatically not a science) is replete with judgment calls and "bet the company" decisions that in retrospect may seem visionary or deranged, depending on the outcome. Corporate directors do not choose between reasonable (nonnegligent) and unreasonable (negligent) alternatives, but face a range of options, each with its attendant mix of risk and reward.[30]

The directors and the board are comparable to a "team." Each director has a different background: Some have management experience, some business or entrepreneurial experience, and some legal or accounting backgrounds. A good friend who is the chair of an audit committee and director of a *Fortune* 500 company advocates that directors and boards should practice and project the five "C's:" Character, Competence, Confidence, Chemistry, and Communication. These characteristics, when practiced, lead to directors and boards that function as responsible and accountable "stewards" of a corporation.

NOTES

1. *Gearhart Industries, Inc. v. Smith International, Inc.* 741 F.2d 707 (1984).

2. *Resolution Trust Corp. v. Norris*, 830 F. Supp. 351 (S.D. Tex.1981).

3. *FDIC v. Harrington*, 844 F. Supp. 300 (N.D. Tex. 1994).

4. In Re Caremark International, Inc. Derivative Litigation, 698 A. 2d 959 (Del.Ch. 1996).

5. ALI *Principles of corporate governance: Analysis and recommendations* (1994), part IV, Duty of care and the business judgment rule.

6. *Smith v. Van Gorkum*, 488 A.2d 858 (Del. 1985).

7. *Brehm v. Eisner*, 746 A.2d 244 (Del. 2000), and In Re Walt Disney Company Derivative Litigation, 825 A2d 775 (Del. Ch. 2003).

8. *Texlon v. Meyerson*, 802 A.2d 257 (Del. 2002).

9. Section 141 (e) Delaware General Corporation Law; Article 2.41D Texas Business Corporation Act.

10. Model Business Corporation Act of 1984, adopted in more than thirty states; standard of conduct is Section 8.30; standard of liability is Section 8.31; and general standards for directors is Section 8.30.

11. ALI *Principles of Corporate Governance* (1994), infra.

12. *Cede and Co v. Technicolor, Inc.* 634 A.2d 345 (Del. 1993).

13. Strine (2003), Derivative impact? Some early reflections on the corporate law implications of the Enron debacle, *Bus. Law, 57,* 1371.

14. In Re Mortgage America Corp. 714 F.2d 1266 (5th Cir. 1983).

15. *Credit Lyonnais Bank Nederland N.V. v. Pathe Communications Co.*, 1991 Del. Ch. LEXIS 215 (Del. Ch. 1991).

16. For an analysis of current doctrines and cases in connection with directors' fiduciary responsibilities when a corporation is in the vicinity of insolvency, see Sheinfeld and Seider (1997, January–February), When your company becomes insolvent, *Corporate Board;* Sheinfeld and Pippitt (2004), Fiduciary duties of directors of a corporation in the vicinity of insolvency and after initiation of a bankruptcy case, *Bus. Law, 60;* and Miller (1993), The fiduciary relationship between directors and stockholders of solvent and insolvent corporations, *Seton Hall L. Rev., 23,* 1467.

17. *Geyer v. Ingersoll Publications Co.*, 621 A.2d 784 (Del. Ch. 1992); *LaSalle Bank National Bank v. Perelman*, 82 F. Supp 2d 279 (D. Del. 2000).

18. *FDIC v. Sea Pines Co.*, 692 F.2d 973 (4th Cir. 1982).

19. The Texas statutes referencing liabilities of directors when a corporation dissolves, and the duties that directors have to creditors when the corporation is unsolvent, are Art. 6.04 and 2.41 Texas Business Corporations Act; see also *Henry I. Siegel Co. Inc. v. Holliday*, 663 S.W.2d 824 (Tex. 1984), and *Smith v. Chapman*, 897 S.W.2d 399 (Tex. App.–Eastland 1995); Delaware General Corporation Law, 8 Del. C. Sections 280–281; see also Hammermesh, The Delaware dissolution statutes: A case study, 12-fall *Del. Law.* 22, and Lin (1985), Shift of fiduciary duty upon corporate insolvency: Proper scope of director's duty to creditors, *Vand. L. Rev., 46,* 1485.

20. *Henry I. Siegel Co. Inc. v. Holliday*, infra; *Guth v. Loft, Inc.*, 23 Del. Ch. 255, 5A.2d 503, 510 (Del. 1939), and *Credit Lyonnais Bank Nederland, N.V. v. Pathe Communications Corp.*, 1991 W.L. 277613 1991 LEXIS 215 (Del. Ch. 1991).

21. In Re: Rego Co., 623 A.2d 92 (Del. Ch 1992); In Re Toy King Distributors, Inc., 256 B.R. 1 (Bankr. N.D. Fla. 2000).

22. *Henry I. Siegel Co. Inc. v. Holliday*, supra.

23. *Henry I. Siegel Co. Inc. v. Holliday*, supra; Bovay v. H. M. Byllesby and Co., 38 A.2d 808 (Del. Supr. 1944); *Amussen v. Quaker City Corporation*, 18 Del. Ch. 28; 156 A 180 (Del. Ch. 1931).

24. Markell (1997), The folly of representing insolvent corporations: Examining lawyer liability and ethical issues involved in extending fiduciary duties to creditors, *J. Bankr. L. and Prac.*, 6, 403.

25. *St. James Capital Corp. v. Pallet Recycling Assoc. of North America, Inc.*, 589 N.W.2d 511 (Minn. App. 1999); *Fagan v. La Gloria Oil and Gas Company*, 494 S.W.2d 624 (Tex Ct. App. 1973).

26. *New York Credit Men's Adjustment Bureau v. Weiss*, 110 N.E.2d 397 (N.Y. 1953).

27. In Re Ben Franklin Retail Stores, Inc., 225 B.R. 646 (Bankr. N.D. Ill. 1998) affirmed in part and reversed in part; 2000 W.L. 28266 (N.D. Ill. 2000) is an excellent decision by a bankruptcy court discussing the fiduciary duty of officers and directors of a debtor corporation and their capability for continuing the corporation's business by fraudulently valuing receivables, thereby inducing creditors to lend more money and furnish more inventory on credit.

28. In Re Toy King Distributors, Inc., 256 B.R. 1 (Bankr. M.D. Fla. 2000) where directors were liable because they violated their duty of loyalty when they acquired creditors claims while serving in a fiduciary capacity.

29. *Pereira v. Cogan*, 2001 W.L. 243537 (S.D. N.Y.) where directors were held liable for breach of their duty of due care because they allowed management to take excessive salary and loans while the corporation was insolvent.

30. In Re United Artists Theatre Company, 315 F.3d 217 2003 W.L. 68020 (3rd Cir. 2003) at 315 F.3d 231.

———— 13 ————

Governance as a Source of Corporate Social Capital

LEE E. PRESTON

The term "social capital" was introduced into economics more than a century ago to refer to the various forms of physical capital (for example housing stock, road systems, etc.) that are of widespread and continuing use and value to societies. More recently the term has been broadened to include established norms and behavior patterns that benefit communities, organizations and/or individuals (Coleman, 1990; Putnam, 1993; Lin, 2001). Attention is now being focused on the importance of social relationships as a source of long-term benefits (i.e., as "capital) in the private sector, particularly within corporations (Leenders and Gabbay, 1999; Adler and Kwon, 2002). The "core intuition" underlying the study of corporate social capital is, as Adler and Kwon put it, "that the goodwill that others have toward us is a valuable resource" (2002, p. 18). Correspondingly, the distrust or ill will of others—referred to in this literature as "social liability"—may be a serious handicap. The questions of greatest current interest are: What does corporate social capital actually consist of? And where does it come from? This essay argues that corporate social capital is any relationship, either internal or external, that facilitates the effective long-term status and operation of the corporation, and that corporate governance arrangements and practices are among its many possible sources. Conversely, of course, governance arrangements and practices can have adverse effects on the firm, and hence become sources of liability.

233

CAPITAL: PHYSICAL, FINANCIAL, HUMAN, INTELLECTUAL, SOCIAL

Conventional economic theory distinguishes three factors of production: land (location, physical space, natural resources); labor (people who work and the time they put in); and capital (all other productive resources, including finance). For many decades economic analysis and its management offshoots focused primarily on *tangible* forms of capital. Contemporary studies, however, recognize the increasing importance of *intangible* capital—characteristics of individuals, groups, and organizations that increase productive capacity, both for specific companies and for the economy as a whole, but that have no specific physical or financial forms (Bounfour, 2003; Hand and Lev, 2003).

The earliest forms of intangible capital to receive serious recognition were *intellectual* capital (Machlup, 1962) and *human* capital (Becker, 1975). The question of whether these valuable resources are or are not "capital" is not debatable. Activities that add to the stock of useful knowledge or that increase the skills of workers—whether they take the form of society-wide educational and research programs (analogous to infrastructure improvements on the physical side), or organizational/professional training and increased "know-how" (analogous to facilities upgrading)—clearly involve *investment*. The benefits that flow from such investments over time are clearly analogous to improvements in revenue and/or efficiency due to additions in physical or financial capital. Also, like other forms of capital, human and intellectual capital can depreciate, both because of the passage of time and because specific skills and knowledge may become obsolete as a result of technological and social change.

Social capital consists of those structures and arrangements that encourage collaborative behavior and hence reduce conflict and improve efficiency within society as a whole or between and within organizations. *Corporate* social capital may involve internal or external relationships: organization-to-individual, organization-to-organization, or organization-to-society. Leenders and Gabbay (1999) emphasize that, although social capital/liability arises from social structures and arrangements, the two are quite distinct. Social structures that contribute to the achievement of organizational goals create *capital;* those that hamper or reduce goal achievement create *liability*. This essay argues that corporate governance arrangements can be an important source of both social capital and social liability. For example, a governance characteristic such as long-term stability in board membership may contribute to familiarity with facts and issues, facilitate communication, promote trust, and so on—and hence create social capital. However, long-serving boards may also be resistant to change and put unwarranted trust in familiar individuals and practices, and hence create social liability.

IS SOCIAL CAPITAL "CAPITAL"?

Critics of the corporate social capital concept have agreed that inter- and intra-organizational relationships are important, but have questioned whether or not they constitute "capital" in any conventional sense. Talmud (1999, p. 109) argues that they do, and points out that social capital has the following features:

- It pertains to the organization as a whole and is not the property of any individual agent;
- It can be accumulated over time;
- It is relation-specific and cannot easily be transformed from network to network;
- It is expensive, involving sunk costs;
- Without proper maintenance, it tends to depreciate over time and may even turn from capital to liability.

These features correspond to the characteristics of tangible capital generally recognized in economics. Hence, although some popular usage of the term "capital" is largely metaphoric, social relationships possessing the above features qualify for recognition as "capital" in the traditional sense.

The valuation of social capital is obviously a serious problem. But similar problems exist with respect to the valuation of physical capital, which may be valued at (depreciated) original cost, replacement cost, or current market value (whether as part of an ongoing operation or as abandoned structures and equipment). The only form of capital that is easy to evaluate is liquid assets, and even the value of these is subject to erosion because of inflation.

The criteria for identifying examples of social capital (or liability) have important implications for discovering its sources. That is: Why do individuals and groups, whether internal or external to the firm, feel goodwill or ill will toward it? Most contributors to the social capital literature—including the authors included in Leenders and Gabbay (1999)—use the term "sources of corporate social capital" to refer to features of the social structure that (a) are beneficial to the firm, and (b) can be modified by the firm's actions and initiatives (that is, increased by "investment" in some form).

Several aspects of social structure that can be reasonably termed "sources of corporate social capital" have been presented in the recent literature:

- Strategic alliances (Todeva and Knoke, 2002);
- Organizational "standing"—i.e., status in the eyes of other organizations (Doreian, 1999);
- Intra-organizational linkages favorable to the development of intellectual capital (Nahapiet and Goshal, 1998);
- Intra-organizational linkages facilitating home-subsidiary coordination (Kostova and Roth, 2003); and,
- Employment practices promoting associability, trust, and shared norms (Leana and Van Buren, 1999).

All of these examples show the sources of social capital to be within the management purview of the firm, something (although intangible) that the firm can buy in larger or smaller quantities, of better or worse quality, and so on.

CORPORATE GOVERNANCE

This essay proposes to add corporate governance to the list of possible sources of corporate social capital recognized in the management literature. Governance arrangements are "capital" in every sense—both within society and within individual organizations. They can produce the collaborative relationships, associability, and trust that characterize the general concept of "social capital" and the other "sources of corporate social capital" listed above. (And, as already noted, governance arrangements can also generate social liabilities—rigidity, distrust, etc.)

In their widely cited volume, Monks and Minow define corporate governance as "the relationship among various participants in determining the direction and performance of corporations" (2001, p. 1). Their primary emphasis is on relationships among share owners, managers, and boards of directors. (For similar viewpoints, see Business Roundtable, 2002; Shleifer and Vishny, 1997.) The editors of the AMR "Special Topic Forum on Corporate Governance" define their subject more broadly as "the determination of the broad uses to which organizational resources will be deployed and the resolution of conflicts among the myriad participants in organizations" (Daily, Dalton, and Canella, 2003, p. 371). Blair defines governance as "the legal rules, institutional arrangements and practices that determine who controls business corporations, and who gets the benefits that flow from them" (2001, p. 2797). Zingales stresses that the corporation necessarily operates through incomplete contracts and sees governance arrangements as the framework for *ex post* bargaining beyond the limits of such contracts (1997, p. 497). My own definition is that corporate governance is "the set of institutional arrangements that legitimates and directs the corporation in the performance of its functions" (Preston, 2003, p. 206). (For additional definitions, see European Commission, 2002, pp. 28–29.) Some specific features of corporate governance that may be critical to its impact are listed in the chapter appendix.

The idea that corporate governance might be a source of social capital is not suggested in any of the sources examined in research for this essay. Hence, it must be carefully justified. We therefore analyze corporate governance according to the detailed characteristics of corporate social capital suggested by Adler and Kwon (2003, pp. 21–22). These characteristics necessarily overlap in various ways, but appear to cover all relevant aspects of the social capital concept.

1. **Long-lived asset.** Governance systems are long-lived features of both the polity as a whole and of any individual firm. They facilitate the amassing of resources for productive purposes and establish relationships among some (although

not all) critical participants in economic life, on both macro and micro levels. Metaphorically, the corporate governance system is the institutional framework of the building within which the corporation conducts its activities. If the physical structures within which the corporation operates are "capital," which they certainly are, then the institutional structure must be "capital" also.

2. *"Appropriable" and "convertible."* Corporate governance systems can be "appropriated" (i.e., used) for diverse purposes (to raise capital; attract personnel; direct management toward or away from certain activities). They may also be "converted" into public reputation, political advantage, etc.

3. *Substitute or complement for other resources.* Governance can substitute for management, or can complement management by enhancing its legitimacy, ratifying its actions, etc. (These are the major themes of Monks and Minow, 2001.)

4. *Requires maintenance.* Governance systems, both within the polity and within individual firms, require maintenance in the form of updating processes and practices, adapting to new regulations and conditions, etc.

5. *Collective good.* Corporate governance systems, both within the entire polity and within any individual firm, involve shared understanding and cooperation among many people. Governance at any level cannot be the property of a single individual.

6. *Based on relationships.* Like many other forms of social capital (and unlike most forms of physical and financial capital), corporate governance necessarily involves relationships; indeed, it requires acceptance and collaboration among multiple participants in order to exist at all.

7. *Investment aspect.* In spite of Talmud's emphasis on "sunk costs," noted above, the fact is that both the investment costs and the flow of benefits (or harms) associated with many forms of social capital are difficult to quantify. The investment costs (and benefits) of corporate governance arrangements are no exception. Some of the operating costs of governance are obvious—director's fees, regulatory filings, shareowner services, etc. But the "behavioral investment" (doing things in certain ways over a long period of time—and the costs related thereto) may be much more important. As for the long-term effects of such investments, they may be much more obvious when they are negative than when they are positive; that is, when the governance system becomes a "liability."

EVIDENCE

In this section we examine the evidence that the corporate governance–social capital relationship suggested here can actually be observed in the world of affairs; that it is not merely a piece of academic jargon.

It is common knowledge that corporate governance arrangements within individual companies affect their appraisal as investment risks, and thus impact the availability and cost of financing. According to the current business press, many fiduciary institutions (which, as a group, account for more than half of the ownership of listed companies in the United States) take governance arrangements into account in making their investment decisions. The criteria used by some major fiduciaries—for example, CREF, CalPERS, NYCERS—are available on their websites and in their publications. In response to this interest—and to the general public concern about governance issues—a "cottage industry" of governance consultation services, including investment rating services, accounting firms, and law firms, has come into being (*Wall Street Journal*, June 6, 2003, p. 1). New lines of "corporate governance software," specifically focused on analysis and improvement in response to the Sarbanes-Oxley Act of 2002 and to changing SEC regulations, have become available.

However, as Daily, Dalton, and Canella (2003, pp. 374–75) conclude from their comprehensive survey, the evidence that governance arrangements are associated with independent evidence of corporate performance in the usual sense is currently inadequate, and the results are certainly mixed. Stanwick and Stanwick (2002) summarize a number of recent empirical studies of the possible association between *some* corporate governance features and *some* indicators of corporate performance. Not surprisingly, some of the studies reveal no association, and some report perverse results. (For example, one study found that having a majority of outside board members, usually considered a "good governance" indicator, is associated with inferior financial performance.) Other studies, however, are consistent with a "good governance–good performance" prediction. It is hard to see how "good governance" could be associated with poor performance. Such a result might well suggest that the performance indicators themselves were inappropriate, or that the association (if any) between the two is simply too complex and path-dependent to be revealed by conventional analysis. (For related viewpoints, see Maher and Andersson, 2002; Vives, 2000.)

Is corporate governance also a source of social capital at the societal level? That is: Does the institutional status of business enterprises, their rights and duties, and the ways in which their activities are directed have significant impact on the overall economic and social development of countries and cultures? The answer has to be *yes*, but the features of governance that are critical to macroeconomic success are difficult to identify; and, governance processes are so deeply embedded in the political and cultural fabric that their specific impact may be unobservable. Nevertheless, it seems clear that the *absence* of legitimate and transparent governance mechanisms for the micromanagerial units within an economic system is a serious liability. An OECD report declares that "good governance" at the micro level contributes to efficient use of capital throughout an economy (OECD, 1999, p. 5). World Bank experts believe that "poor corporate governance has been one of the main stumbling blocks in Russia's uneven transition to a market-based economy" (World Bank, 2003). Establishment of new governance mechanisms has been a major focus of institutional change in the transitional countries of Central and Eastern Europe, and in less developed countries as well (Aoki and Kim, 1995; Berglof and van Thadden, 2000; Tenev and Zhang, 2002). Passage of the 2002 Sarbanes-Oxley Act—regardless of its specific requirements and their impact—suggests that the existence of an association between "good governance" at the micro level and "good performance" at the macro level (which includes appropriate responsibility as well as profitability) is widely accepted in the United States.

IMPLICATIONS

It seems clear that corporate governance should be recognized as a source of social capital, both in the enterprise and in the economy as a whole. Although the impact of favorable governance arrangements and practices may be difficult to specify in detail, the effects of their absence are too conspicuous to be debatable. As a result, many firms are now opening their governance systems to greater outside scrutiny, and also recognizing that their share owners (and other stakeholders) require clearer and more useful information about governance processes (Business Roundtable, 2002). DaimlerChrysler, for example, devoted a six-page section of its 2002 annual report to the subject of governance, and endorsed international adoption of stock market regulations equivalent to those of Sarbanes-Oxley.

If managers want to take advantage of the possibility that governance arrangements can create "social capital" that will improve the firm's overall performance—reduce costs, increase employee loyalty, stimulate investor interest, etc.—the first step is to review existing arrangements. Is the governance system *transparent*; that is, can both insiders and outsiders understand the steps involved in making and implementing corporate decisions? Can stakeholders identify the interests and forces that actually guide and control the activities and policies of the firm? Are there dominant shareholders or blocs, or are top managers actually in control of an organization with diffused ownership? And if the latter (the common situation in larger firms), what kinds of advisory groups are used to assure that the interests of both internal and external stakeholders are appropriately considered in decision-making? What reporting and communications systems enable stakeholders and other interested parties to identify and evaluate the various impacts of the firm?

Expanded legal protections for stakeholders—share owner initiatives, employee access to files, customer and community lawsuits, etc.—have reduced the confidentiality of management in all types of organizations. And widespread use of the Internet has greatly changed the atmosphere of corporate governance. A wealth of corporate and industry data is now freely available, and stakeholder groups focused on a specific issue or interest—environmental impact, product safety, workplace safety, and so on—can be quickly and easily formed. A governance system that recognizes the potential importance of these developments, and finds creative ways to utilize them, can certainly be a source of long-run benefit for the firm.

Responsible and forward-looking governance arrangements and practices can contribute to long-term business success. They form part of the "capital" of the firm. Inadequate or irresponsible governance is clearly a liability for a corporation.

APPENDIX: SOME CRITICAL FEATURES OF CORPORATE GOVERNANCE SYSTEMS

Status of the Corporation

- Incorporation procedures—registration, stock issue, and transfer conditions;
- Reporting and disclosure requirements;
- Tax treatment.

Directors/Boards

- Structure of boards and board-related institutions (for example two-board structures, mandated practices such as codetermination, employee committees, union representation, etc.);
- Qualifications and election of directors;
- Required board committees and their composition.

Management

- Formal reporting, disclosure, and communication requirements—with regulators, share owners, potential investors, creditors, credit rating agencies, and others;
- Takeovers—conditions governing, and permissible responses (poison pills, etc.);
- Definition of and limitations on insider trading;
- Responsibilities toward nonfinancial stakeholders.

Share Owners

- Ownership structure—concentrated or dispersed; role of banks, fiduciaries, other firms;
- Share owner voting rights—protection of minority share owner interests;
- Opportunity and requisite conditions for presentation of share owner initiatives and lawsuits;
- Share owner access to information (including share owner lists);
- Limitations on foreign ownership; foreign exchange convertibility.

Creditors

- Legal status of creditor claims; bankruptcy laws;
- Strength of limited liability principles.

Sources of Governance Standards

- Statute law and related court decisions—national, state, international (for example EU);

- Corporate and securities market regulation (for example SEC);
- Regulation of roles of *other* entities vis-à-vis corporations (for example bank regulation);
- Nongovernmental regulation (for example role of NYSE, NASDAQ, etc.).

REFERENCES

Adler, P. S., and Kwon, S-W. (2002). Social capital: Prospects for a new concept. *Academy of Management Review,* 17–40.

Aoki, M., and Kim, H-K. (1995). *Corporate governance in transitional economies.* Washington: World Bank.

Becker, G. S. (1964). *Human capital: A theoretical and empirical analysis, with special reference to education.* New York: National Bureau of Economic Research.

Berglof, E., and von Thadden, E-I. (2000). The changing corporate governance paradigm: Implications for developing and transition economies. In Cohen, S. S., and Boyd, G., eds. *Corporate governance and globalization.* Cheltenham, UK: Edward Elgar, 275–306.

Blair, M. M. (2001). Corporate governance. In *International encyclopedia of the social and behavioral sciences,* Neil J. Smelser and Paul B. Baltes, eds., Burlington, MA: Elsevier, 4:2797–2803.

Bounfour, A. (2003). *The management of intangibles: The organization's most valued assets.* London: Routledge.

Business Roundtable. (2002). *Principles of corporate governance.* Washington: Business Roundtable.

Coleman, J. S. (1990). *Foundations of social theory.* Cambridge: Belknap Press of Harvard University Press.

Daily, C. M., Dalton, D. R., and Canella, A. A. (2003). Special topic: Forum on corporate governance. *Academy of Management Review,* 28 (3).

DaimlerChrysler. (2002). *Annual report.* Stuttgart, Germany, and Auburn Hills, MI.

Doreian, P. (1999). Organizational standing as corporate social capital. In Leenders and Gabbay, eds., 134–147.

European Commission. (2002). *Comparative study of corporate governance codes.* Final Report. Study Contract ETD/2000/B5-3001/F/53.

Hand, J. R. M., and Lev, B. (2003). *Intangible assets: Values, measures, and risks.* Oxford: Oxford University Press.

Kostova, T., and Roth, K. (2003). Social capital in multinational corporations and a micro-macro model of its formation. *Academy of Management Review,* 28, 297–317.

Leana, C. R., and Van Buren, H. J. (2002). Organizational social capital and employment practices. *Academy of Management Review,* 24, 538–555.

Leenders, T. A. J., and Gabbay, S. M., eds. (1999). *Corporate social capital and liability.* Boston: Kluwer.

Lin, N. (2001). *Social capital: A theory of social structure and action.* New York: Cambridge University Press.

Machlup, F. (1962). *Knowledge: Its creation, distribution, and economic significance.* Princeton: Princeton University Press.

Maher, M., and Andersson, T. (2002). Corporate governance: Effects on firm performance and economic growth. In McCahery, J. A., Moerland, P., Raaijmakers, T., and Renneboog, L., eds. (2002). *Corporate governance regimes: Convergence and diversity*. Oxford: Oxford University Press, 385–418.

Monks, Robert A. G., and Minow, N. (2001). *Corporate governance* (2d ed.). Oxford: Blackwell.

Nahapiet, J., and Ghoshal, S. (1998). Social capital, intellectual capital, and the organizational advantage. *Academy of Management Review, 23,* 242–266.

NYSE begins its huge overhaul. (2003, November 6). *Wall Street Journal,* 1.

Organisation for Economic Co-Operation and Development (OECD). (1999). *Principles of corporate governance*. Paris: OECD.

Preston, L. E. (2003). The truth about corporate governance. In Kochan, T. A., and Lipsky, D. B., eds. *Negotiations and change, from the workplace to society*. Cornell: ILR Press, 205–222.

Putnam, R. D. (1993). *Making democracy work: Civic traditions in modern Italy*. Princeton: Princeton University Press.

Shleifer, A., and Vishny, R. W. (1997). A survey of corporate governance. *Journal of Finance, 52,* 737–783.

Stanwick, P. A., and Stanwick, S. D. (2002). The relationships between corporate governance and financial performance: An empirical study. *Journal of Corporate Citizenship, 8,* 35–48.

Talmud, I. (1999). Social capital and liability: A conditional approach to three consequences of corporate social structure. In Leenders and Gabbay, 106–118.

Tenev, S., and Zhang, C. (2002). *Corporate governance and enterprise reform in China*. Washington: World Bank and International Finance Corporation.

Todeva, E., and Knoke, D. (2002). Strategic alliances and corporate social capital (published in German). In *Kolner zeitschrift fur sociologie und sozialpsychologie*. Cologne: Sonderheft, 42:345–380.

Vives, X. (2000). Corporate governance: Does it matter?" In Vives, X., ed., *Corporate governance: Theoretical and empirical perspectives*. Cambridge: Cambridge University Press, 1–10.

World Bank. (2003). Corporate governance in Russia: Regime change required. *Transition, 14,* 21–22.

Zingales, L. (1998). Corporate governance. In *The New Palgrave Dictionary of Economics and the Law,* 497–503.

Business and Sustainability: Implications for Corporate Governance Theory and Practice

DAVID WHEELER and JANE THOMSON

This chapter describes the increasingly explicit interest of firms in the ideal of corporate sustainability and relates the phenomenon to governance theory and practice. We note the emergence of sustainability and "corporate social responsibility" strategies as means of creating value through the application of stakeholder approaches to strategic management. However, we note the absence of an acknowledgment of these approaches in the corporate governance literature and ascribe this primarily to an ideological schism between normative versions of agency theory and stakeholder theory. We observe that in real terms there are no practical or theoretic impediments to a convergence of these concepts in corporate governance through a more grounded understanding of the way in which resources are mobilized and value is created for firms and their stakeholders. In support of this convergence we present evidence of trends in corporate governance codes and specialist stock market indices, both of which provide legitimacy to the sustainability ideal as a means of uniting the interests of firms and society in ensuring a viable long-term future. We conclude with an exploration of some of the implications of our analysis for corporate governance theory and practice and propose a "resource-stewardship model" to help capture the linkages between firm resources and the creation of sustainable value.

THE SYNTHESIS OF SUSTAINABILITY
AND STRATEGIC MANAGEMENT

The term sustainability, as applied to private sector organizations, implies a strategic commitment to the simultaneous—and potentially synergistic—generation of economic, social, and ecological payoffs arising from the business activities of those organizations (Wheeler et al., 2003). A number of scholars have championed the concept of sustainability as a novel strategic management paradigm, frequently relating it to questions of environmental resource efficiency, stakeholder approaches, and (more recently) market opportunities in developing countries (Porter and van der Linde, 1995; Hart, 1997; Wheeler and Sillanpää, 1997 and 1998; Hart and Milstein, 1999; Prahalad and Hart, 2001; Hart and Christensen, 2002; Prahalad and Hammond, 2002; Aragón-Correa and Sharma, 2003; Hart and Milstein, 2003).

Consistent with the resource-based view (Wernefeld, 1986; Barney, 1991) as a strategic management paradigm, sustainability is frequently grounded in a resource-dependency perspective (Hart, 1995; Sharma and Vredenburg, 1998; Aragón-Correa and Sharma, 2003). Contemporary discussions of "sustainability strategies" also feature neo-Schumpeterian assumptions consistent with the arguments of Christensen and others on the nature of innovation and technological change, again within a strategic management frame (Christensen, 1997; Chistensen and Raynor, 2003; and Foster and Kaplan, 2001). The underlying logic is that within a few decades, when the world's population has grown to 9 billion and is facing even greater economic, social, and ecological stressors, the goods and services produced and sold by corporations, and the very corporations themselves, will need to look very different than they do today (Hart and Christensen, 2002).

In parallel with these academic syntheses there has emerged a good deal of popular literature in the field of strategic approaches to sustainable business practice (Schmidheiny, 1992; Willums and Golüke, 1992; Elkington, 1998; Hawken et al., 1999; Holliday et al., 2002). Descriptions of business cases in these publications have tended to center on large corporations, for example, the memberships of international business organizations such as the World Business Council on Sustainable Development, the International Chamber of Commerce, the United Nations Global Compact, the International Business Leaders Forum, and a wide variety of national business organizations such as Business for Social Responsibility (U.S.) and Business in the Community (UK).

We will now explore why the synthesis between sustainability and strategic management theory and practice is occurring and how that relates to underlying questions of corporate social responsibility and the creation of value.

SUSTAINABILITY, CORPORATE SOCIAL RESPONSIBILITY, AND THE CREATION OF VALUE

Notwithstanding the emergence of rationalist economic "business cases" for sustainability, there is little doubt that a strong driver for many corporations is the desire of external actors to see business constructively engaged in solving global social and environmental challenges (Wheeler, 2003). Political, economic, social, technological, and ecological trends have resulted in significantly increased attention being paid to issues of corporate social responsibility, sustainability, and corporate ethics (Environics, 2002; European Commission, 2001). Thus we can also see "sustainability" as a societal meta-ideal which, like corporate social responsibility, requires a strategic response from businesses in order for them to retain legitimacy (Wheeler et al., 2003).

Conceptual bridges that may be constructed between sustainability and its sister term corporate social responsibility (CSR) depend to a great extent on geographic, cultural, philosophical, and linguistic nuances. However, it is possible to identify common beliefs, behaviors, and norms in many of the world's leading corporations that are consistent with harnessing the power and creativity of the private sector to generate simultaneous economic, social, and ecological gain for the firm and its stakeholders (Watts and Holme, 1999).[1]

Because of their roots in civil society discourse, both terms can carry normative overtones: sustainability frequently being equated with the need for corporations to respond to external environmental pressures, and CSR being associated with responses to external social demands—both of which historically have evoked a reactive corporate posture, either in compliance or philanthropic terms.

Today, leading companies adopting a strategic approach to sustainability or CSR exhibit corporate cultures and capabilities that depend relatively little on questions of regulatory compliance, pressures from advocacy groups, or indeed any other external constraints or demands on corporate behavior (Hart, 1997; Wheeler, 2003). Most leading firms take these activities for granted as part of the baseline "rules of the game" or what Roger Martin describes as the "civil foundation" (Martin, 2002). Instead, leading-edge sustainability (or CSR) strategies tend to be grounded in a recognition of the need to create sustainable value—however, the firm and its stakeholders choose to define value in their marketplaces (Wheeler et al., 2003; Hart and Milstein, 2003). This approach may be summarized in a single quotation from Peter Drucker in which he asserted that "the proper 'social responsibility' of business is to tame the dragon, that is to turn a social problem into economic opportunity and economic benefit, into productive capacity, into human competence, into well paid jobs, and into wealth" (Drucker, 1982). In keeping with Drucker's sentiments, in its report *Tomorrow's Markets,* the Washington-based think tank, World Resources Institute (2002), sought to link a wide array of pressing global economic, social, and environmental issues to market-based solutions and opportunities. In doing this, WRI believed it was appealing to the best instincts of the private sector, creating real space for competitiveness, innovation, and wealth creation. As emphasized by Michael Porter in his foreword to *Tomorrow's Markets,* this aspiration is both meaningful and realistic for private sector organizations.

The aspiration is also consistent with a growing body of evidence that in many sectors wealth creation is dependent on resources that are frequently co-controlled by the firm and its stakeholders (Pfeffer and Salancik, 1978; Barney, 1986 and 1991). And thus "soft" or "intangible" resources such as human capital, intellectual capital, social capital, reputation (especially perceived competence of management), and brands are increasingly valued by the marketplace and factored into stock market prices (Nahapiet and Ghoshal, 1998; Fombrun, 2001; Aaker and Joachimsthaler, 2000; Adler and Kwon, 2002; Wheeler and Davies, 2004). Thus Keith MacMillan long advocated the inclusion of intangible resources such as "goodwill" in corporate governance practice (see for example MacMillan and Downing, 1999).

It is salient to note here that in 2001 the average market to book ratio of firms in the Dow Jones Group Sustainability Index was 3.76. This means that the average market value of these companies in 2001 comprised approximately 80 percent intangible assets. Especially high ratios were quoted for Bristol Myers Squibb (14.98), Sony (7.33), 3M (7.31), P&G (7.02), Unilever (5.79), and Intel (5.41) (Holliday et al., 2002). Given evidence like this and the enormous potential business opportunities to be pursued in a world of 9 billion people, it is unsurprising that hundreds of the world's leading CEOs and their companies now espouse an explicit commitment to some form of sustainability mission or strategy. They also seek to implement those missions or strategies through proactive approaches to protecting and nurturing loyal relationships with stakeholders (Wheeler and Sillanpää, 1997 and 1998).[2]

The nexus between what we might now recognize as socially responsive, mission-based "sustainability strategies" and what would perhaps more traditionally be recognized as stakeholder approaches to strategic management (Freeman, 1984) provides some insight to current practice in many large corporations around the world. For many firms and their leaderships, any formerly conceived conflict between the interests of the firm, its investors, and its other stakeholders (including the protection of the natural environment) is now deemed irrelevant. For them, the "stockholder *versus* stakeholder" and "business *versus* environment" debates are already dead. They understand that whatever the official purpose of the firm, and whatever might be the strictures of company law in Anglophone jurisdictions, value cannot be created without the support of key stakeholder groups and the intangible assets they represent or co-control. They also recognize that "natural capital" cannot indefinitely be converted into economic wealth without significant attendant local and global ecological crises emerging (Holliday et al., 2002). And so it is simply up to management to deliver economic, social, and ecological value as efficiently as possible to the right mix of constituencies at the right time in order to achieve sustainability in every sense—including economic payoffs (Wheeler et al., 2003).

We will return to the relevance of stakeholder approaches to value creation, and therefore corporate governance, later in the chapter. Because, notwithstanding the significant weight of empirical evidence with respect to current trends in corporate strategy and practice, we do not see the same level of acceptance of stakeholder approaches in the field of corporate governance. In particular, an appreciation of the benefits of sustainability strategies and proactive approaches to maintaining and growing the value of stakeholder relationships and other intangible resources does not feature strongly in the North American governance literature. We must now explore why this should be the case, starting with an examination of contemporary approaches to corporate governance around the world.

CONTEMPORARY APPROACHES TO CORPORATE GOVERNANCE

The field of corporate governance is sharply divided between those practitioners and academic commentators who assume that the primary duty of boards, directors, and managers is to investors (because of their rights of ownership of the firm) *versus* those who believe that the duties should be more widely constructed, to take into account the rights both of the firm and its stakeholders. We may describe these two positions as being held by "normative agency theorists" and "normative stakeholder theorists." There are strongly and sincerely held views in both of these camps, but there is no question that the former position dominates the North American corporate governance literature (Daily et al., 2003).

In the first camp, which is largely associated with Anglophone countries where boards are not dominated by banks and other institutional stakeholders, it is not uncommon for commentators to be somewhat uncompromising in their assertion of the primacy of shareholder rights and the need for boards and managements to be held accountable for the financial resources of the investors (Carver and Oliver, 2002; Dimma, 2002; Monks and Minow, 2005).

Some agency theory commentators characterize those who hold a different view somewhat perjoratively as "stakeholder theorists" and/or "social activists" who ("much as happened in the failed communist and socialist experiments of the last century") would seek to undermine the capitalist project (Jensen, 2005).[3] These more ideological perspectives do somewhat ignore the corporate governance realities of most of the rest of the world, where obligations of boards and directors are usually judged in the context of the long-term interests of the company and all of its key stakeholders rather than simply the investors (Charkham, 1995; Wheeler and Sillanpää, 1997; Solomon and Solomon, 2004). Nevertheless, in the second camp, there are indeed those who argue for the more explicit assertion of noninvestor stakeholder rights through their formal inclusion in governance structures and processes. John Parkinson described this perspective as being consistent with the "social institution" model of the purpose of the corporation (Parkinson, 2003). However, it is extremely rare that Continental European or Asian governance perspectives emerge in the North American corporate governance literature, and when they do it is usually as part of an international review of governance practices (see for example Franks and Mayer, 2005) rather than any attempt to explore the comparative merits of alternative models.

There have been attempts in the mainstream management literature to forge approaches that depart to an extent from a strict application of agency theory in a North American context, adopting more of a middle ground. For example, Sundaramurthy and Lewis (2003) discussed the proposition that there may be a need to shift the focus of board responsibilities in order to better balance agency theory and stewardship theory. And Aguilera and Jackson (2003) noted some of the shortcomings of agency theory with respect to embracing the diversity of stakeholders within the principal-agent relationship, the inter-dependencies of firm stakeholders, and the complexity and variation of institutional environments within which governance practices have evolved globally. But neither amounted to a major critique of Anglophone governance models.

Perhaps of more relevance to a discussion of contemporary approaches to corporate governance and sustainability is the *routine practice* of stakeholder-inclusive governance in Continental Europe and Asia, where banks and other institutional stakeholders frequently feature in governance structures and processes (Solomon and Solomon, 2004). It is this practice that those based in the Anglophone world might wish to pay attention to, just in case it provides some opportunities for interesting research and learning.

Three bodies that are obliged to follow a middle path between competing paradigms of corporate governance are the Organisation for Economic Co-Operation and Development (OECD), the World Bank, and the Commonwealth. In each case these organizations have devoted significant resources to researching best practice in governance from a free market perspective without becoming captive of any particular normative position on the ultimate purpose of the firm.

In 1996 the OECD defined corporate governance as "the discipline and control of firms designed to ensure that they are efficiently managed and that the economic welfare of society is maximized" (Clarke and Clegg, 2000). And in its 2004 *Principles of Corporate Governance,* the OECD made explicit the importance of cooperation with stakeholders to corporate sustainability: "The corporate governance framework should recognise the rights of stakeholders as established by law and encourage active cooperation between corporations and stakeholders in creating wealth, jobs, and the sustainability of financially sound enterprises" (OECD, 2004). The OECD also set out six specific prescriptions for protecting the interests of business stakeholders:

- The rights of stakeholders that are protected by law should be respected;
- Where stakeholder interests are protected by law, stakeholders should have the opportunity to obtain effective redress for violation of their rights;
- Performance-enhancing mechanisms for employee participation should be permitted;
- Where stakeholders participate in the corporate governance process, they should have access to relevant and sufficient information on a timely and regular basis;
- Stakeholders, including individual employees, should be able to freely communicate their concerns about illegal or unethical practices to the company board and their rights should not be compromised for doing this;
- The corporate governance framework should be complemented by an effective, efficient insolvency framework and by adequate enforcement of creditor rights.

In the World Bank's 1999 *Corporate Governance Overview,* Sir Adrian Cadbury described governance as "concerned with holding the balance between economic and social goals and between individual and communal goals ... the aim is to align as nearly as possible the interests of individuals, corporations and society" (World Bank, 1999).

Bob Garrett has summarized the work of the Commonwealth Association for Corporate Governance with respect to duties of boards and directors (Garrett and Gould, 2002). Based on "long-established corporate governance values," Garrett describes the work of practitioners in fifty-four Commonwealth countries resulting in the development of ten universal duties:

- Duty of Legitimacy (operating within the law);
- Duty of Upholding the Director's Primary Loyalty (to the company),
- Duty of Upholding the Director's Primary Role (to drive the enterprise forward while keeping it under prudent control);
- Duty of Holding the Company in Trust (fiduciary duty);
- Duty of Insuring Critical Review of Proposals to the Board;
- Duty of Ensuring Directoral Care (in decision-taking);
- Duty of Upholding the Three Values of Corporate Governance (accountability, probity, and transparency);
- Duty of Upholding the Rights of Minority Owners;
- Duty of Ensuring Corporate Social Responsibility;
- Duty of Ensuring Board Learning, Development, and Communication.

The views of the OECD, the World Bank, and the Commonwealth are relevant here because it would be hard for even the most trenchant critic of sustainability strategies or a stakeholder approach to strategic management to assert that these organizations are captive of special interest groups or social activists. All start from an assumption that free markets are important to wealth creation and all subject their recommendations to exhaustive research and practitioner review. One represents mostly richer industrialized countries and the other two both industrialized and developing countries. Thus all three need to balance very carefully their prescriptions between alternative paradigms and governance models.

And so perhaps it is not surprising that the three institutions believe it possible to honor *both the rights of investors and the rights of other stakeholders* who may have legal or governance claims on the firm. And it is interesting that all speak explicitly of aligning the interests of corporations and society; that is, the concept of corporate social responsibility as we defined it earlier with the help of Peter Drucker.

Some individual jurisdictions have traveled even further down the road of reconciling investor and other stakeholder interests in a "win-win" framework for corporate governance. For example, in South Africa, the King Report on Corporate Governance (King Committee, 2002) described a stakeholder-inclusive "modern approach" for corporate governance that exhorted companies "to identify the company's stakeholders, including its shareowners, and to agree on policies as to how the relationship with those stakeholders should be advanced and managed in the interests of the company.... The inclusive approach requires that the purpose of the company be *defined,* and the values by which the company will carry on its daily life should be *identified* and *communicated* to all stakeholders." The King Committee also listed seven characteristics of good governance, which explicitly included social responsibility:

- Discipline
- Transparency
- Independence
- Accountability
- Responsibility
- Fairness
- Social responsibility

Given that (1) hundreds of leading corporations have adopted mission-based sustainability strategies and/or stakeholder approaches to strategic management; and (2) that leading international institutions that have an interest in wealth creation and corporate governance find it relatively simple to reconcile the economic, social, and ecological obligations of the firm; it remains an open question why this should be deemed so antithetical to wealth creation by some commentators on corporate governance. In our view this is the result of a historic misunderstanding of what "sustainable enterprise" or "stakeholder capitalism" might entail. Below, we attempt to trace the source of the misunderstanding, drawing out some of the normative and ideological influences that have obscured the terrain.

AGENCY THEORY AND STAKEHOLDER THEORY REVISITED

The separation of ownership from control—a feature of corporate life that emerged during the twentieth century—raises questions of transaction costs, resource misappropriation, and associated "agency problems" that have long troubled North American commentators on corporate governance and political economy (Berle and Means, 1932; Berle, 1959; Galbraith, 1967). Partly in response to these issues, agency theory emerged to explain the relationship between shareholders, boards, and their appointed managements (Eisenhardt, 1989). One of the most active proponents, if not the "founding father," of a strict "owner/principal" agency theory perspective on corporate governance is Michael Jensen.

In 1976, Jensen was coauthor of a seminal "theory of the firm" article with William Meckling that advocated a clear economic focus for managers to be measured against and held accountable for (Jensen and Meckling, 1976). So it is rather helpful—especially in light of recent spectacular examples of misappropriation of resources in U.S. corporations—that in *Corporate Governance at the Crossroads,* Donald Chew and Stuart Gillan (2005) have assembled a number of articles that include the contemporary views of Jensen. In these articles Jensen covers an impressive array of subjects, embracing economics, politics, political economy, sociology, and psychology, including a rather grandly titled piece: *The Nature of Man* with William Meckling (Jensen and Meckling, 2005).

Jensen's basic position on agency and the importance of long-term "value maximization" and thus the establishment of a single objective for the firm has not changed: "Telling a manager to maximize current profits, market share, future growth in profits, and anything else one pleases will leave that manager with no way to make a reasoned decision" (Jensen, 2005). He advocates maximization of economic performance as the ideal single overriding objective for the firm on the basis that it will effectively unite the interests of investors, boards, and managers. However, in an otherwise uncompromising critique of stakeholder theory and the concept of the "balanced scorecard" of Kaplan and Norton (1996, 1999), Jensen does allow for the possible melding together of a softer form of EVA (Enlightened Value Maximization) with a harder form of stakeholder theory (Enlightened Stakeholder Theory).

In the enlightened version of value maximization, Jensen argues that "we cannot maximize the long-term market value of an organization if we ignore or mistreat any important constituency. We cannot create value without good relations with customers, employees, financial backers, suppliers, regulators, and communities." And in the enlightened version of stakeholder theory, Jensen asserts that in trading off between stakeholders, value creation should be the overriding normative criterion: "Enlightened stakeholder theory adds the simple specification that the objective function—the overriding goal—of the firm is to maximize total long-term value" (Jensen, 2005).

Despite this reasoned attempt to resolve the historic false dichotomy between the interests of investors and stakeholders, Jensen continues to conflate the arguments of "stakeholder theorists" directly with the ambitions of social activists. As Jensen argues, "Special interest groups will continue to use the arguments of stakeholder theory to legitimize their positions, and it is in our collective interest to expose the logical fallacy of these arguments." Moreover, in common with more strident commentators whom he cites approvingly (for example, Sternberg, 1996, 1999), Jensen sees the worrisome possibility that "stakeholder theorists will often have the active support of managers who wish to throw off the constraints on their power provided by the value-seeking criterion and its enforcement by capital markets, the market for corporate control, and product markets" (Jensen, 2005).[4]

Notwithstanding his criticisms of advocates of a stakeholder approach to strategic management[5] and the complete absence of any evidence of managers adopting any normative version of "stakeholder theory" per se—even as a way of escaping their obligations to investors—we wish to acknowledge here that Jensen's analysis has developed since 1976. This progress has been twofold. First, as evidenced by the introduction of the notion of "enlightened value maximization," Jensen explicitly accepts the risk-based argument that doing damage to stakeholder relationships hinders value creation. Second, it would appear that Jensen accepts that stakeholders themselves are capable of exercising sophisticated judgments, even if (under agency theory) boards and managers apparently are not. We will deal with both of these points in turn.

Stakeholder Approaches and the Sustainable Creation of Value

As noted above, it has been argued for some time that there is no necessary conflict between long-term maximization of value for investors and other stakeholders (Freeman, 1984, 2000, 2001; Freeman and McVea, 2001; Wheeler and Sillanpää, 1997 and 1998; Wheeler, Colbert, and Freeman, 2003). Moreover, in a complex global economic business environment, the increasing importance of intangible and relationship-based (that is, stakeholder-mediated) resources to firm valuation means that it is both counterproductive and futile to try to separate the interests of investors and stakeholders (Wheeler, 2003). And as we have noted, this appears not to be a problem for a large number of the world's leading corporations or those international bodies charged with developing guidelines for corporate governance.

It is possible that a lack of familiarity with the current state of the debate in stakeholder theory lies at the root of Jensen's misconceptions of the arguments of its proponents. Such misconceptions have been noted elsewhere (see, for example, the response of Freeman et al., 2004 to Sundaram and Inkpen, 2004). It is true that many stakeholder theorists adopt an ethically normative approach and argue that inclusion of stakeholders in the processes of the firm is an acknowledgment of their rights. This is why so much research has emerged from scholars in the fields of business ethics and corporate social responsibility, many of whom imply or actively assert the importance of a normative core to stakeholder theory (Paine, 1994; Donaldson and Preston, 1995; Donaldson, 1999; Donaldson and Dunfee, 1999; Carroll, 1999; Jones and Wicks, 1999; Margolis and Walsh, 2003).[6]

However, following the original example of Freeman (1984), and summarized more recently by Freeman and McVea (2001), a good deal of stakeholder thinking has long been present in the mainstream management literature, not as business ethics per se but rather as a pragmatic approach to *strategic management* (Kay, 1995; Harrison and St. John, 1996; Wheeler and Sillanpää, 1997). Moreover, a number of empirical studies have been undertaken that explore the correlation between orientation to stakeholders and economic performance (Waddock and Graves, 1997; Agle et al., 1999; Berman et al., 1999).

Stakeholder orientation is frequently manifested in various measures of Corporate Social Performance (CSP). Margolis and Walsh (2001) summarized approximately eighty studies of social and financial performance in the literature and found that around half (53 percent) provided direct evidence of a correlation between financial performance and various measures of corporate social performance (the independent variable). There was no relationship in nineteen studies (24 percent), a mixed relationship in fifteen studies (19 percent) and a negative relationship in only four studies (5 percent).

Despite the evidence of correlations between social performance and economic performance, contemporary advocates of a pragmatic version of stakeholder capitalism do not tend to claim causality in these relationships. But they do note the complete absence of empirical research showing that good social performance leads generally to economic underperformance (a key claim of the normative agency theorists). Equally, they do not seek to create artificial distinctions between the act of value creation and ethical behavior; instead they seek to make sense of the complex multiple challenges and opportunities facing firms from a strategic management perspective (Freeman, 2001). They believe that there is no inherent contradiction between achieving economic and social objectives and that stakeholder capitalism simply "sets a high standard, recognizes the commonsense practical world of business today, and asks managers to get on with the task of creating value for all stakeholders" (Freeman, 2000).

In addition to his misunderstanding of the state of the debate in stakeholder theory, Jensen also fails to transcend the traditional Friedmanesque critique of corporate philanthropy. This critique asserts that the adoption of stakeholder approaches leads directly to firms taking on the social welfare responsibilities of the state. This results in the firm losing efficiency and competitiveness: "A firm that adopts stakeholder theory will be handicapped in the competition for survival because, as a basis for action, stakeholder theory politicizes the corporation and leaves its managers empowered to exercise their own preferences in spending the firm's resources" and "[stakeholder theory] allows managers and directors to devote the firm's resources to their own favorite causes—the environment, art, cities, medical research—without being held accountable for the effect of such expenditures on firm value" (Jensen, 2005).

A number of arguments may be posited against this proposition, the most salient of which are (1) even if we knew what "adopting stakeholder theory" meant in practice, there is no evidence that firms that "adopt" stakeholder theory spend more on corporate philanthropy than those that do not; (2) very few firms donate more than 1 percent of pretax profits to charity, and the trend in professional corporate philanthropy is in any case toward more strategic approaches that align corporate giving with the reputational and marketing interests of the firm; and (3) given the relatively small sums involved (compared with more significant and risk-laden investments such as capital expenditure, R&D, acquisitions, new product launches, and so on) it is unsurprising that there is no empirical evidence of such small investments in reputation management having causal positive or negative impacts on firm performance.

By failing to make distinctions between ethically normative and strategically pragmatic stakeholder approaches, and by exaggerating the importance of corporate philanthropy, Jensen falls into the trap of assuming theoretical uniformity and liberal/left political coherence to stakeholder theory. The plain reality is this: There is no unifying "stakeholder theory" and no ethical or political consensus on the reasoning for inclusion of stakeholder interests in corporate strategy—only empirical evidence that it does no damage and in some cases might be highly beneficial. Jensen conjures a theoretical and political shibboleth that does not exist.

Toward a Unified Theory of Human Judgment and Behavior

Notwithstanding this misunderstanding, just as he has somewhat modified his position with respect to "enlightened value maximization" in allowing for at least some attention to be paid to noninvestor stakeholders, Jensen has also made progress with respect to what motivates real human beings. In *The Nature of Man*, Jensen and Meckling (2005) present five models of human behavior, one of which the authors own and is advocated as integrating "200 years of research and debate in economics, the other social sciences, and philosophy." The "Resourceful, Evaluative, Maximizing Model," or REMM, of Jensen and Meckling is, they assert, superior to the other four archetypes, which are premised only on the individual disciplines of economics, sociology, psychology, and politics. For example, the entire field of sociology is dismissed in a few hundred words as being overly concerned with making allowances for societal victims and underpinned by Marxist and Platonic philosophies: "Marxist politicians understand that the sociological model is the foundation for the centralization of power. Marxism has received wide support in Europe. It has also substantial support among the Catholic clergy [sic] and American academics" (Jensen and Meckling, 2005).

For Jensen and Meckling, the economic and political models represent simplistic versions of ultrarational or ultra-altruistic motivations and behaviors. And the psychology model of human behavior (especially to the extent it is based on the works of Abraham Maslow) is summarily dismissed as being atheoretical and simplistic: "Theory erected on the basis of individuals who are driven by wants, but who cannot or will not make substitutions, will necessarily consist of a series of independent propositions relating particular drives to actions and will never be able to capture the complexity of human behavior." The entire field of organizational behavior and human resource management are included in this summary critique.

So here is a paradox. In claiming to draw on the best of each of four traditional disciplines, Jensen and Meckling's Resourceful, Evaluative, Maximizing Model of human behavior (or REMM), when applied to many real-world situations, seeks to demonstrate that ordinary people are not solely interested in money, income, or wealth. Moreover, ordinary people exercise sophisticated judgments in trading off between a range of benefits available to them today and in the future based on a combination of personal and societal values. How peculiar then, that under the strict application of agency theory, boards and managers of firms are not assumed to be capable of such sophistication, of balancing up the needs of different constituencies in real time with a view to maximizing long-term value for the firm and its stakeholders. Instead, managers need to be given just one deliverable; that is, maximize long-term value for investors, with everything else being subordinate to that.

We will not dwell on this logical contradiction too heavily. Instead we will accept that in formulating REMM, Jensen and Meckling are helping make an indirect case for what happens in the minds of real managers in real organizations. As suggested by Freeman (2000) and subsequently Wheeler et al. (2003) and Freeman et al. (2004), this is not terribly complicated. Real managers in real organizations respond to the need to create value for all stakeholders—however they and the stakeholders like to construct it—in as efficient a way as possible. Indeed, according to the arguments of pragmatic stakeholder approaches, this is what good business has always been about.

Interestingly, we are now beginning to see the emergence of capital market recognition of this truism. The evidence for this resides principally in the nascent but increasingly influential world of sustainable or "socially responsible investment" (SRI). In direct contrast to the narrow measurement and accountability prescriptions of the normative agency theorists, this is the field of investment that seeks to integrate an understanding of *current* "triple bottom line" performance on social, environmental, and economic performance with a view to using these metrics to predict *future* long-term economic performance and sustainability. We will now explore how evidence from sustainable and socially responsible investing lends further weight to the need for a new approach to corporate governance research and practice.

THE CAPITAL MARKETS AND SUSTAINABILITY

Socially responsible investment (SRI) generally involves consideration of social and environmental criteria as well as the economic performance of investments. SRI refers to any or all of the following four areas: (1) positively and negatively screened funds or investment portfolios; (2) shareholder action or corporate engagement; (3) economically targeted investment or community economic development; and (4) social venture capital investment.

The arguments we wish to make here with respect to SRI focus on the first area and specifically *positive screening*. Clear differentiation should be made between negatively screened and positively screened investments. Negative screens (often used in the construction of "ethical funds") apply normatively chosen exclusionary criteria such as no tobacco or military hardware stocks as the precondition(s) on which the investment portfolio is based. Investments are subsequently selected from the remaining universe of potential investments. In contrast, positive screens are applied by specialist investment managers to a pool of conventionally chosen companies (based on financial metrics) which are then selected according to a proprietary mix of corporate social, environmental, and other performance criteria. For example, positive screens may evaluate companies based on issues related to: corporate governance, employee and supply chain diversity, stakeholder engagement, the natural environment, human rights, corporate ethics policies, and so on. In each case an attempt is made to avoid sources of risk and maximize sources of future value. This method is often referred to as "best in class" investing (Mansley, 2000).

SRI in general has enjoyed significant growth in the past decade (Social Investment Organization, 2003; Social Investment Forum 2003; EuroSif, 2003). The main drivers of this growth have been:

Growing Appreciation of Risks

International drivers of sustainability related risks associated with corporate activities include potential involvement in human rights or ecological abuse and exposure to climate change and other liabilities such as chronic illness or disease. These exposures are accompanied by mounting pressures from influential NGOs (World Resources Institute, 2002) and are increasingly driving market confidence in the stocks of the exposed companies. Thus oil and gas companies that are exposed to significant risk from the carbon intensity of their processes, or mining companies that are more exposed to greater than average health and productivity costs for their sector because they have operations in areas of high HIV/AIDS incidence, may be less worthy of investment than companies that are mitigating or managing down these exposures (Austin and Sauer, 2002; Coalition for Environmentally Responsible Economies, 2002).

Increasingly Organized and Individual Stakeholder Interests

Institutional investment professionals find themselves being asked to respond to the values of their stakeholders with increasing frequency. These include religious groups, labor unions, and individuals (Mathias, 2003; Kasemir and Suëss, 2002). In some cases this is coupled with a growing capacity for shareholder activism on social and environmental issues (Biello, 2003). According to Baue (2003), the 2003 U.S. proxy season was a record-breaking year for shareholder resolutions, with more than 1,080 shareholder resolutions filed.

Increasing Transparency

There are new disclosure rules in various countries including the UK, Belgium, Sweden, Germany, France, and Australia that require pension funds and/or mutual funds to be more transparent about their investment policies regarding social, environmental, and ethical (SEE) issues (Feltmate et al., 2001; Yaron, 2001; Social Investment Forum, 2003; Wheeler et al., 2004). In addition, the success of the Global Reporting Initiative in encouraging fuller disclosure on social and environmental performance by leading companies is driving voluntary best practice in this area, bringing to light variances in performance that may drive awareness and sensitivity to risk still further (Global Reporting Initiative, 2002). As of summer 2004, the GRI had 128 "organizational stakeholders" promoting the use of the guidelines, the overwhelming majority of which were large corporations.

Growing Confidence in Performance and Availability of Products

There is growing confidence in SRI products as the performance of SRI funds under management and SRI indices keep pace with or even outperform benchmarks (Feltmate et al., 2001; Mutual Fund Review, 2002; diBartolomeo and Kurtz, 1999). This is accompanied by the increasing number and diversity of SRI products available, enabling investors to hold a balanced SRI portfolio (Social Investment Organization, 2003). As a result of these drivers, socially screened portfolios in the United States grew 7 percent between 2001 and 2002, while the broader universe of professionally managed portfolios fell 4 percent (Social Investment Forum, 2003). Between 1995 and 2003, SRI assets grew 40 percent faster than all professionally managed investment assets in the United States (Social Investment Forum, 2003). SRI has also become the fastest-growing sector of the UK retail funds market, expanding tenfold over the past decade to become an approximately $6 billion industry. Total SRI assets in the UK (including those mobilized for purposes of corporate engagement) increased from £23 billion in 1997 to almost £225 billion in 2001 (Sparkes, 2002). The Canadian Social Investment Organization (SIO) estimates that the sum of all assets in Canada managed according to SRI guidelines as of June 30, 2002, totaled $51.4 billion (Canadian). This represents about 3.3 percent of the Canadian retail mutual fund and institutional investment market (Social Investment Organization, 2003).

Supporting the evidence cited earlier concerning the link between the social and financial performance of firms, similar evidence has emerged from the performance of specialist stock market indices. These include the Domini Social Index (DSI, U.S.), the Jantzi Social Index (JSI, Canada), and the Dow Jones Group Sustainability Index (DJSI, international). The relative performance of these indices—all of which are constructed on a wide range of social, environmental, economic, ethical, and governance-related criteria—versus standard benchmark indices is illustrated below (see Figures 14.1–14.3).

To be clear, neither the empirical studies on corporate social performance cited earlier (Margolis and Walsh, 2001) nor the specialist SRI indices described here demonstrate causality between superior social or environmental performance and economic performance.

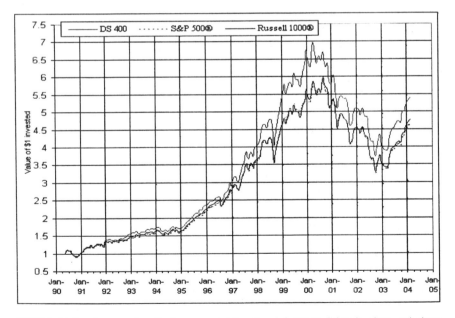

FIGURE 14.1. Comparative Performance of the Domini 400 Social Index (DSI, US) since Inception in May 1990
Source: http://www.kld.com

FIGURE 14.2. Comparative Performance of the Jantzi Social Index (JSI Canada) since Inception in December 1999
Source: http://www.mjra-jsi.com

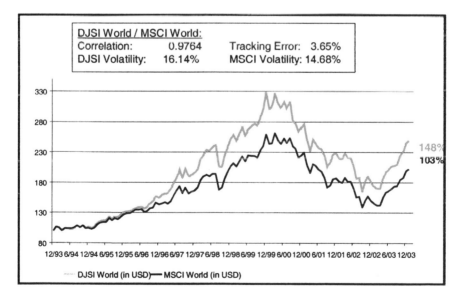

FIGURE 14.3. Comparative Performance of the Dow Jones Group Sustainability Index (DJSI, international) since Inception in 1999 and Backtested Retrospective To 1993
Source: http://www.sustainability-index.com

One theory explaining the phenomenon relates to the numerous political, societal, cultural, stakeholder, ecological, technological, economic, and financial drivers and constraints that create complexity and ambiguity for firms. Thus it is possible that positive correlations between economic performance and corporate social performance are reflective of a third variable, for example, superior management capabilities to navigate complexity in the global business environment (Wheeler, 2003). Others lend support to this notion (Feltmate et al., 2001; Innovest, 2003), describing corporate social performance as a proxy measure for identifying companies with superior quality of management. This is a criterion that mainstream analysts are constantly trying to assess; in SRI it is simply reframed through a sustainability lens.

It is also possible that the performance of SRI funds might be attributed to the extensive research involved. For example, more time is spent analyzing predictive (leading) indicators of future economic performance as opposed to simply assessing current or retrospective indicators of performance: governance, human capital investments, social capital investments, sustainable product investments, and so on.

Whatever the causal factors linking economic, social, and ecological performance of firms, there can be little doubt that markets are responding, thus lending even greater force to the argument that corporate governance practices need to be cognizant of the trend. There is also an implication that narrow (that is, normative) constructions of agency theory may not be sufficient to allow these "sustainability" factors to be captured, thereby placing firms at a competitive disadvantage with respect to raising capital or managing nonfinancial risks (Wheeler and Davies, 2004).

We will now turn to the implications of the pursuit of sustainability using a stakeholder approach to strategic management for corporate governance theory and practice.

IMPLICATIONS FOR CORPORATE GOVERNANCE THEORY

Thus far we have argued that:

1. Sustainability may be defined in terms of competitiveness, value creation, and future-focused approaches to strategic management;
2. In many of the world's leading firms—North American, European, and Asian—there is a de facto acceptance of a mission-based sustainability strategy and the need for a "stakeholder approach" to strategic management in order to drive long-term, sustainable value;
3. In the view of bodies such as the OECD, the World Bank, and the Commonwealth, there is no practical contradiction between the long-term interests of investors and other stakeholders;
4. There is strong empirical evidence that the economic, social, and environmental performance of firms is more often correlated than not;

5. There is strong empirical evidence that taking into account economic, social, environmental, ethical, and governance-related factors in choosing investments does not systematically reduce economic performance of portfolios or the specialist "best in class" indices on which many of them are based.

We have also noted a slight thawing of attitudes in one of the leading proponents of a normative interpretation of agency theory (Jensen, 2005).

In their text *Corporate Governance and Accountability*, Solomon and Solomon (2004) argue that despite the constraints of company law in Anglophone jurisdictions there is no logical or practical constraint to reconciling agency theory with a stakeholder approach. Citing Hill and Jones (1992) and Shankman (1999) together with their own empirical research and a growing body of evidence from the literature, Solomon and Solomon make the point that "there is little inconsistency between the ultimate objective of agency theory and the practice of a stakeholder approach." This leads the authors to argue for a realistic stakeholder approach similar to that advocated by Freeman and Evan (1990) and not dissimilar to Jensen's "enlightened stakeholder theory" (Jensen, 2005). This prescription may be intellectually unsatisfying to proponents of a more normative approach to stakeholder inclusion in business, but as Solomon and Solomon assert: "This is really the only approach to [business] ethics that makes sense in the modern world, given the extant legal and regulatory environment confronting businesses."

Extending the analysis of Solomon and Solomon, this chapter has sought to establish a theoretical and practical case for seeing sustainability and stakeholder approaches to strategic management *in service of value creation: economic, social, and ecological.* The question remains, however: What is the appropriate theoretical frame within which this might occur?

Lynall et al. (2003) have observed the dominance of agency theory, resource dependency theory, institutional theory, and social network theory in Anglophone governance research and concluded that "the lack of empirical support for theoretical models of boards and firm performance calls into question the applicability of existing theories to the phenomena of interest." We agree with this conclusion and, based on our analysis, we wish to propose a contemporary *"sustainable resource-stewardship model of corporate governance"* that we believe integrates the best of agency theory, stewardship theory, and resource dependency theory, and is consistent with the view of Cadbury (World Bank, 1999) that corporate governance is "concerned with holding the balance between economic and social goals and between individual and communal goals... the aim is to align as nearly as possible the interests of individuals, corporations and society."

A visual description of the model is depicted in the accompanying figure.

In this model good governance may be characterized as being concerned with "the relationships among stakeholders in the process of decision-making and control over firm resources" (Aguilera and Jackson, 2003), and thus we

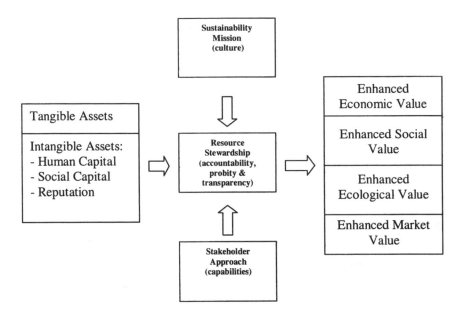

FIGURE 14.4. A Sustainable Resource-Stewardship Model for Corporate Governance

might characterize the primary duty of boards and senior management teams as one of "protecting, growing and helping gain access to resources that might benefit the firm and its ability to create value" (Wheeler and Davies, 2004). We may also note that:

Agency theory (of the non-normative variety) supports this model because it implies that boards and managers act on behalf of investors *and other stakeholders* in growing the value of the firm in market terms as well as with respect to economic, social, and ecological value.

Stewardship theory supports the model because the firm itself is seen as being a bundle of tangible and intangible resources that need to be protected and grown on behalf of a broad range of interested parties in a way that is accountable, transparent, and ethical.

Resource dependency theory supports the model because some of the intangible assets are co-owned by actors external to the firm, and thus it is important that boards and senior teams help draw in and secure those relationship-based assets for the benefit of the firm and its stakeholders.

Institutional and social network theories are consistent with the model because they describe the responses of organizations and their members to external forces mediated by stakeholders, including those of institutional, sectoral, and individual peer groups. These responses, if deemed appropriate, contribute to protecting and growing intangible resources, for example, reputation.

The model is consistent with "sustainability strategies" that in this chapter we have characterized as being aspirational or "mission-based" in nature (rather than strictly concerned with strategic management approaches), and therefore demanding of a corporate cultural empathy in terms of beliefs, behaviors, and norms. And the model is consistent with "stakeholder approaches" to strategic management that require the development and deployment of appropriate capabilities by the firm and its agents if tangible and intangible resources are to be protected, grown, and mobilized (Wheeler, 2003).

The sustainable resource-based model depicted here provides some promising opportunities for future research into the role of governance in achieving sustainability for the firm and its stakeholders. Such research might reasonably address questions of value creation in an era of neo-Schumpeterian creative destruction and growing markets in the developing world; it might also explore in more depth the role of the board in reflecting the interests and insights of stakeholders as co-controllers of resources essential to firm sustainability; and such research might seek to further elucidate those characteristics of governance and strategy that are predictive of future performance in economic, social, and ecological terms.

Specific research questions based on our model might include:

- Do boards and senior management teams as currently constructed reflect cultures (beliefs, behaviors, and norms) that are empathetic to the societal ideal of sustainability?
- Do boards and senior management teams as currently constructed exhibit capabilities associated with stakeholder approaches to strategic management?
- How are board and senior management team cultures and capabilities correlated with the acquisition of tangible and intangible resources?
- How are board and senior management team cultures and capabilities correlated with the protection (risk management) of tangible and intangible resources?
- How are board and senior management team cultures and capabilities correlated with the growth of tangible and intangible resources and their reflection in market valuation?
- What board and senior management cultures and capabilities will contribute to corporate competencies in securing new markets in developing countries?
- What board and senior management cultures and capabilities will contribute to corporate competencies in navigating neo-Schumpeterian forces in both established and new markets?

Answers to these questions would go some way to establishing new insights into optimal board composition for companies wishing to pursue sustainable value through a resource-stewardship role.

IMPLICATIONS FOR CORPORATE GOVERNANCE PRACTICE

With our emphasis on culture and capabilities, and therefore board and senior management team composition, it will be clear that we are not necessarily advocating wholesale structural or legal reform to corporate governance practice. In fact, the evidence is that there is little or no relationship between structures and accountabilities as currently measured and performance (Wheeler and Davies, 2004).

Instead, consistent with the views of Cascio (2004); Letendre (2004); and LeBlanc and Gillies (2004), we believe that the sustained (and thus sustainable) high performance of boards and senior management teams is more likely to be associated with behavioral and skills-based archetypes than specific structural or legal prescriptions, especially those based on normative versions of agency theory or stakeholder theory. In our view, in seeking to guarantee accountability for resources in particular ways, the ideologically normative approaches are likely to end up curtailing the entrepreneurial spirit and effectiveness that is required to generate value of any kind in business.

As implied earlier, we believe that perpetuation of the "stockholder *versus* stakeholder" and "business *versus* environment" dichotomies in the Anglophone management literature are at best a distraction and at worst a potential handicap to practitioner learning and performance. Furthermore, given the emerging international consensus on what firm performance and good governance means with respect to investors, other stakeholders, and the natural environment, the domination of the North American corporate governance literature by simplistic notions of agency accountabilities (which assume the absolute primacy of investor rights in global marketplaces from an Anglophone perspective) are held to be anachronistic and lacking in humility and academic rigor.

Our advice to practitioners leading boards and senior management teams would be simple:

1. Understand what tangible and intangible resources and assets are important to the business today; if they are missing, secure them; if they are at risk, protect them; and if they are important to future value, nurture and grow them.
2. Constantly review strategy to ensure it remains aligned with current and future marketplaces and product needs, taking into account the sustainability drivers of economic, social and ecological change.
3. Constantly review internal firm competencies to ensure they are aligned with current and future marketplaces and product needs.
4. Critically appraise the board and senior management team for their cultural empathy with the societal "meta-ideal" of sustainability and their capabilities with respect to stakeholder approaches—both of which are important to effective stewardship of firm resources and the conversion of tangible and intangible resources into value; if there are missing elements, correct them through processes of recruitment, succession, and personal learning and development.
5. Develop measures, targets and objectives for turning tangible and intangible resources into value for the firm and its stakeholders (including investors).

NOTES

1. The World Business Council on Sustainable Development defines "Corporate Responsibility (sustainable development)" as delivering simultaneously on financial, environmental, and social responsibilities.

2. As of summer 2004 there were more than 160 CEOs and their companies represented in the World Business Council for Sustainable Development and more than 1,700 businesses signed up for the UN Global Compact on corporate social responsibility.

3. On the question of social activism, there is little evidence that advocacy groups pay a great deal of attention to questions of corporate governance and/or company law. One of us (DW) was a member of the Governance subgroup of the UK Company Law Review (CLR) during 1999. It was this subgroup that was requested to accept the decision of the CLR Steering Group that "Enlightened Shareholder Value" should defeat "Pluralism" (i.e., a formal stakeholder governance model) as the guiding principle for the review. Sadly, no middle path option was permitted. Neither the labor movement nor the environmental movement in the UK was active in promoting public discussion on the principles at stake.

4. In fifteen years in the world of sustainability and corporate social responsibility spanning business, consulting, and academia, the primary author of this chapter (DW) has never heard a single corporate manager or social activist use the term "stakeholder theory."

5. At one point Jensen asserts: "Under some interpretations, stakeholders also include the environment, terrorists, blackmailers and thieves." He then cites Freeman (1984) entirely out of context.

6. Of course, this perspective is not necessarily revolutionary; many jurisdictions in the non-Anglophone world explicitly recognize the interests of noninvestor stakeholders in governance processes and structures (Charkham, 1995; Solomon and Solomon, 2004).

REFERENCES

This contribution is dedicated to the memories of Professors Keith MacMillan (1945–2003) and John Parkinson (1955–2003), both of whom devoted significant scholarly efforts to exploring and resolving the governance implications of ideas discussed in this chapter.

Aaker, D. A., and Joachimsthaler, E. (2000). *Brand leadership.* New York: Free Press.

Adler, P. A., and Kwon, S-W. (2002). Social capital: Prospects for a new concept. *Academy of Management Review, 27* (1), 17–40.

Agle, B. R., Mitchell, R. K., and Sonnenfeld, J. A. (1999). Who matters to CEOs? An investigation of stakeholder attributes and salience, corporate performance, and CEO values. *Academy of Management Journal, 42* (5), 507–525.

Aguilera, R. V., and Jackson, G. (2003). The cross-national diversity of corporate governance: Dimensions and determinants. *Academy of Management Review, 28* (3), 447–465.

Aragón-Correa, J. A., and Sharma, S. (2003). A contingent resource-based view of proactive corporate environmental strategy. *Academy of Management Review, 28* (1), 71–88.

Austin, D., and Sauer, A. (2002). *Changing oil: Emerging environmental risks and shareholder value in the oil and gas industry.* Washington: World Resources Institute. Available at http://www.climate.wri.org

Barney, J. (1986). Organizational culture: Can it be a source of sustained competitive advantage? *Academy of Management Review, 11* (3), 656–665.

Barney, J. B. (1991). Firm resources and sustained competitive advantage. *Journal of Management, 17,* 99–120.

Baue, W. (2003, December 17). *2003 proxy season roundup: Shareowner action success measured on and off the record.* Accessed online: http://www.socialfunds.com/news/

Berle, A. A. (1959). *Power without property: A new development in American political economy.* New York: Harcourt Brace.

Berle, A. A., and Means, G. (1932). *Private property and the modern corporation.* New York: MacMillan.

Berman, S. L., Wicks, A. C., Kotha, S., and Jones, T. M. (1999). Does stakeholder orientation matter? The relationship between stakeholder management models and firm financial performance. *Academy of Management Journal, 42* (5), 488–506.

Biello, D. (2003, July–August). A revolutionary season. *Environmental Finance,* 18–20.

Carroll, A. B. (1999). Corporate social responsibility: Evolution of a definitional construct. *Business and Society, 38* (3), 268–295.

Carver, J., and Oliver, C. (2002). *Corporate boards that create value. Governing company performance from the boardroom.* San Francisco: Jossey-Bass.

Cascio, W. F. (2004). Board governance: A social systems perspective. *Academy of Management Executive, 18* (10), 97–100.

Charkham, J. (1995). *Keeping good company: A study of corporate governance in five countries.* Oxford: Oxford University Press.

Chew, D. H., and Gillan, S. L. (2005). *Corporate governance at the crossroads. A book of readings.* New York: McGraw-Hill Irwin.

Christensen, C. M. (1997). *The innovator's dilemma.* Boston: Harvard Business School Press.

Christensen, C. M., and Raynor, M. E. (2003). *The innovator's solution: Creating and sustaining successful growth.* Boston: Harvard Business School Press.

Clarke, T., and Clegg, S. (2000). *Changing paradigms.* London: Trafalgar Square.

Coalition for Environmentally Responsible Economies. (2002). *Value at risk: Climate change and the future of governance.* Boston: CERES.

Daily, C. M., Dalton, D. R., and Cannella Jr., A. A. (2003). Corporate governance: Decades of dialogue and data. *Academy of Management Review, 28* (3), 371–382.

DiBartolomeo, D., and Kurtz, L. (1999). *Explaining and controlling the returns of socially screened portfolios.* Northfield Working Paper.

Dimma, W. A. (2002). *Excellence in the boardroom. Best practices in corporate directorship.* Etobicoke, ON: Wiley.

Donaldson, T. (1999). Making stakeholder theory whole. *Academy of Management Review, 24* (2), 237–241.

Donaldson, T., and Dunfee, T. W. (1999). *Ties that bind: A social contracts approach to business ethics.* Boston: Harvard Business School Press.

Donaldson, T., and Preston, L. E. (1995). The stakeholder theory of the corporation: Concepts, evidence, implications. *Academy of Management Review, 20* (1), 65–91.

Drucker, P. (1982). The new meaning of corporate social responsibility. *California Management Review, 26,* 53–63.

Eisenhardt, K. (1999). Agency theory: An assessment and a review. *Academy of Management Review, 14,* 57–74.

Environics. (2002). *CSR monitor and global issues monitor surveys.* Toronto: Environics.

European Commission. (2001). *Promoting a European framework for corporate social responsibility: Green paper.* Luxembourg: Office for Official Publications of the European Commission.

Eurosif. (2003). *Socially responsible investment among European institutional investors: 2003 report.* Accessed online at http://www.eurosif.org/pub/lib/2003/10/srirept/eurosif-srireprt-2003-all.pdf

Feltmate, B., Schofield, B., and Yachnin, R. (2001). *Sustainable development, value creation and the capital markets.* Ottawa: Conference Board of Canada.

Fombrun, C. J. (2001). Corporate reputations as economic assets. In Hitt, M. A., Freeman, R. E., and Harrison, J. S., eds. (2001). *Handbook of strategic management.* Oxford: Blackwell, 289–312.

Foster, R., and Kaplan, S. (2001). *Creative destruction.* New York: Currency.

Franks, J., and Mayer, C. (2005). Corporate ownership and control in the UK, Germany, and France. In Chew, D. H., and Gillan, S. L. (2005). *Corporate governance at the crossroads: A book of readings.* New York: McGraw-Hill Irwin, 360–375.

Freeman, R. E. (1984). *Strategic management: A stakeholder approach.* Boston: Pitman.

Freeman, R. E. (2000). Business ethics at the millennium. *Business Ethics Quarterly, 10* (1), 169–180.

Freeman, R. E. (2001). *Five arguments in stakeholder thinking.* Paper presented at the Academy of Management, Washington, DC.

Freeman, R. E. and Evan, W. (1990). Corporate governance: A stakeholder interpretation. *Journal of Behavioral Economics, 19* (4), 337–359.

Freeman, R. E., and McVea, J. (2001). A stakeholder approach to strategic management. In Hitt, M. A., Freeman, R. E., and Harrison, J. S., eds. (2001). *Handbook of Strategic Management.* Oxford: Blackwell, 189–207.

Freeman, R. E., Wicks, A. C., and Parmar, B. (2004). Stakeholder theory and "the corporate objective revisited." *Organization Science, 15* (3), 364–369.

Galbraith, J. K. (1967). *The new industrial state.* Boston: Houghton Mifflin.

Garrett, R., and Gould, D. (2002). *The future for boards: Professionalism or incarceration?* In Proc 5th International Conference on Corporate Governance and Direction. See also *After Enron: How can we make governance work?* Henley, UK: Centre for Board Effectiveness, Henley Management College.

Global Reporting Initiative. (2002). *Sustainability reporting guidelines.* Amsterdam, Neth: Global Reporting Initiative. Available at http://www.globalreporting.org (accessed July 21, 2004).

Harrison, J. S., and St. John, C. H. (1996). Managing and partnering with external stakeholders. *Academy of Management Executive, 10* (2), 46–59.

Hart, S. L. (1995). A natural-resource-based view of the firm. *Academy of Management Review, 20,* 986–1014.

Hart, S. L. (1997). Beyond greening: Strategies for a sustainable world. *Harvard Business Review, 75* (1), 66–76.

Hart, S. L., and Milstein, M. B. (1999). Global sustainability and the creative destruction of industries. *Sloan Management Review, 41* (1), 23–33.

Hart, S. L., and Christensen, C. (2002, fall). The great leap: Driving innovation from the base of the pyramid. *Sloan Management Review,* 51–56.

Hart, S. L., and Milstein, M. B. (2003). Creating sustainable value. *Academy of Management Executive, 17* (2), 56–67.

Hawken, P., Lovins, A., and Lovins, L. H. (1999). *Natural capitalism: Creating the next industrial revolution.* New York: Little, Brown.

Hill, C. W., and Jones, T. M. (1992). Stakeholder-agency theory. *Journal of Management Studies, 29,* 134–154.

Holliday, C., Schmidheiny, S., and Watts, P. (2002). *Walking the talk. The business case for sustainable development.* Sheffield, UK: Greenleaf.

Innovest (2003). *New alpha source for asset managers: Environmentally-enhanced investment portfolios.* New York: Innovest.

Jensen, M. C. (2005). Value maximization, stakeholder theory, and the corporate objective function. In Chew, D. H., and Gillan, S. L. (2005). *Corporate governance at the crossroads: A book of readings.* New York: McGraw-Hill Irwin, 7–20.

Jensen, M. C., and Meckling, W. F. (1976). Theory of the firm: Managerial behavior, agency costs, and ownership structure. *Journal of Financial Economics, 3,* 305–360.

Jensen, M. C., and Meckling, W. F. (2005). The nature of man. In Chew, D. H., and Gillan, S. L. (2005). *Corporate governance at the crossroads: A book of readings.* New York: McGraw-Hill Irwin, 87–102.

Jones, T. M., and Wicks, A. C. (1999). Convergent stakeholder theory. *Academy of Management Review, 24* (2), 206–221.

Kaplan, R. S., and Norton, D. P. (1996). *The balanced scorecard: Translating strategy into action.* Boston: Harvard Business School Press.

Kaplan, R. S., and Norton, D. P. (2001). *The strategy-focused organization. How balanced scorecard companies thrive in the new business environment.* Boston: Harvard Business School Press.

Kasemir, B., and Suëss, A. (2002). *Sustainability information and Pension fund Investment.* Belfer Center for Science and International Affairs (BCSIA) Discussion Paper 2002–13. Cambridge, MA: Environment and Natural Resources Program, Kennedy School of Government, Harvard University. Accessed online at http://environment.harvard.edu/gea

Kay, J. (1995). *Foundations of corporate success: How business strategies add value.* Oxford: Oxford University Press.

King Committee. (2002). *King report on corporate governance for South Africa, 2002.* Parklands, South Africa: Institute of Directors in Southern Africa.

Leblanc, R., and Gillies, J. (2005). *Building a better board: What directors, investors, managers, and regulators must know about boards of directors.* Chichester: Wiley & Son.

Letendre, L. (2004). The dynamics of the boardroom. *Academy of Management Executive, 18* (1), 101–104.

Lynall, M. D., Golden, B. R., and Hillman, A. J. (2003). Board composition from adolescence to maturity: A multitheoretic view. *Academy of Management Review, 28* (3), 416–431.

MacMillan, K., and Downing, S. (1999). Governance and performance: Goodwill hunting. *Journal of General Management, 24* (3), 1–11.

Mansley, M. (2000). *Socially responsible investment: A guide for pension funds and institutional investors.* Sudbury, UK: Monitor Press.

Margolis, J. D., and Walsh, J. P. (2001). *People and profits? The search for a link between a company's social and financial performance.* Mahwah, NJ: Erlbaum.

Margolis, J. D., and Walsh, J. P. (2003, June). Misery loves companies: Rethinking social initiatives by business. *Administrative Science Quarterly,* 268–305.

Martin, R. (2002, March). The virtue matrix: Calculating the return on corporate responsibility. *Harvard Business Review,* 5–11. Reprint R0203E.

Mathias, A. (2003, October). Morley wins UK's largest SRI mandate. *Environmental Finance,* 11.

Monks, R., and Minow, N. (2005). The director's new clothes (or the myth of corporate accountability). In Chew, D. H., and Gillan, S. L. (2005). *Corporate governance at the crossroads: A book of readings.* New York: McGraw-Hill Irwin, 151–157.

Mutual Fund Review. (2002, spring). SRI: A brave new world? *Mutual Fund Review,* 6–15.

Nahapiet, J., and Ghoshal, S. (1998). Social capital, intellectual capital, and the organizational advantage. *Academy of Management Review, 23* (2), 242–266.

OECD. (2004). *Principles of corporate governance.* Paris: Organisation for Economic Co-Operation and Development.

Paine, L. (1994). Managing for organizational integrity. *Harvard Business Review, 72* (2), 106–117.

Parkinson, J. (2003). Models of the company and the employment relationship. *British Journal of Industrial Relations, 41* (3), 481–509.

Pfeffer, J., and Salancik, G. (1978). *The external control of organizations.* New York: Harper and Row.

Porter, M. E., and van der Linde, C. (1995). Green and competitive. *Harvard Business Review, 73,* 120–134.

Prahalad, C. K., and Hart, S. L. (2001). The fortune at the bottom of the pyramid. *Strategy + Business, 26,* 2–14.

Prahalad, C. K., and Hammond, A. (2002). Serving the poor, profitably. *Harvard Business Review, 80* (9), 4–11.

Schmidheiny, S., with the Business Council for Sustainable Development. (1992). *Changing course.* Cambridge, MA: MIT Press.

Shankman, N. A. (1999). Reframing the debate between agency and stakeholder theories of the firm. *Journal of Business Ethics, 19,* 319–334.

Sharma, S., and Vredenburg, H. (1998). Proactive corporate environmental strategy and the development of competitively valuable organizational capabilities. *Strategic Management Journal, 19,* 729–753.

Social Investment Forum. (2001). *2001 report on socially responsible investing trends in the United States.* Washington: SIF.

Social Investment Forum. (2003). *2003 report on socially responsible investing trends in the United States.* Washington: SIF.

Social Investment Organization. (2003). *Canadian social investment review, 2002: A comprehensive survey of socially responsible investment in Canada.* Toronto: SIO.

Solomon, J., and Solomon, R. (2004). *Corporate governance and accountability*. Chichester, UK: Wiley.

Sparkes, R. (2002). *SRI: A global revolution*. London: John Wiley & Sons.

Sternberg, E. (1996). Stakeholder theory exposed. *Corporate Governance Quarterly*, 2 (1). Cited in Jensen (2005).

Sternberg, E. (1999). The stakeholder concept: A mistaken doctrine. London: Foundation for Business Responsibilities. Issue Paper No 4. Cited in Jensen (2005).

Sundaram, A., and Inkpen, A. (2004). The corporate objective revisited. *Organization Science, 15* (3), 350–363.

Sundaramurthy, C., and Lewis, M. (2003). Control and collaboration: Paradoxes of governance. *Academy of Management Review, 28* (3), 397–415.

Watts, P., and Holme, R. (1999). *Meeting changing expectations: Corporate social responsibility*. Geneva: World Business Council on Sustainable Development.

Waddock, S. A., and Graves, S. B. (1997). The corporate social performance–financial performance link. *Strategic Management Journal, 18* (4), 303–319.

Wernerfeld, B. (1984). A resource-based view of the firm. *Strategic Management Journal, 5,* 171–180.

Wheeler, D., and Sillanpää, M. (1997). *The stakeholder corporation*. London: Pitman.

Wheeler, D., and Sillanpää, M. (1998). Including the stakeholders: The business case. *Long Range Planning, 31* (2), 201–210.

Wheeler, D., Colbert, B., and Freeman, R. E. (2003). Focusing on value: Reconciling corporate social responsibility, sustainability, and a stakeholder approach in a network world. *Journal of General Management, 28* (3), 1–28.

Wheeler, D., and Davies, R. (2004). Gaining goodwill: Developing stakeholder approaches to corporate governance. *Journal of General Management*, forthcoming.

Wheeler, D., Thomson, J., Woodward, T., and Shokeen, P. (2004). *Comparative study of UK and Canadian pension fund transparency practices*. Ottawa: National Roundtable on the Environment and the Economy.

Willums, J-O., and Golüke, U. (1992). *From ideas to action: Business and sustainable development*. Oslo: International Chamber of Commerce and Ad Notam Gyldendal.

World Commission on Environment and Development. (1987). *Our common future*. Oxford: Oxford University Press.

World Resources Institute, United Nations Environment Program and World Business Council for Sustainable Development. (2002). *Tomorrow's markets: Global trends and their implications for business*. Washington: WRI.

World Bank. (1999). *Corporate governance overview*. Washington: World Bank.

Yaron, G. (2001). The responsible pension trustee. *Estates, Trusts & Pensions Journal, 20,* 305–388.

Index

Abbott Laboratories, 93
Abrams, Frank, 89
Accountability, 41, 178; lack of, 17; most
    effective levers of, ix
Accountable organization, 171
Accounting industry, 64–65
Accounting standards, 216; recognizing
    essential role of, 30
Action Plan (EU), 188–89
Adler, P. S., 236
Advisors, professional, 64
"Agency" problem, 4
Agency theory, 247, 248, 251, 261, 262
Allen, William T., 86
American International Group (AIG),
    211–12
American Law Institute (ALI): *Principles
    of Corporate Governance*, 226; Project
    on Principles of Corporate
    Governance, 92
AMF, 191
Antitakeover defenses: adopting,
    95–97, 109, 124. *See also*
    Poison pill
Antitakeover laws, 59
Aramack Worldwide Corporation, 91
Arthur Andersen, 66, 67
AT&T, 150
Attorney, hiring an, 215. *See also*
    Gatekeepers

Attorney-client privilege, 217
Audit committees, 208; composition, 22,
    56, 147; roles and responsibilities,
    12n.24, 64–65, 68–69, 147, 164–65.
    See also Gatekeepers
Audit function, 67–68, 216; quarantining
    of, 24; Sarbanes-Oxley Act and, 67–69,
    147, 165. *See also* Statutory Audit
    Communication (EU)
Auditor responsibility, conflicts of
    interest and, 193–94
Audit-related lawsuits, 64

Bakke, Dennis W., 89–90
Balanced scorecard, board's, 171–74,
    181n.31; causal relationships in,
    172, 173
Banc of America Securities (BAS), 212
Bankruptcy, 228
Banks, 18
Basu, Kunal, 91
Bebchuck, L. A., 113–14
Berle, Adolf, 52, 53, 108, 123
Best practices, 32, 155; for conduct of
    internal investigations, 214–17;
    voluntary, 5, 6. *See also* Code of Best
    Practice
Bill of Rights, 47
Biondi v. Scrushy, 209–10
Blasius Industries v. Atlas Corp., 126

271

About the Editors and Contributors

Marc J. Epstein is Distinguished Research Professor of Management, Jones Graduate School of Management, Rice University, and was recently Visiting Professor and Hansjoerg Wyss Visiting Scholar in Social Enterprise at the Harvard Business School. Previously, he held positions at Stanford Business School and INSEAD (the European Institute of Business Administration). A specialist in corporate strategy, governance, performance management, and corporate social responsibility, he is the author or co-author of over 100 academic and professional papers and a dozen books, including *Implementing E-Commerce Strategies* (Praeger, 2004); *Counting What Counts: Turning Corporate Accountability to Competitive Advantage*; and *Measuring Corporate Environmental Performance: Best Practices for Costing and Managing an Effective Environmental Strategy*, recipient of the AAA/AICPA Notable Contributions to Accounting Literature Award. A senior consultant to leading corporations and governments for over 25 years, he currently serves as Editor-in-Chief of the journal *Advances in Management Accounting*.

Kirk O. Hanson is Executive Director of the Markkula Center for Applied Ethics and University Professor of Organizations and Society at Santa Clara University. In 2001, he retired from the Stanford University Graduate School of Business, where he served in a variety of teaching, research, and administrative capacities over 23 years. A specialist in ethical behavior of corporations, he writes and presents regularly on the subject. He was the founding president of the Business Enterprise Trust, a national organization created by leaders in business, labor, media, and academia to promote exemplary behavior in business; the first chairman of the Santa Clara County Political Ethics Commission; and has written a weekly column for the *San Jose Mercury News*. He has served on the boards of a variety of organizations, including the Social

Venture Network, the Entrepreneurs' Foundation, and American Leadership Forum Silicon Valley.

Constance E. Bagley is Associate Professor of Business Administration at the Harvard Business School. Before joining the faculty at Harvard in 2000, she taught at the Stanford University Graduate School of Business. Previously, she was a corporate securities partner at Bingham McCutchen from 1984 to 1990, and is a member of the State Bar of New York and the State Bar of California. Her practice currently centers on legal aspects of entrepreneurship and cyberlaw, as well as corporate governance. Her publications include *Managers and the Legal Environment: Strategies for the 21st Century* (4th edition); *The Entrepreneur's Guide to Business Law* (2d edition); *Proxy Contests and Corporate Control: Strategic Considerations;* and *Negotiated Acquisitions.* She has also published articles in such journals as the *Harvard Law Review,* the *Harvard Business Review,* the *Harvard Journal of Law and Technology, Financial Times, Directorship,* the *Stanford Journal of Law, Business & Finance,* the *San Diego Law Review,* and the *National Law Journal.*

David J. Berger is Partner at the law firm of Wilson, Sonsini, Goodrich & Rosati, in Palo Alto, California, where he specializes in the areas of corporate governance, fiduciary duties of directors, and merger and acquisition and securities litigation. He has represented a number of institutional and other investors, as well as directors, in proxy contests and other challenges arising out of control issues. He is a frequent author and lecturer on corporate governance and control issues, and has been a faculty member of the Stanford Director's College and the Duke Director Institute. He has also been a guest lecturer at several law schools and business schools throughout the country, including teaching classes at Stanford, Harvard, and Duke. He is a past recipient of the Martin Luther King, Jr., Visionary award from the Lawyers Committee on Civil Rights, and serves as a director to a number of public service organizations, including the San Francisco Legal Aid Society, the Firearms Law Center, and the Smuin Ballet.

Michael Bradley is the F.M. Kirby Professor of Investment Banking, Professor of Law, and Academic Director of the Global Capital Markets Center at Duke University. His research focuses on issues arising at the intersection of corporate finance and corporate law. He has published numerous academic articles and has provided expert testimony before the Senate Banking Committee, the SEC, the Council of Economic Advisors, and a number of state and federal courts regarding issues of corporate governance.

Sir Adrian Cadbury was Chair of the Cadbury Group from 1965 to 1989, during which time he developed a participative corporate management structure and edited one of the first corporate charters of Business Principles. He was also a Director of the Bank of England from 1970 to 1994, and of IBM (UK) from 1975 to 1994, and from 1984 to 1994 was chairman of PRO NED, a body backed by the Bank of England and designed to promote the appointment of suitably qualified non-executive directors. His most celebrated achievement is the seminal 1992 "Cadbury Code" on corporate governance, which became the model for reform in Europe, Commonwealth countries, and elsewhere. Sir Adrian was also a key member of the OECD Business Sector Advisory Group on Corporate Governance. He currently serves as Chancellor of Aston University and recently retired as a Director of NEC Group. His publications include *Ethical Managers Make Their Own Rules*, *The Company Chairman*, and *Corporate Governance and Chairmanship: A Personal View*.

Jonathan C. Dickey is Partner in the Palo Alto office of Gibson, Dunn & Crutcher, specializing in securities class actions, shareholder derivative litigation, and SEC enforcement matters. He frequently acts as counsel to boards of directors and board committees on securities disclosure and compliance issues, SEC and stock exchange investigations, insider trading, and corporate governance issues. He has served as an advisor to the American Electronics Association on securities class action law reform matters, and was significantly involved in passage of the Private Securities Litigation Reform Act of 1995 and the Uniform Standards Act of 1998. He is a frequent lecturer and author on securities-related and corporate governance topics for such organizations as the American Law Institute–American Bar Association and the Practising Law Institute, and serves as a regular faculty member at the annual Directors' College, sponsored by Stanford Law School. He is a member of the State Bar of California, the American Bar Association, and the Securities Industry Association.

Holly J. Gregory is Partner in the corporate governance practice of the international law firm of Weil, Gotshal & Manges LLP, where she counsels corporate directors, trustees, managers and institutional investors on a range of governance issues, including director and trustee responsibilities, conflicts of interest, board and committee structure, audit committee investigations, institutional investor initiatives, international governance "best practice," and compliance with legislative, regulatory and listing rule requirements. In the public policy arena, she has worked on various corporate governance projects for the OECD, the European Commission, the World Bank, and the U.S. Securities and Exchange Commission. She has lectured widely on corporate governance topics, served as Counsel to the Egon Zehnder International Institutional Investors Advisory Group, and served on the Secretariat of the OECD Business Sector Advisory Group on Corporate Governance. She has authored and co-authored many articles, reports, and book chapters on corporate governance and has served as a featured columnist in Dow Jones' *Corporate Governance* publication.

James E. Heard is Vice Chairman of Institutional Shareholder Services, Inc., a private, for-profit firm that advises institutional investors on corporate governance issues.

Wendy Houle is an Associate at Gibson, Dunn & Crutcher, specializing in securities litigation. She is a member of the State Bar of California, and prior to joining Gibson Dunn & Crutcher, she clerked for the Honorable David O. Carter in United States District Court for the Central District of California.

Jay W. Lorsch is the Louis Kirstein Professor of Human Relations at the Harvard Business School. He is the author of over a dozen books, including *Organization and Environment* (with Paul R. Lawrence), which received the Academy of Management's Best Management Book of the Year Award and the James A. Hamilton Book Award of the College of Hospital Administrators. Other publications include *Back to the Drawing Board: Designing Boards for a Complex World* (with Colin B. Carter), *Aligning the Stars: How to Succeed When Professionals Drive Results* (with Thomas J. Tierney), and *Pawns or Potentates: The Reality of America's Corporate Boards*. Having taught in all of Harvard Business School's educational programs, he has also served in a variety of administrative roles. As a consultant, he has worked with a wide variety of companies in many industries. He is a Director of Blasland, Bouck & Lee, Inc., and Computer Associates International, Inc., and a member of the Advisory Board of U.S. Foodservice and BoardVantage, Inc.

Ira M. Millstein is a Senior Partner at the international law firm Weil, Gotshal & Manges LLP, where, in addition to practicing in the areas of government regulation and antitrust law, he has counseled numerous boards on the issues of corporate governance. He is the Eugene F. Williams Visiting Professor in Competitive Enterprise and Strategy at the Yale School of Management, Honorary Chair of the Yale International Institute for Corporate Governance, and Chairman of the Private Sector Advisory Group of the Global Corporate Governance Forum, founded by the World Bank and the Organization for Economic Cooperation and Development (OECD). He served as Chairman of the OECD Business Sector Advisory Group on Corporate Governance in 1997–1998 and Co-Chair of the Blue Ribbon Committee on Improving the Effectiveness of Corporate Audit Committees (sponsored by the New York Stock Exchange and the National Association of Securities Dealers) in 1998–1999. He was more recently named to the board of the World Trade Center Memorial Foundation and appointed Chairman of the New York State Commission on

Public Authority Reform. An Elected Fellow of the American Academy of Arts & Sciences, he is a frequent lecturer and author on corporate governance, antitrust, and government regulation. Included among his many publications are: *The Recurrent Crisis in Corporate Governance* (co-author), *The Limits of Corporate Power* (co-author), *The Impact of the Modern Corporation* (co-editor), and *The Battle for Corporate Control: Shareholder Rights, Stakeholder Interests, and Managerial Responsibility* (contributing author).

Lee E. Preston is Professor Emeritus in the Robert H. Smith School of Business and faculty ombuds officer for the College Park Campus at the University of Maryland. He is the author or editor of more than 150 academic publications— articles, books and monographs—in the fields of economics, marketing, management, international business and public policy. Prior to joining the University of Maryland faculty in 1980, he was a faculty member of the University of California at Berkeley and of the State University of New York at Buffalo.

Marie-Josée Roy is Associate Professor at the Faculty of Administrative Sciences at University Laval in Quebec City, Canada, where she teaches strategic management, with a research focus on corporate social responsibility and corporate governance. She has written several articles, including "Measuring and Improving the Performance of Corporate Boards," co-authored with Marc J. Epstein, and published by The Society of Management Accountants of Canada.

Myron M. Sheinfeld is Senior Counsel to the law firm of Akin, Gump, Strauss, Hauer & Feld, L.L.P., in Houston, Texas. Since 1965, his practice has focused on reorganization and bankruptcy law, creditors' rights, workout matters, commercial litigation and business transactions. Previously, he served as an Assistant United States Attorney in the Southern District of Texas and law clerk to Ben C. Connally, Chief United States District Judge for the Southern District of Texas. He co-founded the law firm of Sheinfeld, Maley & Kay, P.C., serving as a shareholder until 1996 and as counsel to the firm from 1996 to 2001. He presently serves on the board of Nabors Industries Ltd., a publicly held company. He is the co-editor of *Collier on Bankruptcy* and the co-author of *Collier on Bankruptcy Taxation*, and has taught at the law schools of the Universities of Texas, Michigan and Houston. He has authored articles in *The Corporate Board* and has served on the editorial board of *The Practical Lawyer*.

Jane Thomson is an independent consultant specializing in sustainability and based in Vancouver, BC. She has worked with public and private sector organizations, including Canada's National Roundtable on the Environment and the Economy (NRTEE), Enbridge Gas Distribution, and the Greater Vancouver Regional District (GVRD), on sustainability issues, helping to identify and implement strategic sustainability initiatives. She is also a professional engineer with experience as a mechanical engineering consultant, where she was responsible for design and project management for numerous industrial and commercial clients in Canada and internationally.

Stephen M. Wallenstein is Executive Director of the Duke Global Capital Markets Center, a unique collaboration between The Fuqua School of Business and the Duke School of Law, and Professor of the Practice of Law, Business and Finance at Duke. He is also program director and founder of the Duke Directors' Education Institute, an ongoing series to address the corporate governance failures of diligence, ethics and controls in corporate America. Previously, he served as Visiting Professor of Law at the University of Denver, Adjunct Professor at the American University School of International Service, and as Senior Investment Officer and Senior Corporate Counsel, at International Finance Corporation, where he was responsible for structuring, negotiating, and documenting international business transactions. He has served on the boards and advisory committees of a variety of organizations, presented at workshops and conferences on international corporate governance, and published in such journals as *Law and Contemporary Problems* and *Fordham International Law Journal*.

David Wheeler is Director and Erivan K. Haub Professor in Business and Sustainability at the Schulich School of Business, York University, Toronto. He is also the Founding Director of the York Institute for Research and Innovation in Sustainability, a recent strategic initiative of York University embracing all ten faculties. He has published more than 60 articles and book chapters in a wide variety of academic journals, books, parliamentary inquiries and popular journals, and has delivered speeches at numerous conferences and events. He was principal author of *The Stakeholder Corporation*, the first business text to be endorsed by British Prime Minister, Tony Blair. Prior to his current appointments, he was a member of the Executive Management team of The Body Shop International for seven years.